HORACE GREELEY

AND OTHER

PIONEERS OF AMERICAN SOCIALISM

"I honor the generous ideas of the Socialists, the magnificence of their theories, and the enthusiasm with which they have been urged."—*Ralph Waldo Emerson*, 1883.

"We believe that Government, like every other intelligent agency, is bound to do good to the extent of its ability—that it ought actively to promote and increase the general well being—that it should encourage and foster Industry, Science, Invention; Intellectual, Social and Physical Progress. . . . Such is our idea of the sphere of Government."—*Horace Greeley*, 1850.

A volume in the Hyperion reprint series
THE RADICAL TRADITION IN AMERICA

HYPERION PRESS, INC.
Westport, Connecticut

CHARLES SOTHERAN

From a photograph by Rockwood, New York, 1874

HORACE GREELEY

AND OTHER PIONEERS OF
AMERICAN SOCIALISM

BY
CHARLES SOTHERAN

With a Foreword by W. J. GHENT and
Reminiscences of CHARLES SOTHERAN
By ALICE HYNEMAN SOTHERAN

New York
MITCHELL KENNERLEY
1915

Published in 1915 by Mitchell Kennerley, New York
Copyright 1892 by the Humboldt Publishing Co.;
copyright 1915 by Mitchell Kennerley
Hyperion reprint edition 1975
Library of Congress Catalog Number 75-333
ISBN 0-88355-236-1
Printed in the United States of America

Library of Congress Cataloging in Publication Data

Sotheran, Charles, 1847-1902.
  *Horace Greeley and other pioneers of American
socialism.*

  (The Radical tradition in America)
  *Reprint of the ed. published by M. Kennerley,
New York.*
  Includes index.
  *1. Greeley, Horace, 1811-1872.   2. Socialism in
the United States.   I. Title.*
HX83.S7   1975   335'.3'0924   75-333
ISBN 0-88355-236-1

CONTENTS

v

A FOREWORD

By W. J. Ghent

THIS book, when it first appeared more than twenty years ago, served the useful purpose of reminding some of us that American Socialism had native, as well as foreign, origins. The records of the earlier Socialism had not before been collected. At that time they were, indeed, almost unknown; for the Civil War and the post-bellum scramble for place and pelf had well-nigh obliterated them from the American consciousness.

Since then we have had, from a number of writers, studies of the unrest of ante-bellum days; and that epoch—in particular the period of the 40's, with its unparalleled social awakening—is now better understood. Among these volumes this book deserves a permanent place. With keen satisfaction I learn of its forthcoming republication.

It is not without defects, as Sotheran himself freely admitted. It bears the indubitable marks of the haste with which it was thrown together. Yet it has a prime merit in its store of authentic and valuable material. Sotheran seemed never to have time to finish a task according to the standard imposed by both his judgment and his learning. Hurried, and often harried, he drove his way through a mass of work where few others could have followed him. He was an omnivorous reader. Among men whose paths have crossed mine, I can think of no other who had read so extensively. By instinct and training he was a bibliophile; but he was of that rare species who know the contents of books quite as well as they know bindings and editions.

vii

He was a man somewhat out of his time. It was in the early seventies, shortly after he arrived in America, that he associated himself with the then embryotic Socialism movement. . For more than twenty years he gave his time and labor unselfishly to the cause. With talents that would have won him distinction and means in the *bourgeois* world, he devoted himself to the most unpopular movement in America. During that culminating phase of the old Socialist Labor party in the middle 90's, when the slightest evidence of heterodoxy was brought before the official inquisition, he came under the ban of the censors and was excommunicated. All his long service counted for nothing, and his name was henceforth erased from the Socialist apostolate.

He was too broad a man for the environment he chose. No one could have more at heart the redress of human suffering; but the dogmatic narrowness which for a time characterized the revolutionary movement irked him beyond measure. That intensity of conviction which in other men so often leads to a frowning dourness of temper left no trace on his sunny disposition. Big-bodied, large-minded, warmhearted, was Sotheran; his Socialism was essentially sociable; the word "comrade" meant to him "companion," and his jovial temper radiated good cheer. He would have fared better in these days; but I oftenest think of him as one who, had he lived in the times before Socialism came to trouble men's minds and to upset the world, would have found fitting company with Ben Jonson's inner circle of wits and bookmen.

It is as an honored privilege that I fulfil the request to inscribe my name on his work.

Los Angeles, May 19, 1915.   W. J. GHENT.

REMINISCENCES OF CHARLES SOTHERAN AS PIONEER AMERICAN SOCIALIST
By ALICE HYNEMAN SOTHERAN

TO write of activities carried on in one direction by a character so versatile and prominent in many as was Charles Sotheran, that dominant force in the early American Socialist movement, is a task easy and pleasurable at times. Yet, it is difficult enough at others, to make one echo with approval Robert Louis Stevenson's suggestion of the advantages of the writing of biography as compared with fiction. "Fiction," he wrote, "is too free. In biography you have your little handful of facts, little bits of a puzzle, and you sit and think, and fit 'em together this way and that, and get up and throw 'em down, and say damn, and go out for a walk. And it's real soothing, and when done gives an idea of finish to the writer that is very peaceful."

In gathering together the handful of facts for these reminiscences of Charles Sotheran, the first to come to mind are those which preceded and led to his coming to the United States. Born in 1847 in England, he went to Paris when a boy of nineteen, drawn there by a wish to visit the great Exposition. Although he started with only sufficient money for the expenses of a few weeks' stay, the time went so pleasantly that he remained abroad a whole year, replenishing his purse by writing articles for the London and Manchester Press. These articles were mostly semi-political and character sketches of celebrated people, many of whom he knew intimately. To the Manchester *Free Lance*, the editor of which, John Beresford, was a high degree Mason, he contributed brilliant reviews on the traditions which form the basis for the foundations for exoteric or high grade Masonry. These essays made it patent to the initiates that when Mr. Sotheran took the first degree all of the arcana required for the last were in his possession, and the celerity with which he rose in the Masonic order is one of the many astonishing incidents in his versatile career.

While this account of Mr. Sotheran's connection with Masonry may seem a digression from the main purpose of this article, which is to tell of his activities in the labor movement, it has been told because the part he played in Masonry led to his coming to America, where becoming an American citizen, he was enabled to take part in the Socialist activities of this country. By reason of the articles in the *Free Lance*, James Fraser, Lord Bishop of Manchester, invited him to take charge of the editorial work of his *Annual Calendar*, a book of 250 pages, giving news not only of his Manchester Diocese, but of school, church, and civic organizations of all sorts all over the world. His editorial work attracting the attention of Joseph Sabin, the New York book expert, he arranged with Mr. Sotheran to go to New York with him as Assistant Editor in his monthly magazine, the *Bibliopolist and Dictionary of Books Relating to America*. This position he accepted the more readily since his uncle, head of the firm of Henry Sotheran of London, Paris and Manchester, had large pecuniary interests in the United States and wished him to remain in New York for a season to look after them. Moreover, from youth up he had admired the New World with the love to which his favorite poet Shelley had given expression in the XXIV verse of *The Revolt of Islam*. Like Shelley he looked upon America as the lovely land of Freedom, and he desired to see for himself the workings of Democracy on the large scale afforded by the union of so many states.

It was in the Spring of 1874 that this dream of Mr. Sotheran was realized. In the numerous letters he carried along with him were two which he delivered as soon as he got breathing time after landing. One of these, written by Mr. Sotheran's brother-in-law, Stanley Leigh, B.C.K., M.A., was addressed to Professor Hyslop. The other, written by John Yarker, a Mason of high standing in Great Britain, was addressed to my father, Leon Hyneman, whose reputation as Masonic author, editor, and publisher had become international. Through Professor Hyslop, Mr. Sotheran at once became a member of the New York Liberal Club, then headed by James Parton, the historical writer and husband of "Fanny Fern," who had succeeded its first president, Horace Greeley. As its name argued, the club was a favorite meeting place for thinkers chasing after all sorts of "isms," a proceeding which gained for it the nick-name of the "Home for Hobbies." When my father and I first began to attend its meetings with Mr. Sotheran most of the persons to be met there were professional and literary men and women who had achieved eminence in their special callings. Mr. Sotheran himself spoke frequently. The first of his lectures which I had the good fortune to hear was on Percy Bysshe Shelley as philosopher and reformer. Mr. Sotheran not only claimed preeminence among English poets for Shelley's verse, but he regarded the poet as a philosopher and a political and social reformer, and thus a law-giver to our generation. This conception, expressed over a third of a century ago, has since been confirmed by such eminent students of Shelley as Professors Dowden and Woodbury. Another lecture of this kind was "Mary Wollstonecraft, an Eighteenth Century Reformer," which, prepared at the request of the New York Woman Suffrage Society, was repeated by request before the Liberal Club.

Almost simultaneously with his becoming a member of the Liberal Club, Mr. Sotheran had joined the New York Press Club. Although a Yorkshireman of athletic build, he found no attraction in out-door sports, and was averse to any of the places where games of chance or skill were played. Essentially a "clubbable man," he loved, in words accredited to old Ben Jonson, "to fold his legs under the table, and sitting with men of his own stamp, to throw and catch the ball of conversation." Such social opportunity he found in the New York Press Club, which eschewed politics and was not avowedly ethical. Although young, the club had achieved considerable success and was looked upon as a power. In such a circle of journalists and men engaged in literary pursuits, Mr. Sotheran was completely at home. In less than a year he was elected to the executive committee, along with Gen. Horatio C. King and others of note. It was there that he formed many life friendships.

The next experiment made by Mr. Sotheran in society joining was with the "Sovereigns of Industry." This claimed to be an association of the laboring class without regard to race, color, sex, nationality or occupation, and devoted to mutual aid and self improvement. After a few weeks' investigation he withdrew, saying when he saw me, "It's nothing but a co-operative scheme to dispense with the middleman so as to get tools and goods cheap. It will take something more to secure my services." Meeting me some months after, he called out triumphantly, "Eureka! I've found the very thing I have been searching for ever since the time when, as a boy, I met and talked with Mazzini—an organization built on plans great enough to make life worth living just to work for what it represents." The name of this society which meant so much to him was the *Social Democratic Workingman's Party of North America.* In contradistinction to his other societies, this of the Workingman's Party was educational on lines economic and political. His attention had been called to it by his friends, Dr. Adolf Douai and Osborne Ward. These put him into communication with A. Strasser and J. P. McGuire, men, like themselves, active in the movement. With these he threw himself into the work of the party, striving for its upbuild with the ardor and enthusiasm of youth and the seemingly boundless energy of his nature. In the great dearth of English-speaking members, place was found for him immediately on various committees as delegate to conventions, organizer of an American branch and as speaker at halls and mass meetings. Whenever possible he toured the country as a missionary for the conversion of the people to Socialism. It was my good fortune to hear, through him, accounts of the several conventions when the party name was abbreviated, until in 1877 it was shortened to that of the "Socialistic Labor Party." Subsequently the final syllable of the first word was dropped, and this name has been retained ever since.

After this period, which Morris Hillquit in his admirable *History of Socialism in the United States* has termed the "period of organization," events of interest even to outsiders were constantly occurring. Of this sort is one of the happenings in 1879. Vivid as a proof etching is the picture of an evening in September, when Mr. Sotheran called to tell of a projected trip to the third annual Congress of the National Liberal League, about to convene at Cincinnati. To this, he told us, he was going as president of an Auxiliary League, which had obtained a charter from the National League. "This auxiliary," he exulted, "is composed entirely of Socialists, all of whom are jubilant at the chance which this gathering of Liberals gives them for the spread of their ideals. A convention of liberal thinkers, composed of broad-minded

men, known participators in the fight for the abolition of
chattel slavery, should make it easy for us to draw them into
a fold working for that bigger thing, the abolition of wages
slavery."

On his return from the convention, Mr. Sotheran had much
to tell. He declared that the Socialists behaved splendidly,
and that while all asked for was not granted, through their
persistence some things were gained. One of the most radical
measures was the change made in the sixth paragraph of the
resolutions, which, asking only for "civil and religious liberty," was altered into the demand for "political, economic
and religious liberty." Only upon reading the printed report
of the proceedings of the League did I find that Mr. Sotheran
had himself been the mover of this change, as well as others
of a radical nature in the platform as adopted. Speaking of
the Liberals, he sighed while asserting that they were not
easy to persuade into accepting the Socialist creed. For
instance, Col. Robert Ingersoll as a railroad lawyer could not
swallow the railroad clause. And one of Mr. Sotheran's
anecdotes was in relation to General Morton of New Haven,
also of the railroad interests. When during the discussion
Mr. Sotheran said, "I am about to make a motion in favor
of a resolution insisting on economic protection for national
citizens," it was as though some malignant magician had
changed him instanter into a bull and flashed a red rag
before his eyes. He shouted, "Is this a Socialist congress or a
convention of the Liberal League?" Reassured by the Lib-
eralites, he continued, "Gentlemen, it seems to me we should
waive all minor issues." "A funny thing," continued Mr.
Sotheran, "concerning that congress is that it has been noised
about that we Socialists captured the convention. I've
denied the soft impeachment in the *Truth Seeker*, although in
my opinion the charge will do us no harm."

One other incident drawn from memory's rather tangled skein of things connected with 1879 is that of attending a Socialist convention, convened for the purpose of nominating a State, city, and county ticket. This was the third annual of the S. L. P. and between 1,200 and 1,500 persons, among them a number of women, attended it. Among the well known Socialists present were Alexander Jonas, Edward Nye, Justus Schwab (afterward anarchist), and Frank Skarda. When the nominations were made the president called upon Mr. Sotheran for an address. During a speech which was frequently interrupted by applause he stated, almost at the beginning, that the convention had been called together primarily in ratification of Socialist principles, and secondly to keep the members firmly together in repudiation of any possible compromise with Democrat, Republican, or Greenbacker. He warned them that once the members vote for the candidates of any other political party, disintegration will menace the life of their own. And further, that the candidates of the party had to be voted for straight, "not for the sake of the men chosen from the wage-working class, but for eternal principles and in protest against the present anarchy in society."

Despite Mr. Sotheran's arguments against the Socialists allying themselves with any other political party, the S. L. P. officially decided in 1880 to support the Greenback party. In a caucus, along with other prominent party members, he again made his protest, but without avail. After the election the defections from the Socialist ranks were so numerous that they made his words seem like prophecy.

Another remembrance in connection with bygone days, is that of Mr. Sotheran saying: "When I first took it on myself to fight for the cause of labor, the task I set before me was that of striving to bring the American people to an understanding of the Socialist philosophy, what it will mean to labor, and through labor to the world at large. I knew then," he continued, "as well as John Stuart Mill, that 'no one should attempt anything intended to benefit his age without at first making a stern resolution to take up his cross and to bear it. If he does not begin by counting the cost, all his schemes must end in disappointment'." This was said during the labor troubles of 1877–1880. Several times mass meetings had been called by Socialists sympathizing with the railroad men on strike. At these the police "guardians of peace and order" had indulged in truncheon-wielding carnivals, during which Mr. Sotheran as speaker had been one of the victims. In 1879, as he tells in the preface to his *Horace Greeley*, he was left in Tompkins Square for dead. Meeting him after his recovery, he pretended surprise at my attitude:

"You say you are proud of me!" he exclaimed, "that you think my stand was heroic! Well, most people are taking a different view. Madame Blavatsky, for instance, has sent word that she 'tolerated my heretical opinions when expressed among my equals, but having lowered myself by standing on soap boxes and cart-tails to preach such revolutionary doctrines as the public ownership of railroads to car drivers and conductors, I have placed myself outside the pale of her friendship'. Mrs. W—— is another at whose home in Gramercy Park I once was a 'favored guest among the fair and brilliant throng', while now her doors are closed against the 'wicked Socialist agitator'. Worse, however, than such trifling incidents is the threatened loss of my position with the House of W———n. But, whatever happens, the game is worth the candle, and while it burns, I shall keep my place in its playing. Fortunately my journalistic pen being always ready in the ink-well will serve to keep the family pot supplied with fuel."

One of the by-products, so to say, of Socialist agitation, was the endeavor to carry its propaganda into the trades unions to awaken their members to the necessity for political action. Among my reminiscences of that time is the reading to me by Mr. Sotheran of notes sent him by various bodies, saying that "they wished him to come to their place of meeting and give them a good talk." These usually ended with the words, "Please do not send any one else." One of these meetings to which I accompanied him was a gathering of waiters, desirous of being organized into a union. The room as I see it now was a very small one, and evidently the idea of joining together was new to the minds of its occupants. What their talk was I failed to keep track of, being too busy watching the faces of the men and thinking what the whole business of organization might mean to them in the future.

In the matter of workingmen's organizations Mr. Sotheran was enthusiastic to a degree. In most of his lectures, whatever the subject, he would manage to bring in some note pertinent to that topic. This characteristic impressed me particularly at a lecture delivered by him before the American Branch of the S. L. P. on the "Advent of Socialism." Speaking about the methods of bringing about the co-operative commonwealth he remarked: "Organizations of workingmen are to Socialism what spade and plough are to the farmer. When grouped into unions the ground has been gotten ready for the seed-sowers of political agitation and education. Therefore it is the bounden duty of Socialists to get into the working-class combinations; to agitate among their members, preaching a divine discontent with existing conditions, and through education in Socialist principles showing how to change them."

Another smaller, and as yet insignificant labor body, was that of the New York Central Labor Union. Curiously enough this organization had its rise from a mass-meeting called in 1879 by the Socialists in response to an appeal made by the Irish National Land League, and at which Mr. Sotheran was one of the speakers. A couple of years later, when Parnell was keeping the country in a quiver of emotion over the Irish Land League, the Socialists arranged for another similar mass-meeting at Cooper Institute, which drew a great number of representative trade unionists. To these a suggestion, then and there made, was accepted and carried into effect, viz., for the separate unions to unite and work together under the leadership of one central body. The name selected for this governing body was "The Central Labor Union." Owing its existence in part to the S. L. P., the Central Labor Union remained for years on the most friendly terms with that organization.

Still fresh in my mind is the importance we Socialists in the eighties attached to this grouping of New York trades unions in the Central Labor Union. How we watched its entry into municipal politics, where it made a good showing, and the intense excitement we felt when, in 1886, it joined with the United Labor Party in initiating the famous Henry George campaign. At the start Mr. Sotheran made his usual protest against the Socialists fighting for the election of any other than a party candidate. His words of warning were: "Nothing but harm came from pooling interests with the Greenbackers; and I fear the same results will follow fusing with the Single-Taxers. Should George win or poll a very large vote, all will be attributed to the popularity of the candidate and belief in the land-taxing scheme. So whichever way the election goes the Socialists may find themselves left out in the cold." What did happen was that the United Labor Party, a mongrel body composed of all shades of radicals, intoxicated with the very large vote, 68,000, with a suspicion that all had not been delivered to which they were entitled, felt themselves "the whole show." They discovered their mistake when in 1887 they nominated George for Secretary of State. At this political function the Socialist delegates were refused seats. Angered at this insulting discrimination, the Socialists turned out in force to defeat the Single Taxers. The insignificant vote cast at this election, and the sequent disruption of the United Labor Party, seemed to prove the strength of the Socialists when united on an issue.

Nor out of this fray did the Central Labor Union come unscathed. The mixing with old-party politicians brought a suspicion of corruption that, in the words of Mr. Sotheran, "so disgusted one-half of the members that with one accord they left the union, going in a body to a near-by place where they constituted themselves into a new organization taking the name of the Central Labor Federation." My remembrance of this time is mainly of the part played by Mr. Sotheran as peace-maker in bringing the unions into friendly relations. Henry White, then prominent as the general secretary of the United Garment Workers of America, said to me: "It was mainly through Mr. Sotheran's diplomacy in bringing about harmony and effecting a union of labor forces that the Central Labor Union and the Central Labor Federation had been brought to act together."

As stated in a former paragraph, my personal knowledge of trade union procedure in the early part of 1878 was negligible. But, before the close of that decade, it was permitted me to learn more. It was in 1888 that Mr. Sotheran broached the subject of my joining the Knights of Labor. At the same time he invited Mrs. Laurence Gronlund, who with her husband was then visiting me, to become a member. One of his reasons given was "the desire of building up within that organization sufficient Socialist material to effectually influence their councils." He further explained, "The *Local Assembly*, to which Gronlund and I belong, is composed largely of Socialists and there are in it quite a number of intelligent, brilliant women. There being no sex distinction, women vote, lecture, hold office, and discuss all matters of importance, on an equality with men." This being arranged, we found the assembly to which we had become attached was the rather famous Excelsior Labor Club. Therein were found members of many trades, seriously and sensibly discussing live issues of the day. Among the most notable of the Excelsior's trade union members were Patrick Rock, of the stone masons, and Edward Henckler, of the upholsterers. Many of the members were from the professional class and among the women were the lovely and talented Mrs. Imogene C. Fales, Mrs. Florence Kelley, Alice Woodbridge, Margaret Moore and Leonora O'Reilly.

Under such auspices there is nothing surprising in the fact that for several years thereafter the Socialists exerted a steadily growing sway over the councils of the K. of L. In 1893 they were influential enough to gain control over New York District Assembly 49, and to have some members elected to the General Assembly. This was indeed getting on swimmingly; but by a false stroke they were soon landed in troubled waters. Strong enough to be a determining power in an election, the Socialists used their influence to oust Terence V. Powderly, the General Master Workman of the Order, and to install J. R. Sovereign in his place. As a reward for this action the editorship of the organization's official journal was demanded. This, it was claimed, had been partly promised to Daniel De Leon; and when this alleged agreement was not kept De Leon started such a row in his paper, *The People*, that when sent as delegate by the Socialists to the convention of 1893 the convention refused to seat him.

Through this petty individual matter, the whole of that large aggregation of union labor was placed in antagonism to the S. L. P. The Excelsior Labor Club disbanded, its members seeking places elsewhere. The bitter feelings which existed against Mr. De Leon did not, however, extend to the Socialists as a whole. With many of his fellow-Socialists Mr. Sotheran retained his place in the ranks of the order.

Another great labor organization into which Socialists sought entrance as a field which might be profitable for the propagation of their theories was the American Federation of Labor. Knowing Samuel Gompers and being very friendly toward him, Mr. Sotheran naturally felt pleased when in 1886, the old Federation of Organized Trade and Labor Unions abbreviated its name to the American Federation of Labor, changed its tactics, reorganized, and reëlected Gompers president. For the Socialists the situation looked bright. Many were on the inside track as favorites in the unions. Gompers himself was on such intimate terms with the Socialists that, as Hillquit writes, some papers even went so far as to class him with the Socialists. The phenomenal growth of the Federation, which by leaps and bounds soared into the hundred thousands, gave hope to the S. L. P. of a swift coming future when with red banners flying they could march in and capture, if not the whole Federation, at least a majority of its voters for Socialism. Nor was this a dream of the foolish. In the Unions, which were autonomous, Socialist programmes were discussed, and in convention after convention held in one or the other of the large cities some prominent Socialist would be sure to inject resolutions of a pronounced radical political character.

While the harmonious relations seemed so firm between these two bodies, the Central Labor Federation, anxious to get into that closer touch which would give it a legal voice and vote in the councils of the American Federation of Labor, applied at its annual convention held in 1890 for a charter. To its great surprise and mortification this was refused, for the reason, as Gompers said, "The constitution of the organization forbade alliances with political parties, and among the unions affiliated with the Central Labor Union was the American Section of the Socialist Labor Party, a body committed to political action." Of narrow mental vision, Mr. Gompers failed to see that the Socialist party was not a political party in the ordinary sense, but a great potential force acting solely in the interests of Labor. He could only iterate and re-iterate, "A political party is a political party whatever its ultimate aim may be." Many members of the American Section, Mr. Sotheran among them, were willing to concede that Gompers acted strictly within his rights, puerile as was his interpretation of what constitutes a political party. Unfortunately the editors of the Socialist political organs, *The People* and *Vorwarts*, were not so just. The decisions so angered them that they lost all control over their pens and persisted in violent tirades. By this means they cut the ground that had been gained from under the feet of the Socialists, leaving them without even standing room in the ranks of organized labor.

Memory recalls the bitterness with which the Gompers and De Leon factions discussed this unhappy labor imbroglio. It formed topical talks in the lecture halls at almost every meeting, talks that lasted frequently until the lights were put out. On one of these evenings, I remember a group surrounding Mr. Sotheran, and asking him what his opinion was and his reply, to the effect: that while the charter would have been an excellent thing to make progress with, it was a pity the asking was made before the membership was ripe enough in Socialist doctrine to grant it. To the query, "What about Gompers?" Mr. Sotheran replied:

"Of all people we Socialists must learn to govern ourselves; to take the lesson to heart not to give way to anger and indiscriminate abuse. As to Gompers, against whom attacks have been directed, he is neither, as is claimed, dishonest, a fakir, nor ignorant. On the contrary, for his opportunities he is rather literate, a fairly clever writer, if not much of a thinker, of unquestionable honesty in financial matters, and, so far as we know, in expressions of opinion. Now the great trouble with 'Sammy' is that, like most men who have gotten to a certain point, he imagines the final goal has been reached when his fingers have barely touched a half-mile post.

"Yet withal, Gompers is a man of power; the possessor of a will strong enough to organize and hold large bodies of his fellows to act in unison together; obstinate in his determination to have his own way. I've seen him dominate an adverse audience to the extent of remaining immovable under showers of hisses and cat-calls, and then turn the tables on his adversaries by forcing them to applaud. Thus he stands a rock of adamant against all assaults upon his one pet idea, viz.: to get the country's millions of workers together into trades union bands; forming them into a compact moveable army whose numbers shall render it irresistible in a war for higher wages and better living and working conditions. If he would but listen to reason, the veriest Socialist tyro could point out to him that his millions will lead him to the land of nowhere, while as simple trades union bands they are scattered through cities, towns and villages, living in an environment of armed police, jails, trained militia, hostile judiciary, mayors and governors alike able and willing to invoke the whole resources of the Federal Government to prevent their gaining the things they demand."

The backwardness of the unionists to become participants in working class politics did not abate Mr. Sotheran's hope-

fulness for the future of Socialism. "Socialists," he was wont
to repeat, "are the true optimists. Whatever happens they
keep their minds fixed on the picture of a steady growth of
American radicalism" a hope that appeared justified by the
rise of societies North, South, East and West, whose programmes were founded in part on the teachings of Socialism.
Of such were the "Granges," "Farmers' Alliances" and that
child of Bellamy's novel, the "Nationalist movement."

Now while Socialists enjoyed "Looking Backward" as a
story all knew its teachings were not based upon the economic
foundations of practical Socialism. Yet, when the notion of
municipalization of national industries spread like wild fire
among certain classes of people, and Nationalist clubs were
formed by the hundreds, the Socialists, according to their
wont, proceeded to transform these bodies into propaganda
centres. One of these started in New York City acquired a
large number of members, some of whom, even as Florence
Kelley, Mr. Sotheran and myself, were "true blue" Socialists;
others, such as Henrietta Keyser, were Christian Socialists,
while many were just plain Liberal thinkers. Sad to say, this
club was doomed to be the creature of a day, its fragile life
crushed out in a most malicious and shameless manner.

Mr. Sotheran held that the importance of the
movements was that "unlike the big Federation of Labor,
which deposits its votes with the greatest regularity
in both the Democratic and Republican troughs, the
Nationalists voted with the Populists, the most radical
party outside the Socialist." It was this party which in 1892,
by combining with the Knights of Labor, Farmers' Alliances,
and Single Tax Clubs, cast under the name of the "People's
Party" more than 1,000,000 votes for its Presidential candidate. "The encouraging thing about this," said Mr. Sotheran, "is that these votes were cast by American farmers,

American middle-class men, and American workingmen, all of them presumably believers in a platform declaring for a graduated income tax; Government postal savings banks; government ownership of railroads, telegraphs, and telephones; that wealth belongs to him who creates it, and that the interests of rural and civic laborers are identical. These facts are sign posts showing that politics in America is getting beyond the soup and salad courses and almost ready to digest the strong meat diet of modern scientific Socialism."

I was married to Mr. Sotheran on October 17, 1893, and thereafter shared with him to the full his deep interest in all of his activities. At this time he was deeply impressed with the growth of the People's Party. Many friends of Mr. Sotheran were among the Populists. He frequently attended their meetings, urging the members to study the principles of Socialism and to join the Socialist Labor Party. His hopes were such that he had visions of bringing about a union of the two parties. But, these hopes were not destined to be realized, probably because the leaders of the S. L. P. had lost all conception of their party as one whose main purpose was to reach the people as a whole through agitation and education. Its policy had deteriorated to an exclusiveness resembling that of the would-be-aristocratic "Four Hundred." Or as Hillquit puts it, "Its methods of procedure were those of a religious sect rather than those of a political party of the masses."

Against this narrow-mindedness Mr. Sotheran with numerous other party members vented his disapproval in open criticisms. These criticisms, in place of finding hospitable welcome, were rudely treated as *lèse-majesté*, and the high officials, not having the power to say "Off with the offenders' heads!" were obliged to be content with expelling them from the party ranks. Under this régime, aptly characterized by

Lucien Saniel as "a burlesque reign of terror," not only were the disaffected members thrown out by the score, but whole recalcitrant "sections" were suspended with little ceremony. Exposed to this intolerance as a member of the National Executive Committee, it would have been impossible for one of Mr. Sotheran's temperament to have remained quiescent. Torrents of protest came from him in warnings that "unless present party tactics of personal abuse were made to give way to others more in consonance with the principles of up-to-date Socialism, the S. L. P. would be forced to put up its shutters and go out of business."

Now while Mr. Sotheran had made himself as obnoxious as his expelled confreres by his criticisms of the ruling clique, the position he held in the New York Press Club, which from 1874 he had used extensively in the party service; his position as one of the National Executive Committee, and organizer of the American Section; and his two decades of honored service in the party made the inquisitors hesitate to expel so important a person from their ranks without at least some pretence of ceremony. Reduced to this plight, two measures were open to get rid of their peace disturber. One was to worry him into resigning; this failing, to trump up some charges to give a legal show to a sentence of expulsion. Both were tried. One failed, but the other was carried out. The history of this affair makes curious reading. After a few months (1894) of what he termed "an organized policy of vendetta" confined to four members who persistently annoyed, misrepresented and interfered with his usefulness in the movement, Mr. Sotheran wrote a resignation from the National Executive Committee, but not from the party. This was not sent, as he explained later, but was held back at the urgent request of members of the American Section who found in him an ally too valuable to lose.

This withholding of his resignation, though well meant, proved unwise, for in the mean time, at a board meeting, the motion was made by one of the conspirators "to declare his seat vacant and have his successor appointed." Action was balked by the American Section, which, present in force, voted solidly against the motion.

More successful was the next move. Charges were preferred which read like lines taken from Sullivan opera bouffe. To get a verdict on these charges the methods of saloon politicians were resorted to, *i.e.*, a star chamber session. In defence of such action the conspirators gave this naïvely frank reason: "The New York Section is a 'Kangaroo' court, where Sotheran's friends would have come in force to stand by him as at the last meeting of the Section, when the attempt was made to have his seat on the National Executive Committee declared vacant and his successor appointed."

The charges by which a sentence of expulsion was reached disclose the narrow bounds in which the leaders of the S. L. P. sat entrenched. Foremost was "a too wide tolerance for progressive movements outside the Socialist party." Equal in importance was this next claim, "the utterance of heresy in his Horace Greeley book." And last, but far from least, was the charge of "writing a newspaper article in criticism of the Socialist party, its policy, and some of its members." The amusement Mr. Sotheran's friends derived from reading these formidable statements regarding his iniquitous conduct drew some of the poison from the wound inflicted by his enemies. They laughed at the notion of his "coquetting with the Populists," and said "The charge of heresy sounds as if indited by the clergy of an established church, angry because he would not subscribe to the Thirty-nine Articles of Faith." Mr. Sotheran told them: "Better would it have been for those who made the charge to let their memories hark back

to the time when my book was published and read their own
florid praises printed in their own official organ."

But the real *casus belli* was the newspaper article. This,
written anonymously by a reporter on the staff of the New
York *Sunday Advertiser*, purported to be an interview with a
Populist filled to the brim and running over with grievances
against the S. L. P. Headed "Socialism's Pets," it created
an upheaval of wrath unimaginable to-day when the party
press itself throws its columns open to discussion on all points
of doctrine, management, tactics, new and old, and even of
personalities. For some unknown reason Mr. Sotheran was
credited with being its author the day it appeared. Denials
on his part availed not. Then without investigation to discover who was the actual writer, and with no witness and no
proof other than their own say-so, he was declared to be convicted and expelled from the party without the slim courtesy
of a trial by a jury of his peers.

When Mr. Sotheran received from the Organizer of the New
York Section an account of the Tammany-like proceedings
of the clique, he sat down and wrote to the so-called "National
Board of Grievances" at Boston, where one Anton Krebs
was secretary, an appeal from the "unconstitutional, grossly
unjust and shameful decision." Annexed to this brief was a
copy of his original protest which was first made orally at a
meeting of the "illegal sub-committee" and also presented in
writing to be transmitted to the Section New York.

This protest, which seems to have been utterly ignored both
by the sub-committee and the Section, reads as follows:

"To the Comrades of the Section New York, S. L. P.:

"I hereby enter my protest against your receiving the
report of a sub-committee in any other manner than as the
report of an *initial investigation* and not as the trial of

charges made against me by Comrade De Leon as complainant for the following reasons:

"1. The Central Committee did not have a quorum at its meeting of Wednesday, July 25, and that many members were ignorant of its being in session through not being properly notified.

"2. The Central Committee has no power to try offences against members of the party, who can only be constitutionally tried by a Grievance committee of three elected by the Section in Session and to which grievance the Central Committee only has the right to refer such charges. (Constitution S. L. P., Article 9, Section 2.)

"3. Neither the Central Committee nor the Section thereof has the right to debate charges preferred in writing until such charges have been thoroughly investigated and reported upon to the Section by the Grievance committee elected in accordance with Article 9, Section 2 of the Constitution of the S. L. P.

"4. That therefore all proceedings of the Central Committee's sub-committee improperly elected under protest of members there present and sitting on the De Leon charges in debate are null and void.

"5. That the defendant only received notice of the eight o'clock session of the Central Committee's illegally elected sub-committee after 6 o'clock of the evening of July 28 . . . only thereby giving him two hours, not sufficient time to prepare his defence. . . .

"That he has had no opportunity to call witnesses in his own defence, only being notified two hours before hearing, and has been refused the right to properly cross-examine the complainant and his solitary witness, the whole proceedings being an attempt on the part of the complainant to get the Central Committee to railroad the defendant unconstitutionally and because, as the complainant, when the said sub-committee was elected, asserted, 'the New York Section was a "kangaroo" court where Sotheran's friends would come in force and stand by him' as at the last meeting of the section when he (De Leon) attempted to have Sotheran's seat on the National Executive Committee declared vacant and his successor appointed. . . .

"I rely upon the fair play of the New York Section and that it will not permit a gross outrage to be committed against the defendant, at the demand of the complainant, who as far back as June 3 did not hesitate to use the columns of the official party organ to vilify and traduce the defendant, while serving as a member of the National Executive Committee, whose interests as representing the party he has never failed to further by all means in his power and never neglected his duty while a member of that body.

"The defendant deplores the present difficulties with the complainant, that are simply the results of De Leon's hatred and jealousy. The defendant has been up to the present minute and is still willing, if he can see his way honorably to it, to do all that is possible to bring about peace, even at the sacrifice of himself, as he had already done before De Leon preferred his charges, tendering his resignation as a member of the National Executive Committee.

"In conclusion, he desires to state that his policy as a party member has ever been to defend his brothers against the whole world. In this case he has been the attacked, not the aggressor.

"Yours for Liberty,
"CHARLES SOTHERAN."

That this appeal to the National Grievance Committee had a result similar to that of his protest to the Section New

York caused no surprise to Mr. Sotheran and his friends. For a long time common talk had bruited it around that the N. G. C. was an annex to the "inner circle," the "triangle," as the ruling trio of the N. Y. S. L. P. were termed. With this failure to secure justice, Mr. Sotheran had no other option than to give up the struggle to get back his rights in the party which his own efforts had done so much to bring to the strength it had then developed. Only those who have undergone a similar experience can begin to imagine the feelings of one when alien hands have double barred the doors giving entrance to the sanctuary of his choice. To me the setting down of this portion of Mr. Sotheran's connection with the old S. L. P. is a nerve-racking torture comparable only to that—to use a metaphor of Johnson's—of "treading on ashes from which the fire has not been wholly extinguished." And my sole reason for enduring the pain is to set forth facts for coming writers, who otherwise would only have the *records* of that now discredited organization to use in their researches for Socialist happenings, from which to draw their morals or adorn their tales in historical accounts of the nineteenth century.

Characteristic of the man was the manner in which Mr. Sotheran bore his enforced retirement from Socialist party work. Having used all means available to secure a reversion of the illegal sentence so unjustly obtained, he gave up the fight. Then seeing how the whole nasty business troubled me, he gave comfort in these words: "The manner in which and the place where Socialism's message is taught matter not so much as that the teacher is inspired with its lofty ideals and understands its doctrines. Given these fundamentals, wherever instructor and listener meet, whether it be in greenwood or desert, hut or palace, there, as well as in special lecture halls, stands the temple prepared." Imbued with such sentiments, and feeling the necessity of the born agitator to agitate, he accepted an extremely cordial invitation sent from Populist headquarters. There he was given tacit liberty to use his enormous energy and talents in the propagation of his own theories. In 1896, memorable in political history as the first Bryan campaign, he with the Populists and many another good Socialist went with the crowd into that contest as well as into the Presidential mêlée that followed.

Unable to rest idle during the intervals following election campaigns, Mr. Sotheran busied himself, as a "free lance for Socialism," with social clubs and other material that offered. With Thomas B. Maguire, after the campaign of 1896, he organized a "Speakers' Club," in the Nameoki, a Democratic club composed of those who had taken the platform for Bryan. Maguire was an old-time Socialist and for long years the organizer for District 49 of the Knights of Labor. One of the incidents connected with the Nameoki was its attempted nomination of Charles Sotheran for Assemblyman. This, as a Socialist, he of course refused, putting up in his place a young plumber, who was elected. Under Sotheran's instructions this youth had imbibed a fairly good idea of Socialist doctrine. When his term was ended he came to us saying: "No more Tammany for me! Why, a speaking doll would do as much good as a man. In that Legislature no one has any chance of putting bills of his own through: all he is allowed to do is to follow Croker's deputy and when he pulls the string vote 'Yes' or 'No' as he says 'Thumbs up or Thumbs down.' The plumbing business after this is good enough for me. In that I am at least half a man!"

Another club which Mr. Sotheran frequented during those years, when forced to carry his Socialist torch into alien fields, was the Social Reform Club. This club following in the footsteps of the English Fabians was willing to work with any body of people advocating needed reforms. When twitted by friends for belonging to a reform club, Mr. Sotheran answered that he enjoyed the men he met there such as Ernest Crosby, Henry Leipziger, W. S. Rainsford, John Brisben Walker, W. J. Ghent, and others — fine scholars with whom it was a pleasure to discuss and debate living world issues. Then too, he said, "the audiences which are drawn to listen to the lectures and hear the subjects thrashed out are intelligent, earnest men and women able to throw aside old, worn-out superstitions for new and higher moral truths; people who doubtless later will be found in the Socialist movement."

Next and the last thing to engage the attention of Mr. Sotheran was the proposal to found a People's Institute, *i.e.*, a place where educational lectures on art, science, music, etc., were to be given free to all who wished to attend them. His name is to be found on the prospectus as one of the Institute's incorporators. That the work of the Institute appealed to him he showed by his presence—in spite of his fast-failing health—whenever measures of vital importance to the community were up for discussion. One of these occurred in 1899, when, although very ill, he attended, as one of the vice-presidents, a mass meeting held under the auspices of the Institute, to protest against the giving away in perpetuity the contemplated subway franchise. The scope of the People's Institute was so wide that it enlisted the co-operation at once of many progressive thinkers. Of these the most radical was J. G. Phelps Stokes, who, soon seeing the hopelessness of striving to patch the diseases of the body politic with reform plasters, turned to Socialism. He was made chairman, while the energetic and capable Charles Sprague Smith was its Managing Director. The popularity gained under his management brought from Mr. Sotheran ungrudging praise, in that, as he said, "His energies were given not for his own material success, but for that higher thing as he saw it—the advancement of the common good."

This sketch of Mr. Sotheran's connection with the People's Institute, brings to a close his career among the reformers as Socialist agitator. And, lest we forget, let it be said once more, that these labors were forced upon him. For over two score years his fight had been waged within the ranks of dear Socialist comrades and not until no other choice was left did he transfer his energies to non-Socialist organizations. That work done on these lines in company with his few Socialist comrades placed in the same situation with himself, had been fruit-bearing, was made manifest in the socio-political character of lectures featured regularly on reform club cards and posters; in the greater attention given Socialist matters in the public press, and the growing insistent demand in public libraries for books bearing on Socialism.

Encouraging as, in a way, this was, it was far from satisfying to one like Mr. Sotheran, who had labored for the establishment of other conditions. Often in his home talks he would say: "Nothing in all the world is so soul-inspiring to a Socialist as being in a state of oneness with his party. Working with it deep down in his heart is a feeling different in a higher degree from that experienced by members of other creeds. He, with his comrades, may take issue on points of tactics; but, however partisan the strife in its fervor, the primal bond at its close will remain unstrained. The true Socialist clasping hands with his comrades will agree on fighting to the death for the bringing about the Socialist commonwealth, the realization of the promised heaven on earth of Jesus, the day when little children shall have their inheritance of joy, when Love shall banish hatred, and peace and good will be the portion of all mankind." Inspired with such feelings,

Mr. Sotheran longed with more intensity than most are capable of, for the building of a new Socialist temple, a home wherein he could work once more with comrades in the open. Of this desire he spoke frequently, and together we searched the columns of papers such as the *Coming Nation* and later the *Appeal to Reason*, to find whether there was any probability of such organization being founded. But, nothing was to be met with except accounts of the establishment of Socialist colonies, and to colonization schemes Mr. Sotheran was unalterably opposed.

In this way days wore on until 1897, when tidings came from our old friend, Col. Richard J. Hinton, telling of a new party that was being organized in Chicago. The name of this new party, he wrote, was to be the *Social Democracy of America*. Hinton soon followed his letter, coming purposely to New York to use his personal influence with Mr. Sotheran and some few other friends, former members of the S. L. P., to come into the organization. Memory recalls how Hinton remained as our guest for several days and nights; how he pictured in glowing language the beauties of the scheme he was sponsoring. As we listened our countenances fell, for the plan when unfolded was one of colonization. He told how a large tract of land in Cripple Creek, Colorado, had been secured, and he expatiated upon the attractive homes and stately public buildings which, when erected, would give world-wide publicity to the place. This, with the colony conducted under a strict Socialist régime,—sure of success— would secure its spread throughout the State, and in time enable the pioneers to conquer the entire State government.

To all this Mr. Sotheran listened attentively. Only when his friend stopped to seek his approval did he raise his head to say regretfully: "While I feel sorry for your disappointment, my dear Richard, when I tell you I do not believe in the

colony project, and will not go into it, I'm still more sorry
for myself, for the blighted hopes your letter conjured up of
an organization adapted to the character of the American
people in which I could once more become an ardent useful
worker. As to the isolated community groups based on
Socialistic theories of living, yours will be what these have
ever been and always must be—a failure. The dividing line
—which, thin as a hair separates them from the surrounding
competitive system—cannot prevent this system from break-
ing into and destroying the isolated community groups.
But, my objection to joining your colony is not so much the
idea of failure as a strong conviction that Socialistic work
must be done in places where the world's workers hive; the
Socialist agitator must live in cities, mill-towns, mining districts, to teach the exploited a knowledge of the wrongs they
are up against and show them how to break from slavery into
freedom, how through an intelligent use of the ballot they will
gain the right to live life's highest best."

Hinton, with the courage of conviction, clung to his colony
scheme, but other New York comrades turned a deaf ear to
the colonization plan and he left New York, a keenly disappointed man. He must have been still more discouraged
with the after fate of the Social Democracy, which, while
carrying its point regarding the establishment of colonies,
quietly deceased in setting up two small ones in the State of
Washington.

Fortunately for Socialism, an earnest minority of the delegates to the Social Democracy of America repudiated, as Mr.
Sotheran had done, the colonization idea at the convention
held in Chicago in June, 1898. This minority bolted the
convention hall, and, betaking themselves elsewhere, got
together like practical men, organized a political party, named
it the Social Democratic Party of America, and elected a

national Executive Board, consisting of Eugene V. Debs, Victor L. Berger, Jesse Cox, Seymour Stedman and Frederick Heath. Months passed before news of this important event reached Mr. Sotheran in his quiet home. Then, just as we were giving vent to our delight over the birth of this new Socialist party, rumors came of a squabble in the first national convention wherein the climax of confusion worse confounded arose over the question of fusion between the Social Democratic Party and a seceding faction of the S. L. P. A temporary union was patched up for the campaign of 1900, but it was not till 1901 at Indianapolis that the several elements were united into the Socialist Party. The De Leon faction of the S. L. P. was the only Socialist element of any importance that refused to unite. A significant thing about this 1901 convention was its make-up. Out of the whole number of delegates (124) not more than 25, it is said, were foreign born. Socialism had at last become naturalized, had taken, as was said at the time, "such firm root in the soil that it could no longer be jeer'd at as a foreign exotic, as anti-American in its character, as something evil to be destroyed at all hazards."

This grateful news, through the kindness of his friend, Mr. Ghent—one of the most frequent of his radical visitors—reached Mr. Sotheran during sad days of illness in 1901. He had voted for Debs and Harriman the previous year, and he now took the liveliest interest in the new party. That he did not become an active member was due only to a fear that the S. L. P. might unite with it and become influential in its councils. "Were this possibility eliminated," he prophesied, "it would be the destiny of this fresh young force to create a splendid new era in Socialist politics, since the new party has come into the world armed with the lofty ideals of the utopian era; the scientific knowledge of the Marxian era and the spirit of the struggling, battling, fighting organization era.

Hers will be the era of adjustment and unification; seeing and avoiding the mistakes of the Past and accepting, enlarging all that evolution brings of good." In 1902 when the possibility was gone forever of an alliance with the S. L. P., the noble, generous, and kindly heart of Mr. Sotheran had ceased to beat. How noble in its loyalty to an ideal this great heart was, can best be illustrated by a fact known only to myself: Believing that the hope of the world lay in the acceptance of Socialism, despite the insults—gross in their implications— hurled at him and given nation-wide publicity by De Leon and his two associates, he never wavered in his party allegiance so far as his vote was concerned. After each election he would return home with: "Well, once more I've voted the Socialist Party ticket straight! Socialism is too vast an issue for any man to permit personal grievances, however great their magnitude, to conflict with the imperative duty of striving by all means to hasten the day of its coming."

Mr. Sotheran died on June 26, 1902. When his mortal frame was laid in Mother Earth, to sleep that long, long sleep which knows no waking, the organ of the party to which he had given the best efforts of his best years took no notice of the event. This neglect was held to be because the *genius loci* would say no good, yet dared not blame in face of the eulogistic press comments, all of which rang the same note of sorrow, "that in the death of Charles Sotheran literature and journalism on both sides of the Atlantic suffer a loss which it will be difficult to repair." All paid tribute to his scholarship, his wit, his heart tender as a child's; his open hand ever ready to help a less fortunate toiler over the road which he himself was tramping. There is nothing strange that in the ordinary type of journalistic summing up of Mr. Sotheran's career, no hint was given concerning his active work for Socialism. To the regular newspaper writer, a belief in Socialism was a hallucination that it was a kindness to conceal.

In little more than a decade the practical idealists of the Socialist Party have through their writings, their speeches and their shop-talks among their fellow toilers, caused a vast change of opinion concerning Socialism among the masses. The fruits of this activity are seen in the splendid growth of the Socialist movement, whose aim is to overthrow the whole capitalist system, with all its told and untold horrors, and to erect in its place a sanely ordered government in the interests of the people as a whole. In the midst of the grandeur of this thought, the hopefulness of this, the present outlook, my reminiscences are brought to a close. They have reached only thus far because, carried to my ears, through the ringing of the joybells of approaching victory, has come the knowledge that the great, splendid body of comrades fighting shoulder to shoulder to inaugurate the co-operative commonwealth have given the name of Charles Sotheran that honored place which is its due on the Roster of Pioneer American Socialists.

PROEM.

THIS volume—*Horace Greeley and other Pioneers of American Socialism*—is neither biographical nor scientific, in the full sense of those words. Yet it partakes of both characters, albeit a sociological *olla podrida* with a modicum of seasoning *à la doctrinaire*. It has been written, however, with distinctly positive objects in mental view.

During the many years that I have been a Constitutional State Socialist I have found myself confronted with two serious obstacles blocking the path of my attempts to arouse my fellow American citizens from their political and economic lethargy. One of these hindrances has been willful literary misrepresentation and the other, woful ignorance of Social Science. The latter has been too frequently a result of the former. Strange as it may seem to minds of culture, the great majority of people in the United States still believe that Socialism and Anarchism are one and the same thing, never dreaming that there is a sharp distinction, if not an actual antagonism,—both theoretical and practical,—between the two.

My main object in having taken the Founder of the New York *Tribune*,—and presented him under various aspects, but always as a Socialistic example so to say, in order "to point a moral and adorn a tale,"—was not only to throw light on the darkness I have suggested, but to help in dispelling a few of the mists of unwarranted prejudice.

Horace Greeley, thus exhibited as a central figure, has enabled me to show Socialism in its true colors and as being constructive in its economic philosophy and constitutional in its political action.

I have also proved, in what I consider to be a satisfactory manner, that Socialism, so far from being of comparatively recent foreign importation to this country,—as fallaciously and popularly believed,—is really less European in origin than it is American in evolutionary development.

Organized Industry, as it has recently displayed itself to the community under such semi-Socialistic phases as the Farmers' Alliances, the Knights of Labor and other agricultural and manufacturing solidarities, I think has been demonstrated in the pages of this work to have imbibed much of its inspiration from the agitation undertaken over half a century ago in the Eastern States, through the propaganda then carried on by such agitators with pen and voice as Horace Greeley and his associates—George Henry Evans, Robert Dale Owen, Thomas Skidmore, Albert Brisbane, Parke Godwin, Charles A. Dana and others of the New York and Massachusetts groups of Socialists,

Political developments, furthermore, in the trend of the future Coöperative Commonwealth, such as the Nationalists, the People's Party and similar types, I have traced to the same incentives, which were but outgrowths of the Abolition Movement, that being in its turn the child of the political movement in New York State during 1826–1830, in the Tenth Plank of whose Platform was demanded "the abolition of chattel slavery and of wages slavery."

And it has not been forgotten that a fervent Socialist must be a good Christian from the economic standpoint of those primitive believers who had all things in common.

I have endeavored to make several other important points. One of these is that the very ancient "chestnut" and vulgar notion of Socialists wanting "to divide property up, giving every one an equal share," is the exact opposite of the truth,—for what they actually wish is that national wealth shall belong to the national collectivity, and that every one in the community shall have the absolute ownership, or rather the full value of the products of his or her labor. Another point is that Socialism, when finally accomplished, will, under the new conditions of scientific civilization, mean the greatest possible individual liberty for one and all, with due regard to the body social, economic and political,—and certainly not a continuance of the suppression of individualism under a spurious system of freedom of contract with practical annihilation of one's personality, in that physical and mental purgatory which is the general lot of the millions of the population of this Republic under the present Industrial System of Capitalistic Anarchy. Still another point made is, that "bad times" have always existed in America for most of our *bourgeoisie* or middle class, and more particularly for the whole of the proletariat; and that only those of their particular epoch who have been exempt therefrom were the Plutocrats.

But what has been to me a great delight in the compilation of this volume has been the production of the evidence, that the majority of the best authors of the United States have fought with their good pens on the side of Socialism. Let any one of my readers carefully scan the names of those Pioneers, who illumine the pages of this work, and I defy him or her to specify either creed or party in this country that can produce as the peers of these Socialists, as good citizens or their superiors in intellectual gifts!

What a galaxy of genius was represented by the editorial staff of the New York *Tribune*, when it was a Collectivist newspaper; and even yet more brilliant were the contributors to the Brook Farm *Harbinger*, the immediate organ of the American Socialists of half a century ago, under the editorship of George Ripley and Charles Anderson Dana.

Here are some of them :—Nathaniel Hawthorne, Theodore Parker, Ralph Waldo Emerson, Margaret Fuller, Horace Greeley, James Russell Lowell, John Greenleaf Whittier, William Wetmore Story, Henry David Thoreau,

Albert Brisbane, Parke Godwin, Amos Bronson Alcott, James Freeman Clarke, Thomas Wentworth Higginson, Robert Dale Owen, Frederic Henry Hedge, George William Curtis, the three Channings,—William Henry, William Ellery and Walter,—Orestes Augustus Brownson; and many others could be added whose names are also American "household words."

Yet, with all the possibility of literary enlightenment as to what Socialism was, not only had it, to use the words of Octavius Brooks Frothingham,* "a feeble hand in this country," after the death of the *Harbinger* in 1849, but a gloomier than Egyptian darkness environed it about, except where the sacred fire was kept alive by a few ardent souls like Horace Greeley. And the darkness has continued to our own day, but now the modern Socialist Movement,†— based on Science and Progress,—has come forth like the Phœnix to achieve International triumphs.

But during that period of mental *sheol* adverted to, new generations arose and the great mass of Americans knew not Socialism; and the result of such ignorance among other instances was, that on October 8, 1887, a

---

* *Transcendentalism in New England*, page 331.

† The final official returns of the vote cast by counties in the State of New York for the Socialist Labor Party ticket on November 3, 1891, were:—For Governor, Daniel De Leon, 14,651 votes; for Lieutenant-Governor, Frank Gesser, 14,644; for Secretary of State, Frederick Bennetts, 14,384; for Comptroller, Henry Vitalius, 14,708; for Attorney-General, Henry G. Wilshire, 14,710; for Treasurer, James Withers, 14,824; for State Engineer and Surveyor, Charles Wilson, 14,755 votes.

little over four years ago, in the Empire City of "the home
of the brave and the land of the free,"—where free assemblage and free speech are supposed to be guaranteed,—I
saw several hundred policemen, armed with revolvers and
clubs, but without warrant of law, throw themselves upon
a body of unarmed and peaceable Socialists, whom they
grossly assaulted, although those treated so violently had
not interfered with anybody and were meeting on the
Union Square Plaza lawfully, and in accordance with the
United States Constitution.   And I also distinctly remember how on October 9, 1879, in the presence of half a dozen
"preservers of the peace" and in consequence of my deliv-
ering a propagandist speech at an agitation meeting of the
Socialist Labor Party at Walhalla Hall, Orchard Street, I
was murderously attacked by some thirty to forty members
of the dominant political faction of New York city and
was left lying on the public street for dead.

It can be asked, Why mention these matters here? My
answer is, Because to my mind the acts committed prove
gross public ignorance as to the law-abiding and orderly
character of the Socialists, and show the essential importance of such educational books as this volume, to aid in
having us protected from being bludgeoned to death, or
otherwise assassinated by hired ruffians and political swash-
bucklers.   I will further add, that at the very time both
these shameful occurrences happened, men who years
before had habitually addressed Socialistic agitation meet-

ings themselves, using nearly the same arguments that I had done, and who had been the principal contributors in the 'forties to the *Harbinger*, were editors-in-chief of leading American newspapers. Still there was not an editorial ripple perceived worth the name; not a journalistic voice was raised in protest; and the crimes committed went on unpunished to be repeated again and again! Alleged Public Opinion had apparently followed the legendary example of Rip Van Winkle!

And what did the Socialist editors promise the world at Brook Farm in 1845, nigh upon fifty years ago? They asserted that—

"The interests of Social Reform will be considered as paramount to all others. . . . We shall suffer no attachment to literature, no taste for abstract discussion, no love of purely intellectual theories, to seduce us from our devotion to the cause of the oppressed, the down-trodden, the insulted and injured masses of our fellow-men. *Every pulsation of our being vibrates in sympathy with the wrongs of the toiling millions; and every wise effort for their speedy enfranchisement will find in us resolute and indomitable advocates.* If any imagine from the literary tone of the preceding remarks that we are indifferent to the *radical movement* for the benefit of the masses which is *the crowning glory of the nineteenth century*, they will soon discover their egregious mistake. To that movement, consecrated by religious principle, sustained by an awful sense of justice and cheered by the brightest hopes of future good, all our powers, talents and attainments are devoted.   We look for an audience among the refined and educated circles. . . . ; *but we shall also be read by the swart and sweaty artisan; the laborer will find in us another champion; and many hearts struggling with the secret hope which no weight of care and toil can entirely suppress, will pour on us their benedictions, as we labor for the equal rights of all.''*

The earnest Socialist arguments of George Ripley and Charles A. Dana quoted above,—and they are such as Horace Greeley, George William Curtis, Albert Brisbane and Parke Godwin urged a hundred times and more,— these it is that, with many additional reasons, inspired me to write this book; and although others may have been recreant to their pledges and fallen by the wayside, I devoutly hope my readers will remain steadfast to the cause, whether they accept now or may believe later, the Sacred Truth according to Socialism.

CHARLES SOTHERAN.

New York Press Club,
> November, 1891.

HORACE GREELEY

AND OTHER PIONEERS.

CHAPTER I.

SOCIALISM IS NOT ANARCHISM.

OUR Later Franklin, as the poet John Greenleaf Whittier once designated Horace Greeley, was one of those noble souls associated with what has been styled the renaissance of New England literature, who earliest apprehended and taught the truths of Socialism to the people of the United States of America. He never wearied in the good work of propaganda by both pen and voice. The movement itself may have changed in its methods and assumed a wider scope in the four essentials of "agitation, education, organization and action," but its final objects and fundamental principles remain the same. And when the triumph of the Coöperative Commonwealth will be assured and the Emancipation of Labor accomplished, the work of Horace Greeley will be recognized by grateful generations, and will not be hidden out of sight and mind, as it has been, from the multitude, by those interested in keeping the American proletariat ignorant of economic truth and in the condition of wage-slaves.

The fact that "the editor of the *Tribune* was a Socialist years before the *Tribune* came into existence," has never been denied by friend or foe.   On the contrary the statement just quoted was written by Greeley's biographer, James Parton, who, as well as his wife Fanny Fern, and her brother, N. P. Willis the poet, the great editor's friends, many a time listened to his expositions of Socialism privately and from the rostrum, or perused them in the New York *Tribune* and in his printed works, as did forty to fifty years ago hundreds of thousands of his compatriots throughout the length and breadth of the United States.   In those days social and economic reform was more or less of a fashionable and intellectual "fad," and was rarely sneered at or libeled, for the names of many of America's famous authors and thinkers were identified with the progressive movement, of which the avowed purpose was to reorganize civilization on a Socialistic basis.   Fortunately there is a literature of the subject, which those who run may read, and from its neglected pages, a narrative will be now unfolded for those who have neither the leisure nor the inclination to hunt it out from among the dusty bookshelves.   It is not the present intention, however, to offer a biography, for Greeley's own *Recollections of a Busy Life*, and Parton's admirable *Life of Horace Greeley*, are easily accessible to all and will be found satisfactorily to meet this suggestion of his made in 1846 :—"If, on a full and final review, my life and practice shall be found unworthy of my principles, let due infamy be heaped on my memory ; but let none be thereby led to distrust the principles to which I proved recreant, nor yet the ability of some to adorn them by a suitable life and conversation.   To unerring time be all this committed."

The two works named are voluminous enough to meet

the desires of the most critical, except perhaps as to the social and economic labors of his life now under considera-tion. But nevertheless it may be desirable here to give a few brief biographical data, leaving any others to develop themselves as needed.

Horace Greeley, who was the son of a farmer, was born at Amherst, New Hampshire, on February 3, 1811. He was apprenticed to a printer at East Poultney, Vermont, on April 18, 1826, previous to which time he had either helped at farming or attended school. At the termination of his apprenticeship, he "tramped" westward toward New York City, which he reached on or about August 17, 1831, after picking up a few odd printing jobs at different places on his route. Ten years after settling in the Empire City the farmer-compositor was one of the proprietors and the editor of the New York *Tribune*, of which he issued the first number April 10, 1841, and with which he was asso-ciated for the rest of his life. He was nominated for the Presidency of the United States at Cincinnati, Ohio, on May 3, 1872, by the National Liberal Republican Conven-tion. His life until his death on November 29, 1872, at Pleasantville, Westchester County, in the State of New York, was mainly spent in the great American metropolis, in the City Hall whereof, thousands upon thousands did reverence to his memory, when his corpse lay there in state : it was afterwards carried through the densely crowded streets of Manhattan Island,—with the President, Vice-President and Chief Justice of the United States and the leading men of all classes, beliefs and parties, assisting in the procession to the grave.

What were the causes that made Horace Greeley a Socialist? Why was he so earnest in the cause of indus-trial reform? And, in what, if he was really a Socialist, did his Socialism differ from that of both his predecessors and successors in that line of thought and action?

Pertinent questions these, yet to the minds of possibly ninety-five per cent. of his fellow citizens the idea that Horace Greeley, the whilom editor of the present conservative and aristocratic New York *Tribune*, had anything in common with what a Socialist is unhappily, but popularly conceived to be, would be scouted as both absurd and preposterous, on the face of it. This is not to be wondered at in the present mental, social, political and industrial bondage of the masses, who necessarily think of Socialists much as the average Roman citizen under Nero regarded those primitive Christians* whom he had seen thrown to the lions in the Colosseum. They were, he argued, disaffected and dangerous foreigners, who proposed to destroy the civilization of the mistress of the world; who would make the rich patricians give up all they possessed to the poor plebeians; who shouted such violent demagoguery as that no man of wealth, when dead, could see the Gods face to face in the Elysian Fields; who held that the goods of all should be held collectively and in common; and who in other treasonable ways merited the fate of making sport for a Roman holiday in the Flavian Amphitheater.

Such questions as those suggested would be doubtless, therefore, nonsensical to the great majority, who confuse in their minds, if even they have ever been permitted to know, the difference between Communism and Socialism, to say nothing of that between those extreme opposites,—

---

* The Socialist teachings and lives of the primitive Christians were the principal charges that Tertullian, who died in the Third century, had to defend them against in his famous "Apologia." The cultured Roman of those days cared little for his Pantheon, but a good deal for his wealth and power. The attack on these was, therefore, the greatest of alleged Christian crimes.

Anarchism and Socialism. And given to the rabble a choice, they would naturally select Barabbas rather than Christ in all things.

The broad, general distinctions defined by Noah Webster's "Unabridged," the great American authority, are, under such circumstances, plainly in order and certainly necessary. One's terminology may be misunderstood through popular misapplication and perpetual misinformation, whether it come about in the shape of an entire Papal Encyclical from the Vatican, or a malicious paragraph in a sensational newspaper hawked along the public streets by one of the wretchedly clad, barefooted and hungry waifs of our alleged civilization.

SOCIALISM, Webster defines as :—"A theory of society which advocates a more precise, orderly, and harmonious arrangement of the social relations of mankind than that which has hitherto prevailed."

But there are believers and believers accepting various grades of Socialism, yet who belong to what may be termed the same generic family, as for instance,—the Utopian Socialists, the Theoretical Socialists, the Community Socialists, the Associationist Socialists, the Coöperative Socialists, the Industrial Socialists, the Art Socialists, the Christian Socialists and the Political Socialists, which last style themselves the only "practical" body of the progressive movement, as they unite within themselves all the forces of all, whether idealistic, altruistic, coöperative, economic, collectivist, nationalist or political.

And there is Society itself, which is more or less Socialistic as represented by all the forces immediately controlled by the Government and Congress of the United States, and the administrations of the individual States, their counties and townships. These are Collectively

Communistic in the ownership of considerable real estate, machinery and other wealth. But they are State Socialistic in the exploitation of the different public functions of the "labor" employed by the people,—from the President of the United States down to the scrubwoman in a public building; and which hired "labor" again, as the vast body of office-holders—postmen, school-teachers, firemen, police, printers, clerks and other handicrafts—in numerous ways produce and distribute necessities, or perform needed services for the Social Commonwealth—as now empirically organized under the American Constitution—yet far better than individualistic and anarchic capitalism could undertake them under the competitive system for the Collectivity.

COMMUNISM, the national lexicographic authority tells us, means:—"Community of property among all the citizens of a State; a state of things in which there are no individual or separate rights in property;" etc. And to pursue the matter further, a "Community" is according to Webster:—"A society of people having common rights and privileges, or common interests, civil, political, or ecclesiastical; or living under the same laws and regulations; as a community of monks." Thus there have been Communists and Communists, notably the Conservative Communists or regular orders of the Roman Catholic Church, who have lived as religious communities from the dawn of mediæval Christianity—and the Radical Communists recently represented by those who whilom were besieged in Paris and fought under the red flag of the Commune, as their apologists claim for their municipal liberty, as well as for the rights of Humanity.

ANARCHY, Webster asserts to be :—"Want of government; a state of society when there is no law or supreme power, or when the laws are not efficient, and individuals do what they please with impunity ;"—and an "Anarchist" as :—"One who excites revolt or promotes disorder (*i. e.*, a rioter) in a State." Richard T. Ely,* Professor of Polit- ical Economy in Johns Hopkins University can well be heard from on this point. He writes in his *Labor Move- ment in America* that :—"The Members of the Socialistic Labor Party realize full well that they have little in common with the Anarchists. A pamphlet has recently (1886) been published by the National Executive Committee of this party entitled *Socialism and Anarchy—Antagonistic Opposites.* In the first paragraph the writer says :— 'Socialism and Anarchism are opposites . . . . . . Socialists and Anarchists, as such, are enemies. They pursue contrary aims, and the success of the former will forever destroy the fanatical hopes of the latter.' The Socialists are weak in Chicago because the Anarchists are strong. They claim that if they had had more influence in that city, the horrible tragedy of May 4, 1886, would never have occurred. It is true that they have condemned every proposal of such acts as madness."

Prof. Ely, however, not being a member of the Social- istic Labor Party of the United States and therefore unable to speak *ex cathedra*, Daniel De Leon,† late Professor of

---

* Socialists are under a deep debt of obligation to Prof. Ely for his honest and careful analytical criticism of their movement. It would be as well if all other authors were as conscientious as he has shown himself to be in—*French and German Socialism of Modern Times* and *The Labor Movement in America*, the eighth to twelfth chapters inclusive, of the last named of which de- mand more consideration at the hands of economists and journal- ists, than they have apparently hitherto received.

† Here is, although not of American aboriginal stock, a genuine "old American," who bears the surname of Juan Ponce De Leon, the discoverer of Florida in the Sixteenth Century. Prof. De Leon is a native of Guyana in South America, his ancestors having emi- grated from Spain to America in 1562. When this ardent apostle of Socialism,—who has stumped for the cause from the Atlantic to

International Law at Columbia College, was requested to furnish responses from his personal standpoint to these three queries :—

I. "What is the Socialistic Labor Party?"

II. "How does the S. L. P. differ in principles from the Communists?"

III. "In what way do the members of the S. L. P. vary in doctrine from the Anarchists?"

These are what can be considered the authoritative answers of Prof. De Leon, who has been of late the standard-bearer of the Socialists, having run on their political ticket for the Governorship of the State of New York.:—

I. "The Socialist Labor Party is the practical side of scientific political economy and of the philosophy of history. Fourier, St. Simon and Owen, and before them Harrington, Sir Thomas More and Plato were all Utopian Socialists. The development of industry and the laws of sociology could not in those early days be known. In our own days, sufficient facts are in court to justify conclusions. Socialism, accordingly, has gone through its stage of Utopia and reached the present one where, grounded on facts, not on aspirations, the agitation can be carried on. This is the economic law : Competition destroys profits through the planlessness and wastefulness of competitive production. As soon as this is ascertained by the capitalists they set about removing the evil, and with a correct instinct begin to combine and concentrate their capital. Concentration of capital is equivalent to the perfection of machinery. This has for its effect to reduce the quantities of labor power

___

the Pacific,—graduated from Columbia College in 1878 he took both the prizes in Constitutional and International Law,—the two awarders being William Beach Lawrence, Governor of Rhode Island and editor of Wheaton's *International Law*, and Theodore Dwight Woolsey, President of Yale College and author of the *Introduction to the Study of International Law.*

necessary to production, and in general to reduce the cost of production. Two important things result therefrom. On the one hand, competition becomes harder and harder, and ultimately expires in the trust. On the other hand, wages steadily decline and are furthermore pushed below the point of the exchange value of labor power, owing to the large army of the unemployed which is produced by the displacement of machinery. The statistics of labor in this country, false as they are to a great extent, bear a sad proof of this statement. As a further result of it all, the productiveness of labor is held far below its powers, and want for the many, abundance for the few become inevitable. These being inseparable causes and effects, the land and all other instruments of production must be owned by the people, if involuntary poverty is to be abolished. Already we have Socialism for the few at the expense of the many in the shape of the trusts. We aim to Socialize the trust and establish Socialism for all at the expense of none. There is no valid reason why all the industries of the nation should not be owned by the nation as it owns the Post Office.

II. "Communism differs from Socialism as Federalism differed from Anti-Federalism in this country. To each according to his deed, say the Socialists. The Communists say, from each according to his power, to each according to his needs. The latter principle implies a greater concentration of collective functions than Socialists are ready to accept. But for the same reason that the question of Federalism or Anti-Federalism could not come up until the political Republic was established, there is no occasion to discuss to-day the relative merits of Socialism and Communism until the Industrial Republic is on foot."

III. 'You should not mention the word Anarchist without first defining it. There is quite a variety of them.

"In the first place you have the *bona fide* Anarchists. They are impatient Socialists. They do not believe, as we do, in the efficacy of the ballot but would rush to arms. They are to the main body of the Socialists what the John Brown wing was to the main body of the Abolitionists or Republicans. They entertain for us an inveterate hatred, imputing our deliberation and peaceful methods to cowardice. On the other hand, we feel greatly outraged at their ravings, which, we consider, delay the movement.

"Secondly, you have the *mala fide* Anarchists, of whom Benjamin R. Tucker, of Boston, is the patron saint. Their motto is no *Arch* or Head or Government. Yet their parliamentary practice gives the lie to their preachings. A people's parliamentary practice is the microcosmos of its social institutions. The chairman of these Anarchists has the power to make rulings from which there is no appeal, to the members only the cold comfort is left that they can secede. One-man power, *i. e.*, popular slavery, is the outcome of such principles. We believe in liberty, therefore, in Democracy.

"Then also you have among the Anarchists a set which might be styled the 'Innocents'; They are a tepid crew. They do not want force as do the *bona fide* ones, and they actually do not want any law, government, or arch. They ignore the teaching of history, that where the pen does not write, the sword carves out the law; that where no arch is provided for by statute it is superimposed by the fist or the bayonet, as the case may be. In other words, these, while they mean well, would bring us to where the human race started from, in the inexperience of its infancy.

"These are the three main types. In between them are numerous shades. But with neither shades nor types have we any contact."

There is plenty of other reliable evidence as to the relative positions of those antitheses, Socialism and Anarchy, and which it is necessary, in order to do justice to the good fame of Horace Greeley, to have thoroughly settled before entering at length into his personal advocacy of Socialism.

Prof. De Leon is milder in his utterances than many other Altruistic Socialists, as to the Ultra-Individualistic Anarchists who, as stated, for some inconceivable reason, are confounded as one and the same by both the public and the press. It is correct to state that American Socialists as a rule believe the followers of John Most to be cranks and worse than cranks. They are neither more nor less, it is charged, than monomaniacal destructionists. Destruction of everything, including themselves—that is the Anarchistic doctrine, and for expounding which they should be placed under restraint, the same as other "irresponsible" persons, before they are allowed an opportunity of being dangerous.

Edward Bellamy, the founder of Nationalist Socialism, hit the mark exactly in his delightful *Looking Backward*, when he described them as those who "wave the red flag and talk about burning, sacking and blowing people up, in order, by alarming the timid, to head off any real reforms." It is this excuse, which is generally urged, that keeps the middle-class economic reformers in dread of and away from the Labor Movement, notwithstanding that in their heart of hearts, like Mirabeau, too many of them say, "The people, yes, I love the people, but at a distance." Worse than all, it has terrified and alienated the proletarian masses and hindered large numbers from joining forces with the progressive army of organized industry as originally outlined by Horace Greeley. When this is understood it will be plainly seen that Jay Gould, the Vanderbilts, the

Astors and other plutocrats have no better workers than the Anarchists. Yet "there is balm in Gilead" even in this, for the Monarchs of Capitalism, the Barons of the Stock and other Exchanges galore, the Trusts and Syndicates are, by their concentration of wealth, that mainly consists of the results of labor, and the crushing out of existence of the middle-class, gradually but surely thus helping the Socialists in the organization of capital for the future definitive coöperative civilization.

The Tucker group of Anarchists referred to by Prof. De Leon learned their dogmas from the teacher of the idea that "property is robbery," Proudhon, the mental father of Josiah Warren, of Boston, who taught the theory of the absolute sovereignty of the individual, as did the disciple of the last named, Stephen Pearl Andrews, a native of Massachusetts and the soi-disant "Pantarch of the Universe," who managed to decoy Horace Greeley into a discussion on "Free Love" * in the columns of the *Tribune*, and be it said, to his disgust, for Greeley loved his children and honored his wife,—who was that blessing of blessings, a refined, faithful and loyal lady, in the true sense of the term. He believed in the home and the family. Andrews was the author of the *Basic Outline of Universology* and of the

---

* It has been deemed not only unnecessary, but undesirable to enter in these pages into such questions as either the domestic or other relations of the sexes, which the author for one considers no present vital issue of modern Socialism, except so far as the competition of woman with man industrially is concerned. Yet Bebel has written a volume with which large numbers of Socialists disagree, giving his *personal* views on *Woman and Socialism.* Mary Wollstonecraft's *A Vindication of the Rights of Woman*, (Humboldt Library of Popular Science) can be studied with advantage from the standpoint of an eighteenth century reformer. Those, however, who wish to understand Greeley's views on another aspect of the subject are referred to pages 570–618 of his *Recollections of a Busy Life,* where will be found in its entirety—"Marriage and Divorce, a Discussion between Horace Greeley and Robert Dale Owen."

Science of Society, which he wrote after his conversion to Anarchism by Warren in 1850. A favorite author with the Anarchists is Herbert Spencer,* whom they claim as a teacher, and respecting whom one of the "Chicago Martyrs," Albert R. Parsons, wrote as follows in 1885 in his organ, the *Alarm:*—"Herbert Spencer has done much to break attachment to the principle of authority in attempting to specify the limits of the State."

Bakounine and Proudhon combined are the originators of the teachings of the Communistic Anarchists. These firebrands have got their incendiary work in among the handful of German American labor organizations which, repudiating Socialism, follow the black flag of the International Working People's Association. Their leader is John Most, who everybody knows was hounded out of Europe and has been a chronic jail-bird for his rabid utterances in both hemispheres. Their "ism" is "individualism gone mad," to use the words of the English Socialist agitator Henry Mayers Hyndman,† who thoroughly knows the use of words, being a graduate of Trinity College, Cambridge, and a barrister of the Inner Temple, London.

The Anarchists have no definite platform of principles, but at Pittsburg years ago the Internationalists in convention made one for them, to which many of them more or less adhere. Its principal dogma, in their own words, is

* An analysis of *The Economics of Herbert Spencer* has lately been issued in the Social Science Library, published by the Humboldt Publishing Co., wherein it is claimed among other things that Spencer's land theory forms the basis of Henry George's *Progress and Poverty.*

† H. M. Hyndman was the special war correspondent of the *Pall Mall Gazette* during the Franco-Italian War in 1866. He is the author of half a dozen books or more, principally on Socialism. Although Socialists repudiate leaders, he is the nearest approach to what may be considered one, and is the practical head of the Social Democratic Federation of Great Britain and Ireland, which is probably over a million strong.

"Destruction of the existing class rule by all means, *i. e.*, by energetic, relentless, revolutionary and international action." Their economic ideas are most vague, but many believe in voluntary associations holding property together in common.

Individual Sovereignty is their shibboleth, and at this shrine they sing the pæan: "Do what you please, and no public authority shall be allowed to interfere with any one; there shall be no property, no law, no state, no family, no religion, no anything"—that is Nihilism. Their newspapers are full of violent attacks on religion and marriage, and teach free everything, common property and general promiscuity, as Professor Ely remarks, "in language of unparalleled coarseness and shocking impiety." Their principal thought is expressed in the Internationalist manifesto: "There remains but one recourse—force;" but— "hypocrisy, fraud, deceit, adultery, robbery and murder are held sacred, when beneficial to the revolution," adds the Professor of Political Economy at Johns Hopkins University, who further insists that assassinations committed by them are regarded as executions, and when a few years back Stellmacher and his associates murdered members of the Viennese police, Irving Hall in New York City was packed with Anarchists glorifying their deeds.

Having first looked upon this picture of the revolutionary destructives, we will now look on that of the evolutionary constructives—the conservative, peace-loving, constitutional State Socialists,* with whom, had Horace

* A pleasant picture is given, by an old member of the *Tribune* staff, Ernest Ingersoll, in his *A Week in New York*, of the Labor Lyceum in the Empire City and of "the bright-witted and gay-hearted Socialists," who, as he says, strive "for the propagation of Socialistic truths and the advancement of movements designed to elevate the condition of what Lincoln used to call 'plain people.'"

Greeley been now living, he would have united and helped
them to oppose the leaders,—and their cohorts of office-
holders and heelers,—of the corrupt political parties of the
capitalists, both Republican and Democratic, which in
these times, are mere agents of the Trusts and monopolistic
Corporations.

And American Socialism, if it be nothing else, is a constitutional party or rallying point for loyal American
Citizens to protest against the universal political corruption,
for we are in no better condition to-day in our government
and politics than was the old Roman Empire just before
its fall, as described by James Anthony Froude the historian,
who shows how: "Money was the one thought from the
highest senator to the poorest wretch who sold his vote in
the 'comitia.' For money, judges gave unjust decrees,
and juries gave corrupt verdicts. The elections were managed by clubs and coteries, and those who spent most
freely were most certain of success. The great commoners
bought their way into the magistracies, and from the
magistracies they passed into the senate. Public spirit in
the masses was either dead or sleeping, and the free forms
of the constitution were themselves the instruments of
corruption."

So much ignorance is current as to the means now
urged or employed by American Socialists and Nationalists
to bring about the Coöperative Commonwealth, that it is
important to point out that like other good American
citizens they believe in the ballot. If there be abuses, the
Legislatures, National and State, are there to correct them
in a gradual, but not *laissez faire*, let alone manner. Constitutional amendments are in order when constitutionally
adopted by the people, but the United States Constitution
is broad enough and big enough for all legitimate reforms
with but little alteration.

The theory of the commercial power inherent in the Constitution, as enunciated on various occasions by Alexander Hamilton, Daniel Webster, Abraham Lincoln, and Charles Sumner, as well as the right of eminent domain, have simplified long years ago the future carrying into action of Socialist political and economic demands. These, so far from being Utopian, are so practical that they could with few exceptions and without friction, under favorable administrational conditions, be made statutory in a single session of Congress. In fact, some of the transitional measures, which are deemed by ignoramuses the most radical, were conceded in Europe decades since under the rule of imperial and monarchical despotisms, without the crowns of those whose signatures made them law being in the slightest danger.

But our quondam Democratic Republic is now-a-days more aristocratic, or rather would be so, than the genuine original hereditary aristocracies on the other side of the Atlantic. We now indulge in the dubious luxury of a "Four Hundred," who sport crests and coats-of-arms * embezzled and hypothecated, without rhyme or reason, from their rightful European owners. The plutocracy, through our professional politicians, bribes our voters, governs our lawmakers, "fixes" our statutes, employs armed mercenaries, as well as too frequently controls the scales of American Justice, whose eyes are rarely blinded to a millionaire, when his shekels tinkle in her anxious ears.

This may sound harsh, but to quote the words of

---

* The articles headed "Our Mushroom Nobility," "Our Shoddy Noblemen," "Blue Blooded Citizens" and the like, illustrated with armorial bearings and published in the New York *World* in 1883, were from the pen of the author. They were written at the personal request of the editor, Joseph Pulitzer, who, when a resident of St. Louis, Missouri, belonged, it is said, to the International.

"Brutality and Avarice Triumphant," by that gallant soldier, General Rush C. Hawkins,* a lawyer himself and commander of the Hawkins Zouaves in many a sanguinary fight against the chattel slave-holding South :—"The fact that a considerable number of individuals obtain great wealth by dishonest schemes and cruel practices is of little moment when compared with the effect their financial successes produce upon particular communities and the country at large.   They have established a National Standard, and now only one kind of success is acknowledged.   Morality has no market value."

What has been the result of this new American "National Standard," developed by Jay Gould and the plutocratic Anarchists, who are as dangerous to civilization and the lives and homes of the proletarian working-people as could ever possibly be the dynamite fiends who shout, "Great is Anarchy and Most is its prophet?" James W. Gerard, a blue-blood member of the "Four Hundred" gives us the information direct from that "sacred circle," Describing "Some American Changes," † he says :—

"The result observed is, that society in the large cities becomes a restless, frivolous, underbred minority of wealthy triflers, lavish in ostentation, and gaping after notoriety, which they consider prominence.   The contention for wealth as a means of social eminence has a tendency to become unscrupulous and rancorous; the sympathetic obligations of life are lost sight of, friendship vanishes, simplicity retires, moral standards are disregarded, moral

---

* *North American Review*, June, 1891.   General Hawkins was the Art Commissioner of the United States at the Paris International Exposition of 1889, and is the author of *First Books and Printers of the Fifteenth Century*.

† *Lippincott's Monthly Magazine*, July, 1891.

obliquity does not operate to disqualify, and wealth exerts an undue and unholy influence.

"The Roman satirist has pictured this:

> 'Full lightly shall his morals be explored;
> But all shall ask you, what can he afford?
> How many servants at his sideboard stand?
> What is his style of living? where's his land?
>
> 'O wealth! the day is thine; let honor bow
> Its sacred head to all thy minions now;
> For here, long since, unanimous, we hold
> The sacrosanct divinity of gold.'"

Mr. Gerard, who is one of the monopolist "Land-Lords" of Manhattan Island, then contrasts, "the refined social condition of the first half century of the Republic," with the present time when fortunes are suddenly acquired "through disreputable means and by disreputable people, who thereby acquire prominence and provoke imitation." This, he insists, has brought about a national mediocrity, if not decadence, so plutocrats have come to the conclusion that "America is not good enough" for them and accordingly continued residence in the United States "is *not* interesting to many. There is little temptation for a domicile here by persons of high culture, great learning, artistic tastes, or ultra refinement. Our literature is shallow, art is in its infancy, and science is greatly dependent on what is gathered from abroad. Society, as above described, is deficient in culture, manners are without polish, the art of conversation does not exist, and the art of entertaining consists mostly in display. The people are, on an average, decidedly uninteresting, in their individual features; and a monotony and dullness characterize our lives, our cities, our villages, our abodes, our habits and occupations, that neither provoke curiosity nor awaken interest."

What measures are then demanded by American Socialists and Nationalists for raising the "National Standard of Morality" and arresting the alleged general "decline and fall" of sixty-three millions of real American society, regarded from the standpoint of the proletarian masses, and not from that of members of the dissatisfied classes * who squander most of the money in Europe that they have wrung out of the very life blood of their impoverished compatriots in America? In order to show this and properly to understand Horace Greeley's position relative to these measures later, there will be presented at this point the "Platform" of the Socialist Labor Party of the United States of America, which its members,—after recognizing the general failure of Community Socialism, or Association, as applied to industry by innumerable experiments under present hostile conditions,—endorse and endeavor to carry into successful political action at the polls. They regard these means as the only possibility, in conjunction with economic organization, by which the theories originally promulgated under a different state of things than now, by Greeley, Owen, Fourier, Brisbane, Godwin and the so-called Utopians, can be practically realized. The following "Platform,"—based upon preceding platforms and the knowledge derived from the "progressive" experiences of over a century,—was agreed upon at the last Socialist National Convention held at Chicago, in 1889 :—

---

* Mr. H. G. Wilshire, who edited the American edition of the *Fabian Essays in Socialism*, by G. Bernard Shaw, Sidney Webb, William Clarke, Sydney Oliver, Annie Besant, Graham Wallas, and Hubert Bland, in the Social Science Library, (Humboldt Publishing Co.) asserts in the preface thereto :—"To-day in the United States, 50,000 people, out of a population of over sixty-three millions, own everything worth having in the whole country. Four men, viz. : Gould, Astor, Vanderbilt and Rockefeller, practically control, and, what is more important, are rapidly absorbing the wealth of this 50,000,"

"The Socialist Labor Party of the United States, in Convention assembled, re-asserts the inalienable right of all men to life, liberty, and the pursuit of happiness.

"With the founders of the American republic we hold that the purpose of government is to secure every citizen in the enjoyment of this right; but in the light of our social conditions, we hold, furthermore, that no such right can be exercised under a system of economic inequality, essentially destructive of life, of liberty, and of happiness.

"With the founders of this republic we hold that the true theory of politics is that the machinery of government must be owned and controlled by the whole people; but in the light of our industrial development we hold, furthermore, that the true theory of economics is that the machinery of production must likewise belong to the people in common.

"To the obvious fact that our despotic system of economics is the direct opposite of our democratic system of politics, can plainly be traced the existence of a privileged class, the corruption of government by that class, the alienation of public property, public franchises and public functions to that class, and the abject dependence of the mightiest of nations upon that class.

"Again, through the perversion of democracy to the end of plutocracy, labor is robbed of the wealth which it alone produces, is denied the means of self-employment, and, by the compulsory idleness in wages slavery, is even deprived of the necessaries of life.

"Human power and natural forces are thus wasted, that the plutocracy may rule.

"Ignorance and misery, with all their concomitant evils, are perpetuated, that the people may be kept in bondage.

"Science and invention are diverted from their humane purpose to the enslavement of women and children.

"Against such a system the Socialist Labor Party once more enters its protest. Once more it reiterates its fundamental declaration that private property in the natural sources of production and in the instruments of labor is the obvious cause of all economic servitude and political dependence; and—

"WHEREAS, the time is fast coming when, in the natural course of social evolution, this system, through the destructive actions of its failures and crises on the one hand, and the constructive tendencies of its trusts and other capitalistic combinations on the other hand, shall have worked out its own downfall; therefore be it

"*Resolved*, that we call upon the people to organize with a view to the substitution of the coöperative commonwealth for the present state of planless production, industrial war and social disorder; a commonwealth in which every worker shall have the free exercise and full benefit of his faculties, multiplied by all the modern factors of civilization.

"We call upon them to unite with us in a mighty effort to gain by all practicable means the political power."

Recognizing with Horace Greeley that law and order are necessary as the foundations of the future Social Republic, the American Socialists—"in the meantime, and with a view to *immediate* improvement in the condition of labor," presented the following "Demands" for the approval of their fellow citizens and to be forthwith carried into effect by the aid of legislation :—

"SOCIAL DEMANDS.—1. Reduction of the hours of labor in proportion to the progress of production. 2. The United States shall obtain possession of the railroads, canals, telegraphs, telephones, and all other means of public transportation and communication. 3. The municipal-

ities to obtain possession of the local railroads, ferries,
water works, gas works, electric plants, and all industries
requiring municipal franchises.   4. The public lands to
be declared inalienable; revocation of all land grants to
corporations or individuals, the conditions of which have
not been complied with.   5. Legal incorporation by the
States of local Trade Unions which have no national
organization. 6. The United States to have the exclusive
right to issue money.   7. Congressional legislation providing for the scientific management of forests and water-
ways, and prohibiting the waste of the natural resources of
the country.   8. Inventions to be free to all; the inventors
to be remunerated by the nation.   9. Progressive income
tax and tax on inheritances; the smaller incomes to be
exempt.   10. School education of all children under
fourteen years of age to be compulsory, gratuitous and
accessible to all by public assistance in meals, clothing,
books, etc., where necessary.   11. Repeal of all pauper,
tramp, conspiracy, and sumptuary laws; unabridged right
of combination.   12. Official statistics concerning the
condition of labor; prohibition of the employment of children of school age and of the employment of female labor
in occupations detrimental to health or morality; abolition
of the convict labor contract system.   13. All wages to
be paid in lawful money of the United States; equalization
of women's wages with those of men where equal service
is performed.   14. Laws for the protection of life and
limb in all occupations, and an efficient employers' liability
law.

"POLITICAL DEMANDS.—1. The people to have the
right to propose laws and to vote upon all measures of
importance, according to the Referendum principle. 2. Abolition of the Presidency, Vice-Presidency and Senate of

the United States, an Executive Board to be established, whose members are to be elected, and may at any time be re-called, by the House of Representatives as the only legislative body; the States and Municipalities to adopt corresponding amendments to their constitutions and statutes.   3. Municipal self-government.   4. Direct vote and secret ballots in all elections ; universal and equal right of suffrage without regard to color, creed or sex ; election days to be legal holidays ; the principle of minority representation to be introduced.   5. All public officers to be subject to recall by their respective constituencies.   6. Uniform civil and criminal laws throughout the United States ; administration of justice to be free of charge ; abolition of capital punishment."

The first portion of the second "political demand" given above may sound very radical to many ears, but some of the founders of the American republic thought differently.   Those who object had better study up a desirable work on the question and which is *The Abolition of the Presidency*, by Henry C. Lockwood of the New York Bar.   It gives, so far as his subject is concerned, a fair synopsis of Jonathan Elliott's *Debates on the Adoption of the Constitution.*

Thomas Jefferson, equally with Benjamin Franklin, feared the "monarchical and aristocratical party" which had taken the "place of that noble love of liberty and Republican Government which had carried us triumphantly through the war." Consequently, Jefferson did not believe, says Lockwood, in the presidential form of government.

George Washington's friend, Col. George Mason, of Virginia, who took an active part in the United States Constitutional Convention, said in the course of the debates :—"This government will commence in a moderate

aristocracy; it is at present impossible to foresee whether
in its operation it will produce a monarchy, or a corrupt,
oppressive aristocracy."

The prophecy came true within a hundred years. It
had produced a corrupt, oppressive, aristocratical and
plutocratic oligarchy.

The "Declaration of Principles" of the American
Nationalists is almost identical in spirit with that of the
Socialist Labor Party. The aims of both are most certainly
the same, viz. : "the Nationalization of Industry and the
Promotion of the Brotherhood of Humanity." That this
has been recognized by Nationalists and Socialists is con-
clusively proved by the fact that in almost every instance
where there have been Clubs or Sections of either in the
same localities, they have united for political action at
election time.

There is no true Socialist but who must agree with the
following "Declaration of Principles" of the Nationalists,
for it is the very quintessence of the teachings of Charles
Fourier and Horace Greeley :—

"The principle of the Brotherhood of Humanity is one
of the eternal truths that govern the world's progress on
lines which distinguish human nature from brute nature.

"The principle of competition is simply the application
of the brutal law of the survival of the strongest and most
cunning.

"Therefore, so long as competition continues to be the
ruling factor in our industrial system, the highest development of the individual cannot be reached, the loftiest aims
of humanity cannot be realized.

"No truth can avail unless practically applied. Therefore those who seek the welfare of man must endeavor to
suppress the system founded on the brute principle of

competition and put in its place another based on the nobler principle of association.

"But in striving to apply this nobler and wiser principle to the complex conditions of modern life, we advocate no sudden or ill-considered changes; we make no war upon individuals; we do not censure those who have accumulated immense fortunes simply by carrying to a logical end the false principle on which business is now based.

"The combinations, trusts and syndicates of which the people, at present, complain, demonstrate the practicability of our basic principle of association. We merely seek to push this principle a little further and have all industries operated in the interest of all by the nation—the people organized—the organic unity of the whole people.

"The present industrial system proves itself wrong by the immense wrongs it produces; it proves itself absurd by the immense waste of energy and material which is admitted to be its concomitant. Against this system we raise our protest; for the abolition of the slavery it has wrought and would perpetuate, we pledge our best efforts."

Both Nationalism and Socialism only mean,—when their systems are thoroughly comprehended by an educated and unprejudiced mind,—the practical realization of what John Stuart Mill, * who was a Socialist, put so tersely years ago in his *Autobiography* as follows:—"The social problem of the future we considered to be, how to unite *the greatest individual liberty* of action with a common ownership in the raw material of the globe and an equal participation of all in the benefits of combined labor."

* Mill's views on the progressive moveent will be found in full in *Socialism*, by John Stuart Mill: edited by W. D. P. Bliss, published in the Social Science Library, by the Humboldt Publishing Company.

After reading the pronunciamento of the Nationalists and the definitive platform and transitional demands of the Social Democrats, it can be understood without difficulty, why American Socialists have been the victims of so much misrepresentation and had such false witnessing borne against them. It has been ever thus in the United States, and the political party organs have always, so to say, spat fire and poured vitriol over the leaders of the wrangling factions in the unlovely manner which was peculiarly typical of the first quarter of the Republic's existence, and which George Washington himself objected to when he complained to Thomas Jefferson that he had been attacked in "such exaggerated and indecent terms as could scarcely be applied to a Nero, a notorious defaulter, or even to a common pickpocket."

The Socialist Political Platform and Demands also show how it came to pass that the Anarchists, who believe in no government, no laws whatever, and that consequently—

> "The very best government of all
> Is that which governs not at all,"

were positively refused admittance to the deliberations of the International Socialist Congress held at Brussels in the summer of 1891.

Lucien Sanial, editor of the Socialist official organ *The People*, formerly of the editorial staff of the Paris *Temps*, and the delegate of both the American Socialist Labor Party and the New York Central Labor Federation to the Brussels Congress, officially reported on his return therefrom to his constituents as follows :—"By refusing to recognize and admit Anarchists, it (the Congress) put the stamp of condemnation upon the theory that dynamite in the hands of an otherwise powerless minority, fundamentally opposed to constructive ideas, may at any time effectually destroy the present iniquitous system of wages slavery and permanently accomplish the revolution now in progress, initiated by Socialism, and the final triumph of which must be expected from intellectual evolution alone, promoted by organization, education and political action."

And this policy was punctuated in October, 1891, according to a recent editorial in the New York *Sun*,* which stated:—"The Congress of Socialists, which has just concluded its sittings at Erfurt, did two things which have an important bearing on the political stability and social progress of Germany. It ejected with contumely the Anarchists whose doctrines are irreconcilable with patriotism, and it placed for the first time in its program a declaration in favor of equal rights for women. . . . The repudiation of the Anarchists by the great body of German Socialists means that the latter ask nothing from the Government but the fundamental rights of free assemblage, free printing, and free speech, and that so long as these franchises are conceded to them they will advocate reforms by constitutional methods only. Meanwhile they pledge themselves to remember in the face of possible aggression from without or of separatist tendencies within, that they are Germans first and reformers afterward."

The American Socialists, as Charles A. Dana, an old Brook Farm Socialist himself, doubtless well knows, have always repudiated the Anarchists, notably in 1886. But "a declaration in favor of equal rights for women" was not "placed for the first time" at Erfurt, in the Socialist program. That plank was accepted by the New York Socialists who voted in 1830 for Ezekiel Williams for Governor, and was in the platform printed some years

*The *Sun*, Friday, October 23, 1891.

before then, at the head of their organ the *Workingman's Advocate*, published in the city of New York between 1825 and 1830.

The Anarchists are thus regarded by the Socialist Labor Movement of America and Europe, as the natural enemies of Socialists all the world over.   Anarchism can not subsist in any civilized country.   The only place, or at least "the best place for an Anarchist is in Central Africa, where the 'absolute sovereignty' of his individualism could run riot in conjunction with its logical sequence—pure and simple barbarism conjoined to conditions analagous to the gorilla state." All of which possibilities are certainly hostile to the belief of Socialists that civilization to be assured must recognize with them—

"LOVE AS OUR PRINCIPLE, ORDER AS OUR BASIS, PROGRESS AS OUR END."

And if these fundamentals be not adhered to, then there will never be realized the prophecy of Claude Henri, Count St. Simon, "the Socialist,"—who fought with Lafayette, Rochambeau, Steuben, Kosciusko, Pulaski and other humanitarian foreigners to free the American colonies from British monarchical tyranny, and whose never to be forgotten words were—

"THE FUTURE IS OURS."

CHAPTER II.

CAUSES OF GREELEY'S SOCIALISM.

AMERICAN Socialism having been shown to be altruistic, coöperative and peaceful, and to be absolutely antagonistic to its antithesis Anarchism, which is egoistic, competitive and violent, nothing more need be said on that subject in these pages than to refer the reader to Horace Greeley's lecture on the "Emancipation of Labor" in which he very clearly expresses the opinion that anarchic methods generally lead to reaction culminating in despotism, instancing the French Revolution as a case in point, by showing how Marat and the sanguinary "Sans Culottes" of '93 led to Napoleon and the Empire. Having done with this matter, we will now answer at length two of our former questions, which were :—

What were the causes that made Horace Greeley a Socialist ? And—Why was he so earnest in the cause of industrial reform ?

On Memorial Day, 1889, the comrades of Horace Greeley Grand Army Post stood around Greeley's grave in Greenwood Cemetery,—as is their annual custom when they decorate his last resting place with flowers, evergreens and American flags,—and listened to an address. The orator of the occasion, Col. J. M. Lawson, then told the Post,— which principally consists of journeymen printers and working journalists,—that the youth of Greeley "was an unva-

rying round of study, industry and constant privation, yet
of thorough indifference to the untoward experiences
which marked this period of his life.   He was endowed
with none of the graces of even the crude society from which
he sprung, and his person was destitute of polish, charm or
fascination ; but as he grew to manhood, it began to be
perceived that his was no ordinary intellect, and that, added
to an insatiable thirst for knowledge, he was gifted with a
marvelous memory, a ready, apt and logical utterance, a
subtile sense of discrimination, and a keen insight into the
mysteries of life.   Hence it was that he soon became the
youthful mentor of the village of East Poultney, Vermont,
in fact its town encyclopedia.   It was here, after the most
rudimentary opportunities of the district school followed by
the largest range of reading possible in an intelligent commonwealth of New England, that he entered a printing
office as an apprentice and laid the foundation of his future
editorial career.

   " From the age of fifteen to twenty he was a wanderer
on foot, carrying his humble pack over the hills of New
Hampshire, crossing the dense woods of the Empire State,
and penetrating the uncut forests of Pennsylvania, always
in pursuit of the practice of his craft.   And were these
migrations, like those of the trader and the pioneer, that
he might lay up riches?   Not that—only that his surplus
earnings might go to save the encumbered farm of his
father.   This self-abnegation and generosity were worthy
and conspicuous features of his subsequent life.

   " On the 18th of August, 1831, Horace Greeley, having
descended the Hudson from Albany, arrived in the City of
New York with a capital of ten dollars.   I will not recount
the scoffs and jeers which greeted his uncouth appearance
as he went from printing office to printing office in search

of work ; how most unwillingly and by a mere accident he was put to the test as a practical typesetter.''

And so forth. But poetic, albeit earnest descriptions,— in which the progress from poverty to capital is related,— cannot do justice to his hard, cruel childhood and early manhood, which helped to make him a Socialist. Horace Greeley, "born of republican parentage, of an ancestry which participated vividly in the hopes and fears, the convictions and efforts of the American Revolution," was not the man to feel "thorough indifference to the untoward experiences" which marked his early life. On the contrary, he thought it all out and became an enthusiast of ways and means, not only for the temporary amelioration, but for the final emancipation of the whole human race from every kind of slavery.

As a boy and young man, Greeley knew little other than wretchedness, hunger and bankruptcy. He was even a "tramp" in search of work, after having seen his family driven by the relentless law out of their home to starve or rot. He was profoundly impressed by the tragedy of the death of his mother who, he says—"had for years been worn out by hard work and broken down in mind and body, when toil and trouble had gained the victory over her." He had been born and lived in New Hampshire, the very stony soil of which made the agricultural element a poverty-stricken people. In fact when Greeley was nine years old, in 1820, almost every one in New Hampshire, he asserts, was "hopelessly involved, every third farm was in the sheriff's hands, and every poor man leaving for 'the West' who could raise the money requisite for getting away. Everything was cheap,—dog cheap ; yet the comparatively rich were embarrassed, and the poor were often compulsorily idle, and on the brink of famine."

Horace Greeley had to work on his father's farm almost

from the time he could walk and then, he states, "first learned that this is a world of hard work. Often called out of bed at dawn to 'ride horse to plow' among the growing corn, potatoes, and hops, we would get as much plowed by 9 to 10 A. M. as could be hoed that day; when I would be allowed to start for school, where I sometimes arrived as the forenoon session was half through. In Winter, our work was lighter; but the snow was often deep and drifted, the cold intense, the north wind piercing, and our clothing thin."

His father who was always on the verge of ruin, dealt in lumber, besides being a farmer, and in August, 1820, Greeley tells us, occurred a family catastrophe brought about by the chronic "bad times" and pecuniary shortage in the paternal homestead combined, when, as we are informed, "the sheriff and sundry other officials, with two or three of our principal creditors, appeared, and—first formally demanding payment of their claims—proceeded to levy on farm, stock, implements, household stuff, and nearly all our worldly possessions but the clothes we stood in. There had been no writ issued till then,—of course, no trial, no judgment,—but it was a word and a blow in those days, and the blow first, in the matter of debt-collecting by legal process. Father left the premises directly, apprehending arrest and imprisonment, and was invisible all day; the rest of us repaired to a friendly neighbor's, and the work of levying went on in our absence. It is needless to add that all we had was swallowed up, and our debts not much lessened. Our farm, which had cost us $1,350, and which had been considerably improved in our hands, was appraised and set off to creditors at $500, out of which the legal costs were first deducted. A barn-full of rye, grown by us on another's land, whereof we owned an undivided half,

was attached by a doctor, threshed out by his poorer cus-
tomers by days' work on account, and sold; the net result
being an enlargement of our debt,—the grain failing to meet
all the costs. Thus, when night fell, we were as bankrupt
a family as well could be. We returned to our devastated
house; and the rest of us stayed there while father took a
journey on foot westward, in quest of a new home."

Driven, by this too frequent episode of "competitive
civilization," out of New Hampshire, the Greeley family
migrated to Vermont where life was harder for them than
in the State they had left There, Greeley tells us, the
family "made the acquaintance of genuine poverty,—not
beggary, or dependence, but the manly American sort.
Our sum total of worldly goods, including furniture, bedding,
and the clothes we stood in, may have been worth $200;
but, as we had afterward to pay that amount on old New
Hampshire debts, our material possessions may be fairly
represented by o, with a credit for $200 worth of clothing
and household stuff."

Greeley, when ten years old, had to help his father and
brothers clear off some wild lands near Westhaven, work
which "was rugged and grimy. When we first attacked it,
the snow was just going, and the water and slush were
knee-deep. We were all indifferent choppers, when
compared with those who usually grapple with great forests.
. . . . We had been farmers of the poorer class in
New Hampshire; we took rank with day laborers in Vermont. We were compelled to observe a sterner frugality."
And most of the work amounted to nothing, because the
man for whom it was done "died before we had effected
a settlement; when his estate was declared insolvent, and
we were juggled out of a part of our pay." Other reverses
followed Greeley's father, such as his "wheat being de-

stroyed by the midge;" and as if that were not sufficient, "the water we drank here was so bad that the fever and ague struck down our parents in the Fall, and all of us children next Spring, when we beat a precipitate retreat from 'Flea Knoll,'—where it was said that no family ever remained more than a year," and so ended Greeley's "Martin Chuzzlewit" kind of a time.

As for the "sterner frugality" of the Greeley family, the usual meal, their daily bread, consisted of "a five-quart milk-pan filled with bean porridge—an hereditary dish among the Scotch-Irish—which was placed upon the floor, the children clustering around it. Each child was provided with a spoon, and dipped into the porridge, the spoon going directly from the common dish to the particular mouth, without an intermediate landing upon a plate, the meal consisting of porridge, and porridge only. The parents sat at a table, and enjoyed the dignity of a separate dish." But this fare was most certainly superior to the "bread and water" allowance on a dollar-a-day suggested by Henry Ward Beecher.

Such were Horace Greeley's "school-days," which are supposed to be the happiest part of a human being's life. Was it any wonder that looking back upon them he spoke as follows some years later in a lecture on "Teachers and Teaching?"

"I would not if I could," he said, "conceal from you my conviction that, before Education can become what it should and must be, we must reform the Social Life whence it proceeds, whitherto it tends. To the child daily sent out from some rickety hovel or miserable garret to wrestle with Poverty and Misery for such knowledge as the teacher can impart, what true idea or purpose of Education is possible? How can he be made to realize that his daily tasks concern

the Soul, the World, and Immortality? He may have
drilled into his ears day after day the great truth that 'the
life is more than meat and the body more than raiment,' but
so long as his own food and raiment are scanty and precarious, his mind will be engrossed by a round of petty and
sordid cares. (I speak here of the general fact ; there will
be striking instances of the contrary—brilliant exceptions
which do not disprove, but establish the rule I have indicat-
ed.) But the child whose little all hitherto of life has been
passed in penury and consequent suffering—who lives in
the constant presence, on the very brink, of Want—how
can he have a higher idea of Life than that it is a struggle
for bread, or of Education than that it is a contrivance for
getting bread more easily or more abundantly, or else a
useless addition to his toils and cares? He whose energies
have been, must be, taxed to keep starvation at bay, can
hardly realize that Life has truer ends than the avoidance
of pain and the satisfaction of hunger. The narrow, dingy,
squalid tenement, calculated to repel any visitor but the
cold and the rain, is hardly fitted to foster lofty ideas of
Life, its Duties and its Aims. He who is constrained to
ask each morning, 'Where shall I find food for the day?'
is at best unlikely often to ask, 'By what good deed shall
the day be signalized?' Well did the Divine Teacher
enjoin His followers to 'take no thought for the morrow,'
and difficult will be the work of imbuing the general mind
with any lofty ideal of Life and its ends until this command-
ment can be obeyed in verity, and until such obedience
can be made to comport with the dictates of a reasonable
forecast and with that care for his own household, lacking
which the believer is 'worse than an infidel.'"

And continuing in the same strain he urged that :—

"*Education can never be what it ought until a vast and*

*pervading improvement has been wrought in the Social and
Physical Condition of the destitute Millions of mankind.** In
vain shall we provide capable teachers and comfortable
school-rooms, and the most admirable school-books,
apparatus, libraries, etc., for those children who come
shivering and skulking in rags—who sit distorted by the
gnawings of hunger or suffering from the effects of innutri-
tious or unwholesome food—who must sleep, huddled in
cellars or garrets, unfit even for dog-kennels, hard Necessity
overruling all distinctions of age or sex and crowding
Modesty through the unglazed window to keep company
with exiled Decency outside.   You may fill the hovels of
the famishing with Bibles and Tracts, sufficient to replace
the chairs and tables which famine and the landlord have
sent to the pawnbroker, yet you can not render those who
grow up under such influences religious nor moral; you

---

* Horace Greeley always continued in this belief.   Thus, on
July 8, 1856, he wrote in the *Tribune :*—"We never objected to the
designation of Socialist when it was a term of reproach and oppro-
brium, and we adhere to the convictions under which we earnestly
fought the battle of absolutely Free Common Schools for all the
children of our State.   We assent, with some scruples, to the policy
of State Normal Schools for the education of Common School
Teachers, whose qualifications are too generally meager and questionable.   There, however, we stop.   Free Academies and State
Universities, for the supply of a gratuitous classic or scientific
education to all who see fit (and are able) to claim their advantages, are at war with our idea of the legitimate functions of Government and with that equality which should prevail in the distribution and enjoyment of those blessings.   If our city is to be turned
into a great Communist establishment—for which we consider its
population very ill prepared—let us begin with the satisfaction of
their most urgent and absolute wants before we attempt the satisfaction of those of a more ethereal character.   Let us first guarantee
to every needy man employment and honest bread before we
undertake to glut his intellectual cravings on Greek Tragedies,
Hebrew Roots, and Conic Sections.   In a city where many thousands of children go to bed supperless three months in the year
because their parents have no work and no money, it seems a
mockery and an insult to talk of welcoming all our children to the
advantages of a University Education."

may cram them with Popularized Science and convert them into infant prodigies of intellect and culture, and they will yet be deplorably uneducated, untrained, undeveloped. No stimulation of one or two faculties ever yet produced a true or useful human character, nor ever will. The education which does not begin worthily in the cradle can rarely result in eminent worth or honor. Idly shall you labor to teach the child whose earliest recollections are of torturing hunger or of cloying surfeit that Food is not an end of life but a means of sustaining it—vainly shall you moralize to him, whose youth was rendered bitter and abject by Want, that Wealth is but an added responsibility and not necessarily a sovereign good. The actualization of grosser vice may be shunned from instinct, or fear, or habit; but the soul's native purity and delicacy can not be preserved where a single garret is made to afford the sleeping accommodations of a numerous family, nor can monitorial precepts restore it while the influences which wrought its destruction are still present and potent. It will be idle to expect true, beneficent attainment in school from those who have not the means of decent and comfortable existence at home. You may sharpen their wits; you may awaken in them a dread of shame or pain and a resolution to avoid them. But to impress the solemn injunctions, 'Thou shalt not steal,' 'Thou shalt not covet,' on him who daily casts famine-sunken eyes on the fruit ripening and rotting in the rich man's orchards, and who feels that the fuel which would warm his benumbed limbs is moldering to dust in the adjacent wood, unused and unwanted, this is the impossible task; yet who shall be deemed educated whose heart festers with rebellion against these essential commandments?

"Not until we shall have achieved the emancipation of

the Poor from the slavery of physical and absolute destitution—not till we shall have rendered possible to all,
obedience to the Divine precept, 'Take no thought for the
morrow,'—not till we shall have relieved all who will work
from the terror of constrained idleness and consequent
starvation, can I feel that a secure basis has been laid for
Universal Education.　There will still remain obstacles in
abundance—obstacles originating in perverted appetites,
impetuous passions, narrow-minded parentage, false pride,
mental incapacity, and the like; but before all these I place
the impediments arising from extreme indigence and the
degradations and dangers which have thence their origin.
Let this be removed, and we shall have better opportunity
to appreciate and encounter the residue."

Horace Greeley's "education" finished, next followed
his apprenticeship to the printing trade at the munificent
salary of some forty dollars a year, with board thrown in.*

This was, as already stated, at Poultney, in Vermont.
There he saw a genuine New England chattel slave hunt
under the circumstances thus described by him later:—
"New York had professed to abolish slavery years before,
but had ordained that certain born slaves should remain
such till twenty-eight years old; and the year of jubilee for
certain of these had not yet come.　A young negro, who
must have been uninstructed in the sacredness of constitutional guarantees, the rights of property, etc., etc., etc.,
feloniously abstracted himself from his master in a neigh-
boring New York town, and conveyed the chattel-personal

---

* Horace Greeley did better than the author of this volume, who
had to serve a five years' apprenticeship to printing and publishing,
and only received his board and lodging, but no wages at all.　In
addition to giving his services gratis, his guardian and uncle had to
pay $500 down for the privilege of his nephew being apprenticed,
and had further to find all the clothing, washing and other necessaries requisite, during those five years' apprenticeship.

to our village; where he was at work, when said master, with due process and following, came over to reclaim and recover the goods. I never saw so large a muster of men and boys so suddenly on our village-green as his advent incited; and the result was a speedy disappearance of the chattel, and the return of his master, disconsolate and niggerless, to the place whence he came. Everything on our side was *impromptu* and instinctive; and nobody suggested that envy or hate of 'the South,' or of New York, or of the master, had impelled the rescue. Our people hated injustice and oppression, and acted as if they couldn't help it."

When Horace Greeley's term of five years' servitude to his "master" was over, his "wages slavery" began in earnest. He tramped hungry and foot-sore for a job from Poultney in Vermont to Schenectady in New York, and thence finally to his father's log cabin, where, after a respite of a few days' "holiday" chopping wood, he started again on his search for an honest living. He found work for a week at Jamestown in New York State, but no pay, as the rascally printer who had employed him had no money to give him in payment of his just dues. Then he trudged on again to Lodi in Cattaraugus County, New York, and received $11 per month for six weeks until his "boss" could no longer afford to hire a journeyman and his "freedom of contract" necessarily ended abruptly there. Again, sockless and half-clad, with his entire wardrobe and property tied up in a handkerchief carried over his shoulder on the end of a stick, he wandered on and on, hunting for the opportunity to labor and finding none until he struck the town of Erie in Pennsylvania, where at $15 a month he set type.

Greeley had a rest from tramping for a spell while

working there, but alas! as he says: "At length, work failed at the *Gazette* office, and I was constrained to take a fresh departure. No printing-office in all that region wanted a journeyman. The West seemed to be laboring under a surfeit of printers. One was advertised for, to take charge of a journal at Wilkesbarre, Pa., and I applied for the place, but failed to secure it. I would gladly have given faithful labor at case and press through some years yet for $15 per month and board, or even less; but it was not to be had."

New York City was his only hope, and he turned his steps in that direction in order to make a living and no longer take the chances of a residence in jail for the crime of vagrancy, or in other words for being unemployed and seeking work. His life for about eighteen months thereafter consisted of a series of changes of places with intervals of biting poverty. He worked in job printing offices, as well as in those of the New York *Evening Post*, the *Commercial Advertiser*, and the *Amulet*. But his literary knowledge,—he had always been a great reader of books and "knowledge is power,"—saved him from perpetual wages slavery, for after a brief interval at reporting on the *Spirit of the Times*, he became on January 1, 1833, the printer, publisher and editor of a penny newspaper, the *Morning Post*, and a member of the firm of Greeley and Storey.

It is written in the *Vedas* that "Labor makes known the true worth of a man, as fire brings the perfume out of incense,"—so Horace Greeley's personal experiences as a wages slave, although there were other causes, helped to make him a Socialist. They refined and spiritualized him. It is impossible when reading the passages in his lecture on the "Organization of Labor," where he points out the "victims of social injustice," not to recognize the fact that he pathetically refers to himself and father, although he makes no direct personal allusions. Elsewhere, he over and over again sums up the lack of "Opportunity" in other terms, as in the following passage, which, although written fifty years ago, mentions the possible troubles that will arise among working people in New York from foreign immigration :

"A capable, willing, trustworthy man may earnestly seek employment here for months without finding any. And the reason is very clear : there are more seeking work in the cities than work can be found for ; and, though the business of most cities annually increases, through the growth of the country trading with them, yet the pressure for employment in cities constantly outruns the demand for labor, and if New York were to increase its trade and consequently its population by ten or twenty per cent. a year for the next century, there would at all times be thousands waiting here for chances to do something, and many starved out or impelled to evil courses for want of honest business.

"The gigantic sea of Foreign Immigration incessantly rolling in upon us, bringing thousands each month to our city (some of them most ingenious, expert and capable) who must have work promptly or go to the Poor-House, and who are inured to lower wages and poorer living than Americans will submit to, will keep the general labor market glutted and the average recompense of hired labor low for a term of which I cannot foresee the end."

As a capitalist printer and publisher, Horace Greeley also came in contact with a condition of things that forced him to take a progressive attitude and mentally to exclaim with Ralph Waldo Emerson—"It is high time our bad Wealth came to an end."

Whether it was during the existence of the *New Yorker*,
the *Morning Post*, or the *Log Cabin*, which he edited and
partly owned,—before starting the New York *Tribune* on
April 10, 1841,—he was always a sufferer from capitalist
cupidity and individualistic selfishness.* He never, while
a publisher, appreciated the competitive system.

Describing some years later his troubles, when publisher
of the *New Yorker*, he says in one letter:—"Through
most of the time I was very poor, and for four years really
bankrupt; though always paying my notes and keeping
my word, but living as poorly as possible." And in
another:—"My embarrassments were sometimes dreadful;
not that I feared destitution, but the fear of involving my
friends in my misfortunes was very bitter." He suffered
similarly while the *Log Cabin* was running and made this
appeal when hard pressed by creditors:—"To those who
owe us, therefore, we are compelled to say, Friends! *we
need our money*—our paper-maker needs it! and has a
right to ask us for it. The low price at which we have
published it, forbids the idea of gain from this paper: we
only ask the means of paying what we owe. Once for
all, we *implore* you to do us justice, and enable us to do
the same."

Greeley when editor of the *Tribune* was once attacked
editorially by a contemptible newspaper scribe,—who probably never paid his own tailor's bills until he was forced by
a judgment,—on account of his clothes looking shabby and
being out of style. In the course of his scathing response,
he stated:—"The editor of the *Tribune* is the son of a
poor and humble farmer; came to New York a minor,

* Jonas Winchester and Thomas McElrath, two of his partners,
had nothing selfish about them. They were high spirited, noble
gentlemen—and good abolitionists to boot.

without a friend within 200 miles, less than ten dollars in his pocket, and precious little besides; he has never had a dollar from a relative, and has for years labored under a load of debt, (thrown on him by others' misconduct and the revulsion of 1837) which he can now just see to the end of. Thenceforth he may be able to make a better show, if deemed essential by his friends.''

Horace Greeley looked askance at all "business" methods. He says in his *Recollections:*—"To be hungry, ragged and penniless is not pleasant; but this is nothing to the horrors of bankruptcy. All the wealth of the Rothschilds would be a poor recompense for a five years' struggle, with the consciousness, that you had taken the money or property of trusting friends,—promising to return or pay for it when required,—and had betrayed their confidence through insolvency. I dwell on this point, for I would deter others from entering that place of torment. Half the young men in the country, with many old enough to know better, would 'go into business'—that is, into debt—to-morrow, if they could. Most poor men are so ignorant as to envy the merchant or manufacturer whose life is an incessant struggle with pecuniary difficulties, who is driven to constant 'shinning,' and who, from month to month, barely evades that insolvency which sooner or later overtakes most men in business; so that it has been computed that but one in twenty of them achieve a pecuniary success. For my own part,—and I speak from sad experience,—I would rather be a convict in a State prison, a slave in a rice-swamp, than to pass through life under the harrow of debt.''

He absolutely hated commerce, as existing under our present semi-anarchic social system. In his lecture on "Life, the Ideal and the Actual," he thus attacks it:—

"But perhaps the most imperative of the influences of practical life to narrow and distort the man is that exercised by Traffic. To obtain More for Less—this is the aim and the impulse of Trade. The game of the counter, like that of the boxing-ring, places two persons opposite each other at proper distance, and bids them shake hands and begin. That each *may* be a gainer by the bargain is of course practicable; (though which of them naturally cares for this?) that both may be honest men is freely conceded. The criticism impeaches not the men, but the attitude in which they are pitted against each other. Where Wealth is the object of general and eager desire, where Labor is loathed and Luxury coveted—it is too hard on frail Human Nature to place it where a slight departure from rectitude may win its thousands. The temptation *may* be resisted— it doubtless often is; for Trade has furnished its full quota of the upright and more than its share of the benevolent of our race; but while these may probably have owed to Commerce the *means* of being liberal, I doubt whether any have been indebted to it for their *integrity.* Of that, a man must carry all into a life of buying and selling that he expects to bring out again, and he can hardly afford to commence business on a small capital either. If a man of unsettled or weak principles ever trafficked five years without becoming a rogue, he must present a striking evidence of the sustaining, saving mercy of an overruling Providence."

Elsewhere Greeley said:—"Do you ask *why* the rate of mercantile profit is too high? Count the number of stores in any county, and you have a ready answer. There are five to ten times as many persons employed in and subsisting by trade as there need or should be. As the taxes of a nation must be in proportion to the number and salaries of those quartered on its treasury, so the profits of trade must be graduated by the number they are required to support." And as to one particularly favorite capitalistic trick, he remarked : "The meanness, the dishonesty, the iniquity, of squandering thousands unearned, and keeping others out of money that is justly theirs, have rarely been urged and enforced as they should be. They need but to be considered and understood to be universally loathed and detested."

Another reason for Horace Greeley's Socialism can be found in his study of the general environment of the rest of the world besides himself.

The evils complained of in our time were just as bad in the United States seventy years ago and have been continuously since, as they are now. There was quite as much poverty and as many unemployed in the country relatively to its population as there are now, if not more.

We can go back over a hundred years, if need be, for that excuse of superficial minds—"Bad Times,"—as if there had ever been anything else for the proletariat and, for the matter of that, for the majority of the middle class also, but "Bad Times" under the competitive, capitalist system of the United States.

McMaster in his *History of the People of the United States* asserts, when speaking of the working people, that in the year 1784 :—"Their houses were meaner, their food was coarser, their clothing was of commoner stuff, and their wages were, despite the depreciation that has gone on in the value of money, lower by one-half that at present."

How the people of Horace Greeley's native State, New Hampshire, suffered from poverty in 1820 has already been shown by his own evidence. He also tells us of the circumstances of the wage earners of Manhattan Island in 1831, when he first became a resident of New York City. Writing of that period, over a quarter of a century later, he says :—"Our city stood as if besieged till Spring relieved her ; and it was much the same every Winter. Mechanics and laborers lived awhile on the scanty savings of the preceding Summer and Autumn ; then on such credit as they could wring from grocers and landlords, till milder weather brought them work again. The earnings of good mechanics did not average $8 per week in 1831–32, while they are now double that sum ; and living is *not* twice as dear as it then was. Meat may possibly be ; but Bread is not; Fuel is not ; Clothing is not ; while travel is cheaper. Winter is relatively dull now (1868), but not nearly so stagnant as it formerly was. In spite of an inflated currency and high taxes, it is easier now for a working-man to earn his living in New York, than it was thirty to forty years ago."

Byllesby, who wrote the first American Socialistic work,* of which the author is aware, asserts that on January 1, 1826, there were in the city of New York "at least one-fourth of the journeymen in its different mechanic arts destitute of settled employment."

And a still more remarkable American Socialistic volume † of over four hundred pages, written by Thomas

Observations on the Sources and Effects of Unequal Wealth ; with Propositions toward Remedying the Disparity of Profit in Pursuing the Arts of Life, and Establishing Security in Individual Prospects and Resources. By L. Byllesby. New York : Published by Lewis J. Nichols, 1826. The back of the title testifies to it having been copyrighted "on the 26th day of January, in the fiftieth year of the Independence of the United States of America," by Lewis J. Nichols, and deposited in the District Court Clerk's office, of the Southern District of New York.

† *The Rights of Man to Property! Being a Proposition to Make it Equal among the Adults of the Present Generation ; and to Provide for its Equal Transmission to Every Individual of each Succeeding Generation, on Arriving at the Age of Maturity. Addressed to the Citizens of the State of New York, Particularly, and to the People of other States and Nations, Generally.* By Thomas Skidmore. New York : Printed for the Author by Alexander Ming, Jr., 106 Beekman Street. 1829.

Skidmore, and published in 1829, refers to the proletariat of
New York State as "depressed by poverty and its ten-
thousand evils," whose labor is the sole resource they
have "to maintain their existence, degraded as it is by
the slavery in which they are plunged," and that their
"sufferings are continually augmenting," making them
"slaves and worse."

Six years after his arrival in New York, Greeley asserts
that things had gone from bad to worse, for "the commercial revulsion, which was rather apprehended than fully
experienced in 1834, was abundantly realized in 1837.
Manufactories were stopped, and their 'hands' thrown
out of work. Trade was almost stagnant. Bankruptcies
among men of business were rather the rule than the exception. Property was sacrificed at auction—often at
sheriff's or assignee's sale—for a fraction of its value ; and
thousands, who had fondly dreamed themselves millionaires, or on the point of becoming such, awoke to the fact
that they were bankrupt. The banks were, of course, in
trouble,—those which had been Government depositories,
or 'pets,' rather deeper than the rest. Looking at the
matter from *their* point of view, they had been first seduc-
ed into a questionable path, and were now reviled and
assailed for yielding to their seducers."

Such facts as these led to Horace Greeley becoming a
Socialist, but above all, the horrors of the year 1838 in
New York city. He narrates the story himself in his autobiography. So also does his biographer, James Parton,
and as follows :—

"The editor of the *Tribune* was a Socialist years before
the *Tribune* came into existence.

"The Winter of 1838 was unusually severe. The
times were hard, fuel and food were dear, many thousands

of men and women were out of employment, and there was
general distress.   As the cold months wore slowly on, the
sufferings of the poor became so aggravated, and the number of the unemployed increased to such a degree, that the
ordinary means were inadequate to relieve even those who
were destitute of every one of the necessaries of life.   Some
died of starvation.   Some were frozen to death.   Many,
through exposure and privation, contracted fatal diseases.
A large number, who had never before known want, were
reduced to beg.   Respectable mechanics were known to
offer their services as waiters in eating-houses for their food
only.   There had never been such a time of suffering in
New York before, and there has not been since.   Extraordinary measures were taken by the comfortable classes to
alleviate the sufferings of their unfortunate fellow-citizens.
Meetings were held, subscriptions were made, committees
were appointed ; and upon one of the committees Horace
Greeley was named to serve, and did serve, faithfully and
laboriously, for many weeks.   The district which his committee had in charge was the Sixth Ward, the ' bloody '
Sixth, the squalid, poverty-stricken Sixth, the pool into
which all that is worst in this metropolis has a tendency to
reel and slide.   It was his task, and that of his colleagues,
to see that no one froze or starved in that forlorn and polluted region.   More than this they could not do, for the
subscriptions, liberal as they were, were not more than
sufficient to relieve actual and pressing distress.   In the
better parts of the Sixth Ward a large number of mechanics lived, whose cry was, not for the bread and the fuel of
charity, but for WORK !   Charity their honest souls dis-
dained. Its food choked them, its fire chilled them. Work,
give us work ! was their eager, passionate demand.

    "All this Horace Greeley heard and saw," Parton con-

tinues. "He was a young man—not quite twenty-six—
compassionate to weakness, generous to a fault. He had
known what it was to beg for work, from shop to shop,
from town to town; and, that very Winter, he was struggling with debt, at no safe distance from bankruptcy.
Why must these things be? *Are* they inevitable? Will
they *always* be inevitable? Is it in human wisdom to devise a remedy? in human virtue to apply it? *Can* the
beneficent God have designed this, who, with such wonderful profusion, has provided for the wants, tastes, and
luxuries of all his creatures, and for a hundred times as
many creatures as yet have lived at the same time? Such
questions Horace Greeley pondered, in silence, in the
depths of his heart, during that Winter of misery."

There was another brave soul also thinking over these
things, Parke Godwin, the son-in-law of the poet, William
Cullen Bryant, with whom he was associate editor of the
New York *Evening Post.* Like his friend Horace Greeley,
Godwin declared himself a convert to Socialism and in 1843
produced his famous pamphlet *Democracy, Constructive and
Pacific,* on pages 50–51 of which is reprinted an article from
the *Evening Post* entitled "Poverty in the State of New
York," to which he added this note :—"New York is one
of the richest, if not the richest agricultural State in the
Union, yet 1 in 17 of its inhabitants are supported by charity. In the city of New York, the Alms-house has administered relief, in the year 1843, to 40,000 persons ! This is
at the rate of 1 to 7½ of the population." It should be
noted that this statement was printed some three or four
years before the Irish potato famine and before the emigration from down-trodden Erin came pouring over here as
a consequence, in overwhelming numbers.

Later we have official information as well as philanthropic. Fernando Wood, Mayor of the city of New York, in his "Inaugural Address to the Common Council" in the year 1855, speaks in unmistakable language to the City Fathers as follows :—

"To tolerate profligate outlays of the public money, whilst nearly one-tenth of our whole population are in want of the necessaries of life, is as shocking to humanity as it is injustice to a large and valuable class of our suffering fellow citizens.

"Surely we are admonished that if this rate of taxation be continued, more of it should be devoted to the relief of the poor, whose industry bears most of its burdens, and who are now ringing into our ears their cries of distress.

"Labor was never so depressed as now. Employment is almost entirely cut off, and if procured, its remuneration is totally inadequate, owing to the high price of articles of subsistence. The prices of labor and of food bear no relative equality.

"In ordinary times of general prosperity capital possesses advantages over labor.

"Capital can always protect itself, and it is only at periods of inflation, when capital is directed to speculation in the products of labor, that the operative is appreciated, and his industry rewarded by competent compensation.

"But now, when capital either timidly retreats, through fear, to the bank-vaults, or is diverted to the oppression, for gain, of those who employ labor, his condition is sad enough. Does it not behoove us, not only individually, but in our corporate capacity, to throw ourselves boldly forward to his relief?

"This is time to remember the poor!

"Do we not owe industry every thing? It is its products that have built up this great city.

"Do not let us be ungrateful as well as inhuman. Do not let it be said that labor, which produces every thing, gets nothing, and dies of hunger in our midst, whilst capital, which produces nothing, gets everything, and pampers in luxury and plenty."

Matters have not improved since Greeley's lamented death nigh on twenty years ago, for "poverty, hunger and dirt" meet one's every footstep on Manhattan Island. The crucifixion of the proletariat goes on in the murderous sweating shops, the fetid tenements and the vile dives permitted by American civilization.

Liberty in the harbor of New York has her back turned upon the city where the corrupt political hirelings of plutocratic despotism debauch everything. And it is no wonder that even the pulpit is aroused and clergymen speak with denunciatory voice, as did the Rev. Thomas Dixon a few Sundays ago* before his Baptist Congregation in the big hall of the Young Men's Christian Association of New York, as follows :—

"The present ruler of New York is Filth. Filth unutterable! Filth indescribable! Filth supreme! Streets piled with rubbish strewn with disease-infested garbage, heavy with dirt, or impassable with mud. What is the result?

"This great city, with its teeming millions, is threatened with an epidemic of diphtheria. The horrors of such a possibility are enough to make the stoutest heart tremble. Diphtheria, grim and horrible phantom that haunts those little pattering feet and laughing eyes!

"This dread disease has played sad havoc already in the tenements of our filth-ridden districts. There is a poor

---

* September 19, 1891, and reported in full in the New York *Herald*, the day following.

man and woman in this congregation who buried their only
little one from one of these pest holes within the past few
weeks. He told me that every child in that tenement had
diphtheria—and every one of them died except those that
were able to get away. The cellar of this house reeked in
mud and filth, and was let to those poor people at the
price of blood by the city of New York as landlord! The
building is owned by the city of New York. The
administration of the city of New York is guilty of
infanticide.

"Whence this reign of filth and carnival of disease?
The answer is easy. Filth in the streets means filth in the
City Hall. All streets lead to the City Hall. A fountain
of filth at the heart of the city is certain to pollute every
vein and artery. Filthy streets! Filthy politics!

"The water supply of the city is declared by experts
to be unfit for human use. The water supply of a great
city lies at the root of the city's life. To let this fountain
of life become a pool of filth marks the outermost limits of
the pendulum of social degradation.

"Yes, dearly beloved, how often have some of you said:
'I will have nothing to do with politics!' So you have
withdrawn and let the rascals run it. You have had
nothing to do with politics, but politics has had something
to do with you. It has filled the air you breathe with
powdered stone and sickening stench, poisoned the water
you drink and covered the ground on which you walk with
the slimy mantle of disease and death!"

The agitation against chattel slavery was another of the
numerous causes which made Horace Greeley a Socialist.
From his early childhood, and until the hour of his death,
he had been confronted with either the curse of slavery,
both chattel and wage, or the compensating consequences

thereof. Greeley states in his autobiographical *Recollections* that being "an eager, omnivorous reader, especially
of newspapers, from early childhood, I was an ardent
politician when not yet half old enough to vote. I heartily
sympathized with the Northern uprising against the admission of Missouri as a Slave State, and shared in the disappointment and chagrin so widely felt when that uprising
was circumvented and defeated by what was called a
Compromise." This took place in March, 1820, when
James Monroe was President and Greeley was just turned
nine years of age. His account of a slave hunt in Vermont
during his apprenticeship has been narrated.

But what Horace Greeley hated in later years as a
native American, was the hypocrisy of our Democratic
Republic basing its existence and laws upon the Declaration of Independence with its opening sentences reciting
man's "unalienable rights" to "life, liberty and the
pursuit of happiness," and then allowing the chattel slavery
of the negro race to be sanctioned under the Constitution
of the United States. And Greeley knew thoroughly and
felt as keenly this national disgrace as did Wendell Phillips,
when speaking before Theodore Parker's Fraternity in the
Boston Music Hall on February 17, 1861,—with a murderous New England mob outside,—his inspired oratory
brought forth these bitter words of scorn against the
United States Constitutional Convention :—

"In 1787, slave property, worth, perhaps, two hundred
millions of dollars, strengthened by the sympathy of all
other Capital, was a mighty power. It was the Rothschild
of the State. The Constitution, by its *three-fifths slave
basis*, made slaveholders an order of nobles. It was the
house of Hapsburg joining hands with the house of Rothschild. Prejudice of race was the third strand of the cable,

bitter and potent as Catholic ever bore Huguenot, or Hungary ever spit on Moslem. This fearful trinity won to its side that mysterious omnipotence called *Fashion,*—a power which, without concerted action, without either thought, law, or religion on its side, seems stronger than all of them, and fears no foe but Wealth.''

And this repudiation of the real democratic principle, as well as the bondage of the nation to Capitalism, and as a consequence forgetfulness of the rights and duties of Humanity, cost the American people,—dollars, yes,—but more than that ; during the Civil War between the years 1861 and 1865 over 413,000 lives either slain on the battle-field, or by deadly wounds thereafter, or by consequent disease therefrom, or otherwise—all brought directly about by the chattel slave holding capitalists. But every one of those then ''done i' the death'' might have been spared for many long years as wealth producers, had the makers of the United States Constitution been true to the Declaration of Independence signed eleven years before, and recognized the colored people as men and brothers with ''inalienable rights'' instead of degrading them into slaves, chattels to be bought, sold and speculated in by capitalists.

Horace Greeley foresaw what might happen, and hence was more confirmed in his belief that the capitalistic system was all wrong. He also watched what was going on around him and the violent acts of that portion of his fellow-countrymen who ''loved rum and hated niggers.'' Greeley was twenty-six years old when the poet-editor Elijah Parish Lovejoy was murdered by a pro-slavery mob on November 7, 1837, at Alton, Illinois, for publishing an Abolitionist newspaper, and as Wendell Phillips said a month afterwards in Faneuil Hall, Boston, taking ''refuge under the banner of liberty,—amid its folds ; and when he fell, its glorious stars and stripes, the emblem of free institutions, around which cluster so many heart-stirring memories, were blotted out in the martyr's blood." Truly on that occasion Anarchy showed a red flag.

After this foul crime had been enacted in consequence of Lovejoy's daring "to argue the incompatibility of slavery with the Golden Rule," Greeley's faith was more stimulated than ever against human slavery, for he remarks : "If I had ever been one of those who sneeringly asked, 'What have we of the North to do with Slavery?' the murder of Lovejoy would have supplied me with a conclusive answer. A thousand flagrant outrages had been, and were, committed upon the persons and property of men and women guilty of no crime but that of publicly condemning Slavery; but these were usually the work of irresponsible mobs, acting under some sort of excitement; but Lovejoy was deliberately, systematically, hunted to his death, simply because he would not, in a nominally Free State, cease to bear testimony as a Christian minister and journalist to the essential iniquity of slaveholding. It was thenceforth plain to my apprehension, that Slavery and true Freedom could not coëxist on the same soil."

When asked later, in 1859, by a Missouri Abolitionist for propagandist arguments as to why the abolition of slavery was a national necessity, Greeley furnished among others the following: "Because, in the order of nature, every adult human being has a *right* to use his own God-given faculties—muscles, sinews, organs—for the sustenance and comfort of himself and his family. Consequently, it is *wrong* to divest him of the control of those capacities, and render him helplessly subservient to the pleasure and aggrandizement of another. Slavery is palpably at war with the fundamental basis of our government,—the inalienable rights of man. It is a chief obstacle to the progress of republican institutions throughout the world. It is a

standing reproach to our country abroad. It is the cause
of exultation and joy on the side of the armed despots.
Slavery is the chief cause of dissension and hatred among
ourselves. It keeps us perpetually divided, jealous, hostile.
If it were abolished, we should never dream of fighting
each other, nor dissolving the Union. Slavery makes a
few rich, but sinks the great mass, even of the free, into
indolence, depravity, and misery. It prevents the accumulation of wealth. It renders land a drug. For these and
other reasons, I am among those who labor and hope for
the early and complete abolition of human, but especially
of American slavery."

Horace Greeley detested white slavery as well as
colored slavery, wages slavery as well as chattel slavery,
and between them he could see little distinction,—as we
will show later,—hence the arguments given above. But,
for these views which made him a Socialist "dyed in the
wool," the New York *Herald*, after grossly attacking him
in various editorials, on account of his Socialism, among
other things, wound up with the Anarchist threat that: "If
we decide to hang the Abolitionists, poor Greeley shall
swing on the post of honor at the head or tail of the lot.
We promise him that high honor." James Parton records
that "These efforts were at length crowned with some
degree of success. The *Tribune* office was assailed by a
mob during the Draft Riots of July, 1863, and its editor
would certainly have been put to death but for the
precautionary measures of his friends."

And there was still another American of international
reputation who was transformed into a Socialist through
the same causes and that was Wendell Phillips. It was
his voice, in conjunction with that of William Ellery
Channing, that rallied the Abolitionists of New England in
1837 when Lovejoy was martyred, but it was his own eyes

that two years before, on October 21, 1835, had seen a crowd of "gentlemen of property and standing" endeavoring like cowardly ruffians to break up a meeting of anti-slavery ladies then in session in Washington and State streets, Boston, in order to "snake out that infamous foreign scoundrel, Thompson," acknowledged by John Bright to have been "the liberator of the slaves in the British colonies," and "bring him (Thompson) to the tar kettle before dark." This plan failing, William Lloyd Garrison, the leader of the Emancipationist Movement, was "snaked out" instead, and Wendell Phillips saw that heroic reformer dragged through the streets of Boston, "his person well nigh denuded of clothing," and around his waist a rope with which, after being tarred and feathered, he was to be strangled to death at a lamp-post, from which fate he was saved by the Mayor of Boston who had him locked up in jail. For narrating these facts twenty-five years afterwards, December 21, 1860, in "cultured Boston," another mob which howled "Crush him out!" "Down with the Abolitionists!" "Bite his head off!" and the like, endeavored to seize Wendell Phillips and murder him, but he was rescued from the fate of the martyr Lovejoy,—and the right of free speech and free assemblage was "vindicated" in the Old Bay State.

Wendell Phillips ten years later, in 1870, when running as the candidate of the Labor Reform Party for the Governorship of Massachusetts, publicly announced himself a Socialist, declaring that—

"The wages system demoralizes alike the hirer and the hired, cheats both and enslaves the workingman, (while) the present system of finance robs labor, gorges capital, makes the rich richer, and the poor poorer, and turns a republic into an aristocracy of capital."

CHAPTER III.

AMERICAN SOCIALISM ANTEDATES GREELEY.

HORACE GREELEY'S conversion to a belief in Socialism was owing in a great measure, in addition to the causes already stated, to the fact that he came in contact with and studied Community Socialism, which had been established in the United States before the Declaration of Independence;—as well as Political Socialism, that had been carried into active campaign work at the polls in the State of New York about the time he was concluding his apprenticeship in Vermont over sixty years ago.

By this American Political Socialism, in which friends of his were active participants, modern European Socialism has been partially developed in its evolution, as was also the Abolitionist Movement, of which it was a political outgrowth and to which all the political efforts of American Socialists were devoted for over thirty years. And when the final triumph occurred in 1863 by the Emancipation Proclamation of Abraham Lincoln, it came mainly about through the personal work of two Socialists—Robert Dale Owen and Horace Greeley.

The Origin of American Socialism must be looked for in the primeval period, thousands upon thousands of years ago, before the dawn of history.

The American aborigines not only believed in the collective tribal ownership of the means of life, but in the personal ownership of the products of individual labor. They were identical in this respect with modern Socialists, who never were guilty of that popular fallacy of the ill-informed, that Socialism means an equal division of the individual personal property directly earned by the honest labors of other people. The American Socialist, Wilshire, can be safely quoted respecting this. He says:—"Socialism means anything but the *division* of the ownership of the means of production. Socialism contemplates the absolute *concentration* of the ownership of the wealth of the country into the *collective* control and ownership of the people themselves. The only division of things that Socialists propose, is the fair division of commodities produced, but not by any means do they propose the division of the ownership of the machinery that produced those products. For instance, the people will collectively own the land, the grain elevators, the flour mills and the bakeries, while the people individually will own the product: the bread."

Thomas Jefferson furnishes some interesting evidence on this subject, relative to the North American Indians. He was somewhat of a Socialist * himself, but had as little

---

* This is decidedly hard on the American Socialists, who are constitutionalists, and do not believe in unnecessary revolutions by force, when the ballot and legislation are available for reform, whereas Thomas Jefferson favored a kind of chronic, or rather occasional revolution. He was at heart a Jacobin and had in theory a decidedly Anarchist trend. Thus referring to the Massachusetts Rebellion of 1786-87 led by Captain Daniel Shays,—whose followers complained that "the governor's salary was too high, the senate aristocratic, the lawyers extortionate and taxes too burdensome to bear,"—Jefferson, the Democratic idol, said:—

"God forbid that we should ever be twenty years without such a rebellion. What country can preserve its liberties, if its rulers are not warned from time to time that the people preserve the spirit of resistance? Let them take arms. What signify a few lives lost? The tree of liberty must be refreshed from time to time with the blood of patriots and tyrants. It is its natural manure."

in common with the blatant pseudo-Democracy of our
period as corrupt so-called Republicanism has with the
spirit of Abolitionism, whose laurels it has filched.   In a
work prepared by himself* in 1812 for the use of counsel
in a suit in the United States District Court of Virginia
and in which he was a defendant, Jefferson writes :—"That
the lands within the limits assumed by a nation, belong to
the nation, as a body, has probably been the law of every
people on earth, at some period of their history. A right
of property, in moveable things, is admitted before the
establishment of government. A separate property, in
lands, not till after that establishment. The right to
moveables is acknowledged by all the hordes of Indians
surrounding us. Yet, by no one of them has a separate property, in lands, been yielded to individuals. He
who plants a field, keeps possession till he has gathered
the produce; after which one has as good a right as
another to occupy it. Government must be established,
and laws provided, before lands can be separately appropriated, and the owner protected in his possession. Till
then, the property is in the body of the nation, and they,
or their chief, as trustee, must grant them to individuals,
and determine the conditions of the grant."

The noble red man, the genuine American, had his
lands therefore Socialized or Nationalized, in identically
the same manner as Michael Davitt proposed to have the
lands of Ireland †—the property collectively of the people

* *The Proceedings of the United States in Maintaining the
Public Right of the Beach of the Mississippi, adjacent to New
Orleans, against the Intrusion of Edward Livingston.* New York,
published by Ezra Sergeant, 1812.

† The American Socialists were about the first to point out to
the Irish people the fallacy of compromise measures in relation to
the land question of all countries. "Nationalize the 'old sod' of
Ireland" was the advice of their progressive thinkers. The Irish

and to be held for the people, by the people and through the people as their own tenants.   This is the very opposite of the Irish National Land League theory, which would still perpetuate the capitalization of land under the old competitive system with landlords and capitalists,—"*ad sæcula sæculorum.*"

The erudite Dr. William Robertson, in the third volume of his *History of America*, quotes the sixteenth century Spanish American chronicler Antonio de Herrera to this effect :—"The state of property in Peru was no less singular than that of religion, and contributed likewise toward giving a mild turn of character to the people.   All the lands capable of cultivation were divided into three classes.   One was consecrated to the Sun, and whatever it produced was applied toward celebrating the public rites of religion. The other belonged to the Inca, and was set apart as the provision made by the community for the support of government.   The third and *largest* share was reserved for the maintenance of the people, among whom it was parcelled out.   No person, however, had a right of exclusive property, (exclusive forever, is here meant,) in the portion allotted to him.   *He possessed it only for a year*, at the expiration

National Land League was founded on October 21, 1879.   Within a month thereafter and before Charles Stewart Parnell visited the United States to raise funds for the new organization, the following call for a meeting was made by large posters throughout New York City :—"Land and Liberty for the People of Downtrodden Ireland.   Grand Mass Meeting of Sympathy with the Irish People in their Struggle against Tyranny to be held under the Auspices of the Socialist Labor Party on Friday, December 5, 1879, at 8 o'clock, P. M., Germania Assembly Rooms, 291–293 Bowery. Patrick Ford, Dr. A. Douai, Alexander Jonas, John Swinton, Henry Drury, Osborne Ward, Charles Sotheran and other citizens will address the Meeting.   The Committee."   And says the New York *People* from which the above is taken :   "The meeting duly took place and was duly reported at length in the *Irish World,* which in those days was a very advanced newspaper."

of which, a new division was made, in proportion to *the rank, the number, and exigencies* of each family. *All* those lands were cultivated by the joint industry of the community. The people, summoned by a proper officer, repaired in a body to the fields, performed their common task, while songs and musical instruments cheered them to their labor."

So much for indigenous American Socialism, but the first foreign Community Socialism imported to America may have been brought over from the Pacific Coast of Asia by those Buddhist missionaries whose records tell us they landed here centuries before the arrival of Christopher Columbus at the Island of San Salvador in 1492. Those Buddhist apostles were ascetic devotees, "Sramanas" or "Bikshus" whose successors still worship the "Light of Asia," and have control of the education of China and Thibet. They are the monks of Buddhism and live in monasteries, "Viharas," where they have a collective ownership of property, read the sacred scriptures of the divine Buddha to the people, and strive to attain "Nirvana" by a holy life of altruism.

Another form of Community Socialism was imported to the Three Americas from Europe, at the end of the Fifteenth and beginning of the Sixteenth Centuries, by those Christian "religious," who came along with or followed in the wake of the Spanish discoverers. Their conventual monasticism, conjoined to the common ownership of goods practiced by the apostles and the primitive Christians, was first adopted under the direction of St. Antony, of Thebes, in the Fourth Century. The Benedictines, Dominicans and other regular Orders of the Roman Catholic Church, whose members founded Communist monasteries and nunneries in America, were developed later.

But the palm of the earliest, yet empirical American Political and Economic Socialism combined, must be conceded to the Fathers of the Company of Jesus, who accomplished a work that even their enemy, Voltaire, called "one of the triumphs of Humanity." This was the Christian Socialistic system of Paraguay founded among the American Indians and probably partially developed from the tribal manners of the natives, by the Jesuits in the Sixteenth Century. We are told that "The legislation, the administration, and the social organization of the settlement were shaped according to the model of a primitive Christian community, or rather of many communities under one administration ; and the accounts which have been preserved of its condition, appear to present a realization of the ideal of a Christian Utopia."

Prof. Ely calls attention to the fact that the "oldest American charter" under which the first English settlement, Virginia, was made on American soil helps us to realize various forms of early Socialism and Communism. He says :—"One condition stipulated by King James was a common storehouse into which products were to be poured, and from which they were to be distributed according to the needs of the Colonists, and this was the industrial Constitution under which the first inhabitants of Jamestown lived for five years." Capt. John Smith having had a good deal of trouble with some of the idle, and probably wealthier settlers, who wanted to live on the labor of others, he informed them in good old-fashioned Anglo Saxon that "he that will not work shall not eat." "Dream no longer," said he.

"Dream no longer, of this vain hope from Powhatan, or that I will longer forbear to force you from your idleness or punish if you rail. I protest by that God that made me, since necessity hath no power to force you to gather for yourselves, you shall not only gather for yourselves, but for those that are sick. They shall not starve.''

The New England Pilgrims who landed on Plymouth Rock on December 21, 1620, had, says Prof. Ely, "a somewhat similar arrangement which they had entered into with London merchants, but the issue of the experiment was not more successful, and it was partially abandoned ; not wholly, for a great deal of land was long after held in common, and, indeed, to-day, there are small parcels of this land still common property. As is well known, the Boston Common is but a survival of early Communism, as in fact its very name indicates.''

Horace Greeley was always interested in "dryasdust" particulars like these, which can be seen in the references in his lecture on the "Social Architects," to Plato's *Republic* and Sir Thomas More's *Utopia*. It is, therefore, not the fact, as once suggested, that he never bothered his head about them at all. He was, however, more particularly observant of the American Socialistic Communities of the Shakers, the Harmonists, the Separatists and the Owenites—all of whom he refers to in the *Social Architects* and elsewhere in his writings, and many members of which he knew personally. He eulogizes them all.

The Shakers are the earliest in American origin of those named. They came to this country in 1774 and started Communist colonies soon after, some of which successfully flourish, socially and economically, until this day, as do the Harmonists and Separatists. They have all been well written up by Ely, Noyes, Nordhoff and other authors, in whose works will be found full particulars concerning them. It is generally conceded that they show the perfect success of Community Socialism under favorable conditions, equally with the Catholic conventual regular Orders, after which they seem to have been economically modeled in some particulars, although in others they resemble the Buddhist, but are quite different in their religious rites and observances from both of those ancient examples of Socialism.

The secret of their success is to be found in their unity of faith and absolute harmony in all other matters. They are better business men and women in many respects than the average manufacturer and merchant, who live "in the world," for the reason they are united in a community of interest, not making profits out of or swindling each other, within the law; and what goods produced by themselves they sell to the outer world are honest in manufacture, neither being adulterated, nor short in weight, nor in measure, etc., and are further sold at a reasonable advance on the actual cost.

They are altruists. They live for others and strive after the highest ideals vouchsafed them. They are neither sordid nor grasping, and try to live good lives according to their own lights. With them egoism is a vice and selfishness a sin. And as a rule, they really "do unto others as they would be done by," and follow the precept "Love thy neighbor as thyself." Although, living, perhaps, in metaphysical abstractions and transcendental cloudland, they have "faith" in their principles, "charity" for a misguided world and "hope" that the rest of the people of the globe will some day accept their particular form of Socialism as the perfect life.

Horace Greeley knew the Shakers and loved them. He was a warm personal friend of Elder Frederick William Evans, of Mount Lebanon Community, and of his brother, George Henry Evans, to whom the American Socialist and

Abolitionist Movements are under the deepest obligations. The *Autobiography of a Shaker* by Elder Evans, originally published in the *Atlantic Monthly*, is full of the most interesting facts associated with the early American Labor Movement. The Evans Brothers were Englishmen by birth and emigrated to this country in 1820 with their father, who had been an officer in the British army under Sir Ralph Abercromby, the commander of the Egyptian expedition that coöperated with the British fleet, under Lord Nelson. George was born in 1805 and Frederick in 1808. They were both strong Land Reformers and the earliest in this country. Prof. Ely says :—" George Henry Evans became a friend of Horace Greeley, and followed with active interest the political movements of the country up to the time of his decease, which occurred about 1870. The younger brother, Frederick W. Evans, joined the Shakers at Mount Lebanon in 1831, and now one of their leading men is familiarly known among them as Elder Frederick. He still maintains his radical social views, and they form part of his religion. One of the three days I passed with the Shakers at Mount Lebanon, in the Summer of 1885, was fortunately a Sunday, and I had the pleasure of listening to an address from Elder Frederick. I must confess that it sounded strange to me to hear the views I had associated with Henry George preached as part of a religious system ; and it was a surprise to me to learn, that the Elder had been preaching them for fifty years and more."

Elder Evans tells us in his *Autobiography* that he " early became a convert to the Socialistic theories which, about the year 1830, were so enthusiastically advocated by their respective adherents, as the grand panacea for all the wrongs perpetrated by Church and State. To all my other

radical ideas I now (about 1828) added Socialistic Communism ; and I walked eight hundred miles (starting from New
York) to join a Community at Massillon, Ohio." Next,
"about a dozen of us,—young men,—looking into the causes
which had destroyed so many Communities (some of us had
been in five or six different ones, and were well acquainted
with the whole movement), concluded to found another
Community, upon a proper basis, purely philosophical."

After further traveling, including a visit to England,
the Elder proceeds : "I returned to New York in January,
1830, when we perfected our plans for the new Community;
and I was deputed to travel for information, and to find a
suitable location in which to start. At this time we had in
New York a Hall of Science, and Robert Dale Owen and
Fanny Wright were its great lights."

Later, in 1831, the year that Horace Greeley came to
New York, Elder Evans joined the Shakers, where among
the other brothers, was one whom he specially notices—
"Abel Knight who had been a Quaker, then a Socialist,
and whose house in Philadelphia had been the head-quarters
of Communists; a man of standing in all the known
relations of life ; he was a brother indeed, and a father
too."

Before the year 1800 the Shakers had Socialistic Communities in New York, Massachusetts, Ohio, Kentucky
and other States. In 1886 they had, Prof. Ely states,
"seventeen societies and about seventy communities, as a
society may include several 'families,' or communities. The
largest society, at Mt. Lebanon, comprises nearly four
hundred souls, and it is there that Elder Frederick W.
Evans, the best known of the Shakers, resides. Their
numbers have declined in recent years, but they claim, all
told, still some four thousand members, while their property

is of great value. . . . . One who has been
some time with them, estimates their property at twelve
millions of dollars at least."

Elder Frederick W. Evans, it can be stated in addition,
has during his long life contributed to seventy different
publications. He has been a great lecturer and delivered
his well known lecture on "Religious Communism" in
St. George's Hall, London, in 1872.* He also published
in 1871 a volume entitled *Shaker Communism.*

The Harmonists, to whom Greeley makes many references in his printed works, settled in Pennsylvania in 1807,
four years before the birth of the editor of the *Tribune.*
They were Community Socialists, who came to the United
States from Germany in consequence of religious persecution. These Harmonists first settled at a place called by
them Economy, near Pittsburgh. Then they removed to
a tract of 27,000 acres lying above the Wabash River in
Indiana, to which they gave the name of New Harmony.
Later they returned to Pennsylvania where they still
flourish, and according to Prof. Ely:— "their present
wealth is estimated at sums ranging from ten to forty
millions of dollars. This is mostly the results of their
manufactures of woolen cloth, flannel goods, carpets, silk
and wines, as well as through their raising of flax, grain and

---

* The author, like many others doubtless, has to recognize his
personal interest in Socialism, partly, through the acquaintance of
Elder Evans. They first met in 1876 at the Rosehill Methodist
Episcopal Church, New York City, where the Universal Peace
Union was in session. Both made addresses, that of the writer
being printed in Philadelphia with the title—"A Peace Address,
Delivered before the New York Branch of the Universal Peace
Union, Monday, January 17, 1876, by Charles Sotheran,"—whose
first actual knowledge of Community Socialism was gained a quarter of a century ago within the walls of one of the houses of learning
of the Order of Charity. And they were very pleasant and never
to be forgotten days that were spent at St. Marie's College.

live stock." These Communists, who lead a celibate life, have been called Rappists after George Rapp, who was their leader when they came to America. He died in 1847 at Economy. Greeley was always fond of quoting them in his lectures; and Byllesby, the New York Socialist author, gives in his work printed in 1826, some twenty pages concerning them, mostly reprinted from Melish's *Travels in the Western Parts of Pennsylvania*, published in 1811.

Horace Greeley also dwells considerably on the Separatists, a religious sect of Community Socialists, who emigrated from Wurtemburg, in Germany, when Greeley was six years of age. By the pecuniary assistance of the Philadelphia Quakers, whose peace views they hold, they were enabled to establish themselves in 1817 at Zoar, Tuscarawas County, Ohio, where they still live. They are devoted Socialists and strongly object to "the industrial and social system of the outside world." Prof. Knight, a friend of Prof. Ely, visited the Separatists a few years ago and was told by one of them, in answer to his question:

"We all live comfortably, we don't have to worry about money matters, we are all on an equality, and we are sure of being taken care of when we are too old to work. Can you say the same for everybody where you live?"

Both Greeley and Byllesby devote much attention to the Owenite Socialistic Community system, the former particularly in his lecture on the "Social Architects." Byllesby's work on the *Sources and Effects of Unequal Wealth* was written in consequence of the importance attached in the United States to the economic views of Robert Owen at the beginning of this century, and which he had carried into practice, years before he advocated Political Socialism.

Horace Greeley knew Owen intimately, and in 1851, when in London, he celebrated the old Socialist Reformer's eightieth birthday with him and other friends at the Colbourne Hotel.

"I cannot," Greeley wrote at the time, "see many things as he does ; it seems to me that he is stone-blind on the side of Faith in the invisible, and exaggerates the truths he perceives until they almost become falsehoods ; but I love his sunny, benevolent nature, I admire his unwearied exertions for what he deems the good of humanity ; and, believing with the great apostle to the Gentiles, that 'Now abide faith, hope, charity ; these three ; but the greatest of these is charity,' I consider him practically a better Christian than half those who, professing to be such, believe more and do less."

Robert Owen, who was born five years before the Declaration of Independence, was a Political as well as an Economic Socialist. His name is usually, however, only connected with the latter. Three years before the birthday celebration in which Horace Greeley participated, Owen went to Paris during the Revolution of 1848 to help Louis Blanc and others in the direction of Political Socialism, just as twenty years before he had gone to Mexico on a visit of propaganda. He never lost faith in his industrial belief,—for once a Socialist always a Socialist,—and when eighty-seven years of age a few weeks before his death on November 17, 1858, he attended the convention of the Social Science Association at Liverpool—"with all his schemes as fresh and complete as ever," as recorded in Chambers's *Encyclopædia*.

Owen in 1799 transformed his cotton-mills at New Lanark on the Clyde into a coöperative enterprise, taking his men into partnership with him. Being a philanthropist by nature, it struck Owen, says a capitalist authority, "that much degradation, vice and suffering arose from the disorganized manner in which the progress of machinery and manufactures was huddling the manufacturing population together. He introduced into the New Lanark Community education, sanitary reform, and various civilizing agencies, which philanthropists, at the present day, are but imperfectly accomplishing in the great manufacturing districts (of Great Britain). The mills became a center of attraction. They were daily visited by every illustrious traveler in Britain, from crowned heads downward, and it was delightful not only to see the decency and order of everything, but to hear the bland persuasive eloquence of the garrulous and benevolent organizer.

"A factory," the same writer continues, "was, however, far too limited a sphere for his ambition. He wanted to organize the world ; and that there might be no want of an excuse for his intervention, he set about proving that it was in all its institutions—the prevailing religion included— in as wretched a condition as any dirty demoralized manufacturing village. Such was the scheme with which he came out on the astonished world in 1816, in his *New Views of Society, or Essays on the Formation of the Human Character;* and he continued in books, pamphlets, lectures and other available forms, to keep up the stream of excitation till it was stopped by his death." *

---

* Although Robert Owen did not first visit the United States until about 1825, after his purchase of New Harmony, Indiana, from the Harmonists or Rappites, yet his philanthropic labors were recognized in this country, years before then. One of the earliest notices of Owen will be found in the "concluding appendice" to the *Pleasures of Contemplation*, by Thomas Branagan, published at Philadelphia in 1817, in which the author remarks : "I have read with much interest pieces in the *Aurora*, wrote with the view of correcting the present mode of civilization ; but the author,

Robert Owen purchased in 1826 the colony of New Harmony, in Indiana, from the Harmonists, with dwellings for one thousand persons, and there founded a Socialistic colony. But it was not a success. Evans writes in his *Autobiography*, published in 1869: "I understand that Mr. Emerson, in a recent lecture in Boston, made some statements relative to communities, the causes of their failure, etc. Robert Owen published his view of the causes of failure at New Harmony, as follows: 'There was not disinterested industry; there was not mutual confidence; there was not practical experience; there was not unison of action, because there was not unanimity of counsel. These were the points of difference and dissension, the rock upon which the social bark struck and was wrecked.'"

Ralph Waldo Emerson did, however, in his heart of

---

whose name is Mr. Owen, though deserving a statue of gold for his excellent and benevolent remarks, little thought how futile it was to attempt to prevail upon those who live in elegant idleness upon the corruptions of society, freely to forego their ill-gotten prey." Another appendix to this interesting volume is by a Quaker, one Doctor C. C. Blatchley, of New York city, and which has a separate title, dated 1817, commencing—*Some Causes of Popular Poverty.* The good physician in his twenty-five pages opposed "the enriching nature of interests, rents, duties, inheritances, and church establishments." Thus he asserted: "If they who benefited general society were the only persons rewarded for their diligence, ingenuity, and labor, industry would be rewarded and thrive; and indolence (the luxurious, the lazy, the idle, the extravagant and injurious) be punished by poverty." And again: "Money goods and lands are intended to be used; and they who cannot occupy and use them should let those hold and improve them who can and desire to. But the avaricious spirit of the world, which craves *what justly belongs to others*, will be opposed to such principles and practice, and object many plausible difficulties that I cannot now attend to obviate and remedy. I hope the humane will obviate them." Dr. Blatchley whose mind, nigh upon seventy-five years ago, was assuredly "Socialistically bent," concluded what he had to say, with the well known verses from the Christian Apostle St. James, denouncing the rich of the First Century who kept back "the hire of the laborers."

hearts believe in Socialism, even if he did not live the community life of good old Elder Evans. In 1883, writing on Socialists with whom he had been intimately acquainted, Emerson in his "Historic Notes of Life and Letters in Massachusetts," published in the *Atlantic Monthly* says : "These reformers were a new class. Instead of the fiery souls of the Puritans, bent on hanging the Quaker, burning the witch, and banishing the Romanist, these were gentle souls, with peace and even with genial dispositions, casting sheep's-eyes even on Fourier and his houris. It was a time when the air was full of reform. Robert Owen, of Lanark, came hither from England in 1845, and read lectures or held conversations wherever he found listeners, —the most amiable, sanguine and candid of men. He had not the least doubt that he had hit on a right and perfect Socialism, or that all mankind would adopt it. He was then seventy years old, and being asked :

"'Well, Mr. Owen, who is your disciple? How many men are there possessed of your views who will remain, after you are gone, to put them in practice?'

"'Not one,' was his reply.

"Robert Owen," Emerson proceeds, "knew Fourier in his old age. He said that Fourier learned of him all the truth he had ; the rest of his system was imagination, and the imagination of a banker. Owen made the best impression by his rare benevolence. His love of men made us forget his 'Three Errors.' His charitable construction of men and their actions was invariable. He was the better Christian in his controversy with Christians, and he interpreted with great generosity the acts of the Holy Alliance and Prince Metternich, with whom the persevering doctrinaire had obtained interviews.

"'Ah,' he said, 'you may depend on it, there are as

tender hearts and as much good will to serve men in palaces as in cottages.'"

Ralph Waldo Emerson then writes:—"And truly, I honor the generous ideas of the Socialists, the magnificence of their theories, and the enthusiasm with which they have been urged. They appeared the inspired men of their time. Mr. Owen preached his doctrine of labor and reward to the slow ears of his generation with the fidelity and devotion of a Saint."

But the philosopher of Concord, writing with American revolutionary and literary memories clustering around him "as thick as the leaves of Vallambrosa" and on the spot where—

". . . . . . . once the embattled farmers stood,
And fired the shot heard round the world,"

doubtless recorded correctly Owen's statement that "not one" would put his theories into practice when he was gone. But that belief will not be verified. There are to-day in the two hemispheres, millions of Socialists,—every one of whom is a missionary,—who are still sowing the same seed as he did,—but with scientific additions and newer machinery,—to transform this globe of ours into an earthly paradise.

So much for the present, of that American Economic Socialism which antedated the Socialism of Horace Greeley.

Before discussing the Political Socialism which confronted Greeley as a young man, when he arrived in New York, over sixty years ago, we will glance at the conditions that preceded the early Independent Political Labor Movement of the United States.

The Declaration of Independence, with its terse, yet

grand sentences, was never realized by the proletariat of the United States, fully half a century after it was written, to be a document that in certain particulars could apply to their own condition. It was read in the schools from time to time, and, amid a din of gunpowder and fireworks, was recited as the prelude to the rhetorical efforts of "distinguished" Fourth of July orators. And there it ended, for its liberty-stirring phrases were to the average mechanic or laborer something which only referred to the expulsion of a foreign despotism from "Columbia, Happy Land!" It had nothing apparently to do with the particular environment or condition of the lowly bread-winners.

So with the Constitution of the United States and the Constitutions of the different States, for their Articles and Sections and Clauses were to the working people simply glittering generalities. They were affairs with which only statesmen and politicians had to do, and such were not of their class. It is true, Roger Sherman had been a shoemaker, but when the Revolution broke out, he was a Judge, having graduated from the politician grade into the ranks of the superior middle-class aristocracy. Two or three other signers, like him, had been workers once at the bench, but they never would have had their names affixed to the Declaration of Independence, if they had not had property qualifications to enable them to be enrolled among the representatives of the United States, on July 4, 1776.

Particularly was this the case in the State of New York,— where Greeley resided almost continuously from 1831 until 1872,—for although the National Constitution meant universal suffrage, it was not until 1821 that at the State Constitutional Convention, we hear of a limited extension of the electoral franchise, with blue bloods of the Martin Van Buren type strongly objecting to its being permitted to all male citizens.   Thus the result was, that it was not until 1830 that the workingmen of the State even thought of nominating a Governor of their own, and then only to be side-tracked, as they were over and over again in the few miserable lesser nominations they made for long years afterwards.

Governors, State Senators and Assemblymen all belonged to the wealthy and middle classes, never to the masses.   Take the roll of New York's Governors, from the first holder of the position, after the Constitutional period, in 1789, following the close of the Revolution, until 1831, the year of Greeley's arrival in New York city. Not one of the proletarian class, or who immediately even came out of it, is on the list.

George Clinton, who was twice elected Governor, in 1789 and 1801, was a lawyer by profession and the son of Col. Charles Clinton, who was a Judge before the Revolution.   The next occupant of the gubernatorial chair was John Jay, an aristocrat of aristocrats, whose mother was a Van Cortlandt and wife a Livingston, thus connecting him with both the Dutch patroons and British Lords of Manors, who owned huge sections of the State.   Morgan Lewis was elected in 1804 Governor of New York and was the son of one of the largest landed proprietors of Long Island. Following him and elected in 1807 was Daniel D. Tompkins, whose family were big Westchester County landowners. John Tayler, who was acting Governor in 1816, when Tompkins became Vice-President of the United States, was a merchant originally, but threw that overboard when he went into political life, forty years of which he spent in the New York Legislature.   De Witt Clinton, was the next Governor in 1817—he was re-elected in 1824—and was the son of General James Clinton and nephew of Governor

Geo. Clinton, already named. In 1822 Joseph C. Yates was Governor, being sandwiched in between De Witt Clinton's two terms and like him, was a lawyer by profession, having been a Judge of the Supreme Court previously. Martin Van Buren, who was elected Governor of the State in 1828 and later became President, was likewise a lawyer, and his father was a rich land owner of old Knickerbocker stock.

All of these Governors were thus either of wealthy and landed families, or lawyers, and hence had nothing whatever in common with the proletarian wage-earners of their period, except to help in keeping them dependent on their own capitalistic associates.

Native-born American workingmen—very much like the great majority of their descendants now—during the administrations of Washington, John Adams, Jefferson, Madison, Monroe and John Quincy Adams could, for combining for defensive industrial purposes, without hardly a murmur, be arrested, jailed, tried, convicted and fined or sentenced to hard labor. Disfranchised, they saw the first elections under a new constitutional government take place in 1789, when the polls were kept open for weeks and voters brought from distant places to turn the scale of victory. They were comparatively docile and patient and allowed the infamous capitalistic conspiracy laws against labor to harass their lives out and they said naught to ameliorate their own condition. Yet they would rage furiously, as they did in 1793 and 1794, against the crowned heads of Europe when the young movement began of the Democrats, who were originally so-called, as Houghton tells us, in reproach because "the party in power claimed to be Federal Republicans, and when they were accused of being monarchists and enemies of free institutions, they repelled the charge and 'stigmatized the Republicans as

Democrats,' an appellation assumed by the ferocious
Jacobins who had so lately filled France with frenzy, terror
and bloodshed."

In those days to be called a "Democrat" was considered quite as insulting and infamous as being styled now-
a-days an "Anarchist," and it was not half so respectable
in the public opinion as even now is thought to be that
grossly misrepresented individual "a Socialist." But
fashions and opinions change. A few years hence, within
perhaps a quarter of a century, society will wonder that
there ever existed such disreputable persons as millionaires
and capitalists.

But to revert to the early days of the Republic. Then
these Democratic proletarians, like those of Wythe County,
Virginia, would declare the "constitution wanted mending,"
and that "if this was not done Washington might become
the greatest despot on earth." But their own industrial
bondage was as nothing to them for fully thirty years thereafter, and even then, at the polls they sided with their
oppressors, except for a year or two, and then the capitalists
gobbled up their leaders.

There was, however, with the great majority of Americans
a sentiment of intense sympathy with the aspirations of the
French Revolution, and a feeling of terrible indignation
when the reactionary Directory, in the interests of the
bourgeoisie, had guillotined on May 24, 1797, the two
Socialist martyrs, Francis Noel. Babeuf, better known as
"Gracchus" Babeuf, and Augustin Alexander Darthé, for
preaching political and social equality in a Republic and,
at the same time working for the return of the people of
France to the purely constitutional administration, laid
down by their legal Constitution.

Babeuf had dared to formulate the needs of French
citizens in the following fifteen articles :—

"I. Nature has given to each individual an equal right to the enjoyment of all the goods of life.

"II. The end of society is to defend this equality, often assailed by the strong and wicked in the state of nature; and to augment, by the coöperation of all, the common enjoyments of all.

"III. Nature has imposed on each person the obligation to work; nobody could, without crime, evade his share of the common labor.

"IV. Labor and enjoyments ought to be common.

"V. There is oppression wherever one part of Society is exhausted by labor, and in want of everything, whilst the other part wallows in abundance, without doing any work at all.

"VI. Nobody could, without crime, exclusively appropriate to himself the goods of the earth or of industry.

"VII. In a veritable society there ought to be neither rich nor poor.

"VIII. The rich, who are not willing to renounce their superfluities in favor of the indigent, are the enemies of the people.

"IX. No one can, by accumulating to himself all the means, deprive another of the instruction necessary for his happiness. Instruction ought to be common to all.

"X. The end of the French Revolution is to destroy inequality, and to reëstablish general prosperity.

"XI. The Revolution is not terminated, because the rich absorb all valuable productions, and command exclusively; whilst the poor toil like real Slaves, pine in misery, and count for nothing in the State.

"XII. The Constitution of 1793 is the veritable law of Frenchmen, because the people have solemnly accepted it; because the Convention had not the right to change

it ; because to succeed in superseding it, the Convention
has caused the people to be shot for demanding its execution ;* because it has hunted and massacred the deputies,
who performed their duty in defending it ; because a system
of terrorism against the people, and the influence of
emigrants, † have presided over the fabrication and pretended acceptation of the Constitution of 1795, which nevertheless, had not a quarter of the number of suffrages in its
favor that the Constitution of 1793 has obtained ; because
the Constitution of 1793 has consecrated the inalienable
right of every citizen to consent to the laws, to exercise
political rights, to meet in assembly, to propose what he
deems useful, to receive instruction, and not to die of hunger ; rights which the counter-revolutionary Act of 1795
has openly and completely violated.

"XIII. Every citizen is bound to reëstablish and
defend in the Constitution of 1793, the will and happiness
of the people.

"XIV. All the powers emanating from the pretended
Constitution of 1795 are illegal and counter-revolutionary.

"XV. Those who have used violence against the
Constitution of 1793 are guilty of High Treason against
the nation."

And then resulted their trial, at which, as described by
Buonarroti, the anarchical minded tribunal sentenced Babeuf
and Darthé,—both of whom had opposed Robespierre and

* On the First Prairial of the Year III., and the days following,
Bourbotte, Duroy, Duquesnoy, Goujon, Romme, and Soubrany
were put to death. Peyssard was deported and Forestier condemned to prison.

† The men of the popular party were publicly massacred, or
thrust in heaps into dungeons. A great number of emigrants, and
more especially all who had deserted after the Revolution of the
31st of May, had been recalled since the 9th Thermidor of the
Year II.

the Terrorists,—to "Die!" and in these words seven of their associates, Buonarroti, Germain, Cazin, Moroy, Blondeau, Meneissier and Bouin,—to transportation with hard labor :—

"Go and drag along a miserable life, far from your country, in burning and murderous climes."

Mignet, the French Historian, writes :—"They none of them belied their character; they spoke like men who were neither afraid to avow their designs nor to die for their cause. At the beginning and end of each examination, they hummed the air of the 'Marseillaise.' This ancient song of victory, joined with their confident demeanor, struck the spectators with astonishment and seemed to render them still more formidable. Their wives having followed them before the tribunal, Babeuf in finishing his defense, turned toward them and said,—

" 'They might follow them to the very place of execution, for their punishment could not make them blush.' "

Buonarroti, their fellow "conspirator," and who was condemned to transportation, in his *History of the Conspiracy for Equality*, writes of these Socialist Martyrs :—"Their courage never belied itself; and strong in conscience they marched resolutely to the scaffold, as to a triumph. Immediately before receiving the stroke of death, Babeuf spoke of his love for the people, to whom he recommended his family. A general mourning prevailed when those generous defenders of equality lost their lives."

Before 1797 was over Napoleon Bonaparte was made by the Directory,—the murderers of these heroes,—Commander-in-chief of the French Army, and before another year was ended, on the 18th Brumaire, he was First Consul and Ruler of France.

Twenty-two years after the judicial assassinations of Babeuf and Darthé another occurrence happened which stirred up the indignation of thinking minds in America. This was the "Massacre at Peterloo," on September 6, 1819, by cavalry, of a number of unarmed men who were peaceably agitating * for the rights of labor. That celebrated poem the "Masque of Anarchy," written by Percy Bysshe Shelley, † who although born in luxury and the heir to great wealth and title, was a Socialist,—attracted the attention of all the friends of true liberty, more particularly his closing lines calling the "heroes of unwritten story" to

> "Rise like lions after slumber
> In unvanquishable NUMBER !
> Shake your chains to earth, like dew
> Which in sleep had fall'n on you ;
> 'YE ARE MANY—THEY ARE FEW.' "

As Babeuf and his brother Socialists endeavored to bring their countrymen to the "veritable" spirit of the French Revolution, so, emulating them, a little band of cultured thinkers in New York city essayed to make their fellow American Citizens have carried into practical effect

---

* American Socialists have had some bitter experiences in this direction. While this volume was being prepared the United Central Labor Federations of New York, Brooklyn and Hudson County, New Jersey, passed resolutions denouncing an outrage by the police and politicians on a mass meeting of Socialists held in New York city on October 17, 1891, where Prof. De Leon was addressing his fellow citizens. One of these resolutions recited that "The brutal attack upon a mass-meeting of thousands of American citizens (Socialists) at Union Square, New York city, on October 8, 1887, by the police, still remains unpunished although still other infamous attacks on free speech are committed in defiance of Article 1 of the Constitution, which gives citizens the right peaceably to assemble and have full freedom of speech for a redress of grievances."

† *Percy Bysshe Shelley as a Philosopher and Reformer.* By Charles Sotheran. New York, 1876.

the principles of the true spirit of the American Revolution, based upon the Declaration of Independence.

Life-long friends of Horace Greeley were among those who played the principal part in this early Political Socialistic Movement of which Elder Evans is the historian. After narrating the story of his own childhood up to his twelfth year in 1820, he refers in his *Autobiography* to his brother George H. Evans, with whom he spent the next ten years of his life and who was a radical in civil government, but "made his mark upon the page of history, which has recorded the current of thought as it flowed down from the *founders* of the American government, upon principles more nearly realizing the abstract truisms affirmed in the Declaration of Independence than were ever before advanced.

"George started the land-reform movement in this country, on the basis of the principle laid down by Jefferson, that 'the land belongs to man *in usufruct* only.' And *that idea* was, doubtless, entertained by all the signers of the Declaration of Independence. George was contemporary with Horace Greeley in his younger days; and, at the time of starting the New York *Tribune*, they were fast friends. This school of mind had progressed up to the Community theories of Fourier and Owen, and the attempts to realize them in various places in Europe and America were most rife about the year 1830. The right *to be* and the right *to land*, each included the other; we held that they were identical; and hence we waged a fierce and relentless war against all forms of property accumulation that owed their origin to land monopoly, speculation, or usury."

Elder Evans then proceeds to state:—"While still an apprentice at Ithaca, G. H. E. published *The Man*. Afterwards I combined my means with his, and we published, successively, *The Workingman's Advocate*, *The Daily Sentinel*, and, finally, *Young America*, besides a great variety of other publications, including *The Bible of Reason*, etc., etc. ; none of which, in a pecuniary point of view, was successful ; for G. H. E. was a poor financier, and we had a tremendous current to stem.   But that these publications had a controlling influence upon the American press, may be inferred from the very frequent quotations in other papers from the editorials of *Young America*, and also from the fact that six hundred papers indorsed the following measures, which were printed at the head of *Young America :*—

"I. The right of man to the soil : Vote yourself a farm.

"II. Down with monopolies, especially the United States Bank.

"III. Freedom of the public lands.

"IV. Homesteads made inalienable.

"V. Abolition of all laws for the collection of debts.

"VI. A general bankrupt law.

"VII. A lien of the laborer upon his own work for his wages.

"VIII. Abolition of imprisonment for debt.

"IX. Equal rights for women with men in all respects.

"X. ABOLITION OF CHATTEL SLAVERY AND OF WAGES SLAVERY.

"XI. Land limitation to one hundred and sixty acres,—no person, after the passage of the law, to become possessed of more than that amount of land.   But, when a land monopolist died, his heirs were to take each his legal number of acres, and be compelled to sell the overplus, using the proceeds as they pleased.

"XII. Mails, in the United States, to run on the Sabbath,

"These and similar views and principles we held and propagated to the very best of our ability; for our whole hearts and souls were in them. This Spartan band was few in number; but there were deep thinkers among them; and all were earnest, practical workers in behalf of the down-trodden masses of humanity."

The abolition of "wages slavery," as well as of "chattel slavery." That is the key-note to the whole movement, —as well as it was of Babeuf's,—and it eventuated into a "Workingmen's Party Convention" coming together in 1830 at Syracuse, in New York State. Ezekiel Williams was nominated for Governor and—"received less than 3,000 votes." The New York City and County Workingmen's ticket was run on a fusion with the Whigs, and resulted in the election of Silas M. Stilwell, Gideon Tucker, Ebenezer Ford and George Curtis. Thurlow Weed, in his *Autobiography*, from which these details are learned, goes on to show that between 1831 and 1834 the "Workingmen" were comparatively quiescent, but in 1835 they elected to the State legislature Thomas Hertell and Job Haskell, a carman, of whom Weed sneeringly writes:— "Job was inflated with his success and tried to be a reformer but failed." Thurlow Weed reprints a newspaper interview of September, 1873, in which he stated:—"About forty-five years ago an attempt was made to organize a workingmen's party in New York; in fact the party was organized. It had papers published in its interest, plenty of men who devoted all their energies to its success, and really did an extensive work. It elected one (or more) of its candidates to the legislature. That party I regarded as dangerous. . . . . . The party was put down after an existence of a single year."

But Thurlow Weed was mistaken in the latter part of

his statement, as the anti-slavery movement,—better known as Socialism,—is not yet put down, much less was it in a single year, for "it will not down," or be "downed." Whereas it was then confined to a single State of the American Union, now it belongs to the whole world. It is the International Socialist Labor Movement.

The "Spartan Band," to which Elder Evans referred was not "snuffed out," because, as he asserts, "It was war between abstract right and conventional rights. We held the Constitution to be only a compromise between the first principles of the American government, as they were set forth in the Declaration of Independence, drawn up by Jefferson, and the then existing vested rights of property-holders and conservatives of all sorts, secular and religious ; and we contended that the mutual, well-understood intention and design of the founders of the government was, that, as soon as was possible, the Constitution should be amended, so as to conform more and more to the ideal pattern set forth in the declaration of rights inherent in humanity, it being a question *only* as to *how long* an acknowledged *wrong* should be permitted !"

Then the Elder goes on to say :—"Our little party gradually and steadily increased, and acquired the title of 'The Locofoco Party' in the following manner : On the evening of the 29th of October, 1835, a great meeting was to be held in Tammany Hall, by the Democratic party (which was then and there split into two, and in which the Radical Land Reformers triumphed, taking with them a large portion of the party). The conservative leaders came up the back stairs into the hall, and secured the fore part of the meeting, and elected a chairman and committee. But these were finally entirely outvoted by the thousands of workingmen who crowded into and filled the hall, ejecting

Isaac L. Varian, whom the monopolists had installed, and putting in Joel Curtis as chairman. Then the conservatives retired in disgust down the back stairs as they came in, and revengefully turned off the gas, leaving the densely packed hall in total darkness. The cry was raised, 'Let there be light,' and 'there was light'; for locofoco matches were ignited all over the room, and applied to candles, when a fine illumination ensued, creating great enthusiasm, which finally resulted in the election of Andrew Jackson and B. M. Johnson as President and Vice-President of the United States. For it was soon found that the Locofoco party held the balance of power; and they offered their entire vote to whichever of the parties would put at the head of their great papers the twelve measures above enumerated, and the offer was accepted by the Democratic party."

It was a fortunate thing for the Progressive Movement that there were among its membership those who did not allow their individualities to be lost in that Democratic Party of which Horace Greeley wrote in the following terms in 1854:—"Our Democracy has now, with a corrupt Christianity, reduced the United States to a great conspirator against human liberty. Aggression, annexation, slave-extension are all contained and approved in the so-called Democracy and so-called Christianity which coalesces with it. We need men—not trading priests, nor trading politicians, nor trading merchants—but men—men who see what Christianity is in its sublime morality, and what Democracy is according to the organic spirit and the political instrument which underlie the whole theory and practice of this Government—the Declaration of Independence, in a word. We need journals—not echoes, not subscriber-hunting, popularity-cherishing organs—but presses

of light and liberty. We need advocates of principles and
enemies of truckling and corruption. Our great men so
called have failed to reduce a great political truth to
practice during this century. They have dallied with the
evil. If in the South, they have held with the grip of
exasperated avarice to their bondmen ; if in the North, they
have been careful not to offend their Southern brethren,
lest they should not get the regular nomination. And
what has all this South done which has so lorded it with
her one hundred or two hundred thousand negro-drivers,
over this country?"

But the good men, the true and the tried, managed to
have put in the Locofoco platform stirring "words" for
the protection of all, and the repeal of bad laws, but above
all, the demand that all men must contribute to the
necessities of society. They further had declared
"unqualified hostility to any and all monopolies by legislation, because they are violations of equal rights of the
people ; hostility to the dangerous and unconstitutional
creation of vested rights or prerogatives by legislation,
because they are usurpations of the people's sovereign
rights ; (and that) no legislative or other authority in the
body politic can rightfully, by charter or otherwise, exempt
any man or body of men in any case whatever, from trial
by jury and the jurisdiction or operation of the laws which
govern the community," etc.

Yet they were only "words" after all to those "professional labor politicians," who had crept into the ranks
and whose acts led that keen sighted old political lobbyist,
Thurlow Weed, to say in after years about them :—"There
are now, as there have been in the past, spasmodic organizations of workingmen, with organs, candidates and party
platforms ; but in all the past the result has been almost

invariably the same. The representatives of those organizations, or the men elected to office, have, after election, sold out to the highest bidder, corporation, party or individual, wherever was to be obtained the highest price for treachery.'' And so even into the early American Progressive Movement, as the legend tells us into the Garden of Eden, there crept the serpent—which was followed by the Temptation and then the Fall of the Locofocos,—who practically allied themselves through the Democratic Party with the natural enemies of their Socialistic originators—the slave-holding capitalists.

But many of the measures inaugurated by the ''Spartan Band,'' mainly through their agitation in the ranks of the Abolition and Land Reform Movements, were finally taken hold of, by the popular recognition of their necessity, and as Elder Evans proudly recorded, ''during the last thirty-eight years (1831--1869, have been) accomplished the following among our progressive purposes, viz. :—

''II. The United States Bank overthrown.

''III. Freedom of public lands to actual settlers secured.

''IV. Homestead laws in nearly all of the States.

''VI. General bankrupt laws passed by the United States.

''VII. Lien of laborers upon work to a great extent secured.

''VIII. Abolition of imprisonment for debt, in most of the States.

''X. Abolition of chattel slavery in the United States entire.''

Mighty good work indeed for a handful of reformers who, first starting as Socialists, developed into Abolitionists, and with the assistance of Horace Greeley and other anti-slavery advocates saw chattel slavery destroyed, after they had been persecuted for thirty long years for waging war against it.

Robert Owen had gone to the great majority without seeing all the colored slaves emancipated, but while working in the Political Socialist Movement, he had rejoiced at the Emancipation of the Negro Slaves consummated in the State of New York on July 4, 1827 ; and then with his son, Robert Dale Owen, determined to continue working for the freedom of white and colored slaves alike by legislation, and accordingly the emancipation of slaves, white and black, was put in the Workingmen's Party Platform.

Robert Dale Owen had the satisfaction, however, of knowing on January 1, 1863, when Lincoln's Emancipation Proclamation took effect, that not only what he had been one of those to inaugurate over three decades before, had been accomplished ; and that directly through his personal advocacy and influence, the Martyr President had been led to sign that document freeing four millions of human beings from bondage.

The witness to this was Salmon P. Chase, the Secretary of the Treasury and afterwards Chief Justice of the Supreme Court of the United States, who acknowledged that Robert Dale Owen's letter to Lincoln advocating the policy of emancipation as sanctioned by the laws of war and dictates of humanity, "had more effect in deciding the President to make his Proclamation than all the other communications received."

But most certainly to Horace Greeley was also due a great deal of that honor as well. In August, 1862, he addressed in the New York *Tribune* an open letter to Abraham Lincoln. It was shortly after General McClellan's retreat from the Chickahominy, which followed his defeat by the rebel forces. His appeal to the Chief Executive was headed "The Prayer of Twenty Millions," and in the course of it he requested the President to write to the United States Ministers in Europe and ask them "to tell you (Lincoln) candidly, whether the seeming subserviency of your policy to the slave-holding, slavery upholding interest is not the perplexity, the despair of statesmen and of parties, and be admonished by the general answer."

President Lincoln publicly replied to this public appeal of Horace Greeley as follows :—

"EXECUTIVE MANSION, WASHINGTON,
August 22, 1862.

"HON. HORACE GREELEY :—

"DEAR SIR :—I have just read yours of the 19th, addressed to myself through the New York *Tribune*. If there be in it statements or assumptions of fact which I may know to be erroneous, I do not now and here controvert them. If there be in it any inferences which I may believe to be falsely drawn, I do not now and here argue against them. If there be perceptible in it an impatient and dictatorial tone, I waive it in deference to an old friend, whose heart I have always supposed to be right.

"As to the policy I 'seem to be pursuing,' as you say, I have not meant to leave any one in doubt.

"I would save the Union. I would save it the shortest way under the Constitution. The sooner the national authority can be restored, the nearer the Union will be 'the Union as it was.' It there be those who would not save the Union unless they could at the same time *save* slavery, I do not agree with them. If there be those who would not save the Union unless they could at the same time *destroy* slavery, I do not agree with them. My paramount object in this struggle *is* to save the Union, and is *not* either to save or destroy slavery. If I could save the Union without freeing *any* slave I would do it ; and if I could save it by freeing *all* the slaves, I would do it ; and if I could do it by freeing some and leaving others alone, I would also do that. What I do about slavery and the colored race, I do because I believe it helps to save this Union ; and what I forbear, I forbear because I do *not* believe it would help to save the Union, I shall do *less* whenever I shall believe what I am doing hurts the cause, and I shall do *more* whenever I shall believe doing more will help the cause. I shall try to correct errors when shown to be errors ; and I shall adopt new views so fast as they shall appear to be true views. I have here stated my purpose according to my views of *official* duty, and I intend no modification of my oft-expressed *personal* wish that all men, everywhere, could be free.

"Yours, A. LINCOLN."

Greeley thereupon published the subjoined reply :—

"DEAR SIR :—Although I did not anticipate nor seek any reply to my former letter unless through your official acts, I thank you for having accorded one, since it enables me to say explicitly that nothing was further from my thought than to impeach in any manner the sincerity or the intensity of your devotion to the saving of the Union. I never doubted, and have no friend who doubts, that you desire, before and above all else, to re-establish the now derided authority, and vindicate the territorial integrity, of the Republic. I intended to raise only this question,— *Do you propose to do this by recognizing, obeying, and enforcing the laws, or by ignoring, disregarding, and in effect defying them ?*

" I stand upon the law of the land. The humblest has a clear right to invoke its protection and support against even the highest. That law—in strict accordance with the law of nations, of Nature, and of God—declares that every traitor now engaged in the infernal work of destroying our country has forfeited thereby all claim or color of right lawfully to hold human beings in slavery. I ask of you a clear and public recognition that this law is to be obeyed wherever the national authority is respected. I cite to you instances wherein men fleeing from bondage to traitors to the protection of our flag have been assaulted, wounded, and murdered by soldiers of the Union, unpunished and unrebuked by your General Commanding,—to prove that it is your duty to take action in the premises,—action that will cause the law to be proclaimed and obeyed wherever your authority or that of the Union is recognized as paramount. The Rebellion is strengthened, the national cause is imperiled, by every hour's delay to strike Treason this staggering blow.

" When Fremont proclaimed freedom to the slaves of rebels, you constrained him to modify his proclamation into rigid accordance with the terms of the existing law. It was your clear right to do so. I now ask of you conformity to the principle so sternly enforced upon him. I ask you to instruct your generals and commodores, that no loyal person—certainly none willing to render service to the national cause—is henceforth to be regarded as the slave of any traitor. While no rightful government was ever before assailed by so wanton and wicked a rebellion as that of the slaveholders against our national life, I am sure none ever before hesitated at so simple and primary an act of self-defence, as to relieve those who would serve and save it from chattel servitude to those who are wading through seas of blood to subvert and destroy it. Future generations will with difficulty realize that there could have been hesitation on this point. Sixty years of general and boundless subserviency to the slave power do not adequately explain it.

"Mr. President, I beseech you to open your eyes to the fact that the devotees of slavery everywhere—just as much in Maryland as in Mississippi, in Washington as in Richmond—are to-day your enemies, and the implacable foes of every effort to re-establish the national authority by the discomfiture of its assailants. Their President is not Abraham Lincoln, but Jefferson Davis. You may draft them to serve in the war; but they will only fight under the Rebel flag. There is not in New York to-day a man who really believes in slavery, loves it, and desires its perpetuation, who heartily desires the crushing out of the Rebellion. He would much rather save the Republic by buying up and pensioning off its assailants. His 'Union as it was' is a Union of which you were not President, and no one who truly wished freedom to all, ever could be.

"If these are truths, Mr. President, they are surely of the gravest importance. You cannot safely approach the great and good end you so intently meditate by shutting your eyes to them. Your deadly foe is not blinded by any mist in which *your* eyes may be enveloped. He walks straight to his goal, knowing well his weak point, and most unwillingly betraying his fear that you too may see and take advantage of it. God grant that his apprehension may prove prophetic!

"That you may seasonably perceive these vital truths as they will shine forth on the pages of history,—that they may be read by our children irradiated by the glory of our national salvation, not rendered lurid by the blood-red glow of national conflagration and ruin,—that you may promptly and practically realize that slavery is to be vanquished only by liberty,—is the fervent and anxious prayer of

"Yours truly,

"HORACE GREELEY."

"NEW YORK, August 24, 1862."

Socialism triumphed over statecraft within a month, when Abraham Lincoln signed the Emancipation Proclamation.

And later was heard the voice of Wendell Phillips throughout the land telling his fellow-citizens that the chattel slaves having been freed, next in order was the emancipation of the wages slaves,—as had been demanded over thirty years before by the originators of the movement, at some of whom we will now glance.

Robert Dale Owen was one of the most earnest of the "Spartan Band" who helped the Political Socialist propaganda begun by George H. Evans and Frederick W. Evans, both of whom were converts to his father Robert Owen's Social System. He was not only a philanthropist, but an author of repute, as the list of his works will attest. Before his death at Lake George, in 1877, he had been a Member of Congress and United States Minister at Naples. After finishing his education in Switzerland, Robert Dale Owen accompanied his father to America in 1825, and aided him at the Owenite Colony of New Harmony, Indiana, where was published the *Gazette*, afterward the *Free Inquirer*, a weekly journal devoted principally to the cause of Socialism, which he edited in later years with Frances Wright D'Arusmont, the famous author of *A Few Days in Athens* and other works. He paid a brief visit to Europe in 1827 and returned the same year. In 1828 he threw himself into Political Socialistic work in New York city, lecturing at the Hall of Science, editing his paper and otherwise agitating and organizing the masses assisted by Fanny Wright, after whom the "Workingmen's Party," was nicknamed the "Fanny Wright Party." He remained in New York until 1832 when he returned to New Harmony.

Frances Wright, who was the "Hypatia" of the movement, was one of the most remarkable women of this country and commanded a great deal of public celebrity until her death at Cincinnati in 1852. Her father was a friend of Adam Smith who wrote the *Wealth of Nations*, and of numerous other eminent literary and scientific people,— hence possibly her enthusiasm as a propagandist of political, economic and social reform. In 1825, after her return from a visit to Paris, on the invitation of Lafayette, she purchased a tract of 2,000 acres of land in Tennessee, which the Franco-American patriot held in trust for her. She colonized upon it a number of slave families, that she had freed, but the laws of the State of Tennessee being opposed to her "free" settlement, it was disbanded and the lands were restored to Lafayette, the slaves being subsequently sent to Hayti. Then Frances Wright worked for the freedom of the wages slaves of New York as already stated. Between 1833–1836 she lectured publicly in the principal cities of the Union on Socialism and Abolition. Later she returned to New Harmony, where she helped Robert Owen, and still later went to France, married Monsieur D'Arusmont, from whom she separated not long after and came back to America. Joseph Rodman Drake, the author of the *Culprit Fay*, and who died in 1820, was one of her intimates and gives her a place in *The Croakers*.

Horace Greeley had another friend, who was one of the

principal founders of the New York Workingmen's Party,—
Orestes Augustus Brownson, a very famous American lit-
terateur. He was born in Vermont in 1803 and died at
Detroit in 1876. He made the acquaintance of Robert
Owen, accepted his schemes of industrial reform and then
went into the foundation of the progressive party, "the
design of which was to relieve the poorer classes by political agitation," as its Socialism is modestly explained by a
leading authority. In the organization of the Locofoco
party he played a leading part. Dr. Brownson was the
author of several volumes still in request, and was the editor
of the Boston *Quarterly Review*, afterward merged into
the New York *Democratic Review*, and of *Brownson's
Quarterly Review*. Although a Universalist minister, and
later on, through the influence of William Ellery Channing, a Unitarian, he became a Roman Catholic. Some of
his writings were brought to the attention of the Pope as
heretical, but after a report of Cardinal Franzelin, who
scrutinized those complained of, he was ordered "to be
more moderate in his views."

Parke Godwin printed in the Appendix to *Democracy,
Constructive and Pacific*, a statement made by Dr. Brownson
in 1844 which explains his exact position as a Socialist :—

"The Industrial System, which has transformed the
serf into the operative and prepared the way for Modern
Feudalism, which we insist is no advance on the Feudalism
of the Middle Ages, is beginning to attract the attention,
not only of radicals and Socialists, but of politicians and
statesmen. Its effects in reducing labor to a state of complete servitude to capital, and, therefore, the operative to
the proprietor, is beginning to be seen, and to be felt, in
the unspeakable misery and distress of the laboring classes.
The great fact can no longer be concealed or denied, *that*

the present economical system of what are called the more advanced nations of Christendom, places labor at the mercy of capital, and every increase of wealth on the part of the few is attended by a more than corresponding increase of poverty and distress on the part of the many. Here is the fact. Men may gloss it over as they will, ascribe it to this cause or to that; but here is the fact. The richest nation in the world is the poorest; abundance superinduces want, and, with the general increase of wealth, the mass of laborers find themselves reduced to the starving point, and rapidly falling *below* it. This is the fact our Social Reformers see, and seek to remedy. Our own labors for twenty years have been devoted almost exclusively to the great work of ascertaining the means by which labor may be emancipated, and the acquisition of wealth prevented from becoming a public curse."

Among the first of the American Social Architects who saw the evils of the competitive system was L. Byllesby, who wrote in 1826. His volume, already alluded to, was one of the economic text-books of the early New York Socialists, who united for political action. He wrote it for his fellow citizens of New York and with a fear, as he says, for "his own prospects" because he had done so,— like one or two journalists now barely "existing" in Gotham, who have been blacklisted in certain offices because of their "unpopular" views, Socialism not being at present a fashionable "fad." But "nil desperandum,"— porridge à la Greeley is healthier than "paté-de-foie-gras" and—cheaper too! Byllesby points out "the pernicious effects of the present mode of obtaining wealth," the "absolute necessity for a revision of the present system," that "those who labor do not have the enjoyment of the products of their labor" and that "labor alone is the source of wealth."

Wealth, this earliest of American Socialists defines as follows :—" *Wealth* is, properly and only, an excess of the *Products of Labor*, either for the subsistence, or the pleasure and happiness, of mankind, beyond what is necessary for immediate use. So much of the products of labor as is necessary for immediate consumption, is only a *supply*, and not *wealth*, as a supply is requisite to maintain bodily vigor, until more of such products may be obtained ; but all excess over a *supply* is *wealth*.

"Money is not, intrinsically, wealth ;—it is only an accredited representative of it. In a situation where the products of labor did not exist, gold, silver, etc., would be as insignificant as any of the meanest articles of creation. But the products of labor would be equally valuable, in all situations, were there no such things as gold and silver in existence ; neither are *lands* intrinsically wealth."

Byllesby showed New Yorkers sixty-five years ago the evils resulting, even at that time, from the introduction of labor-saving machinery owned by capitalism under the competitive system, and then in a modest and timorous manner called attention to some of the remedies essential. The four principal features of the system proposed, in which he follows more or less Robert Owen's theories, whom he criticises however, were :—

"First, Such an arrangement as will secure to the producer the full products and control of the fruits of his labor, from the incipience to their consumption.

"Second, That all exchanges of products will be based on principles of reciprocity or equal quantities of labor for other equal quantities.

"Third, That no one consume the products of labor without yielding exact compensation therefor, in some shape or other, unless incapacitated ; and,

"Fourth, The consequent evasion of those uses of
money from which it has been customary to derive
interest."

The most important Socialist work developed by the
New York Workingmen's Labor Movement of the early
part of this century, was *The Rights of Man to Property*,
which was printed for the author by Alexander Ming, Jr.,
106 Beekman St., New York, 1829, upon the title page of
which "Altered from Mr. Jefferson's Declaration of
Independence" we read—

"I hold these truths to be self evident: that all men
are created equal; that they are endowed, by their Creator,
with certain unalienable rights; and that among these are
life, liberty and PROPERTY."

That author was Thomas Skidmore, a New York
citizen of means, who lashed the principal New York real
estate owners of those days, the Astors and Lorillards, with
a scourge such as they have never writhed under before, or
since. He was a State Socialist of Socialists and not only
showed the defective character of our present governmental
methods and laws, but explained how the future Coöperative
Commonwealth, as projected by himself, should be organized,
or as he puts it—

"How to organize this new government in such a
manner as to compel all men, without exception, to labor
as much as others must labor, for the same amount of
enjoyment; or in default, thereof to be deprived of such
enjoyment altogether."

The title of Skidmore's book may be misleading to many,
but the contents are as plain as plain can be When he
speaks of the "inequality" of property, he does not mean
it in the popular sense made use of by superficial people.
He held "that as long as property is unequal; or rather,

as long as it is so enormously unequal, as we see it at present (1829), those who possess it *will* live on the labor of others, and themselves perform none, or if any, a very disproportionate share, of that toil which attends them as a condition of their existence, and without the performance of which, they have no *just* right to preserve or retain that existence, even for a single hour."

Skidmore believed "that all men should live on their own labor, and not on the labor of others." He also argued that if the then "present possessors of enormous property have no just title to their possessions; and if it is apparent, as I trust it is, that when property is enormously unequal the men of toil, of all countries, can never have the full enjoyment of their labor; it will be conceded, no doubt, that I have shown enough to justify my fellow citizens in pulling down the present edifice of society, and to induce them to build a new one in its stead."

The author of *The Rights of Man to Property* further believed in the collective ownership of property by the people, in fact just as the people of New York city, to whom he was more particularly addressing himself sixty years ago, now hold the Public Parks; the New York and Brooklyn Bridge and its railway; the streets; the schoolhouses, court houses, City Hall, and other public buildings the property of all the citizens; the Croton Water and so forth. But as a Collectivist he applied it, like the modern Socialists do at present, more particularly to labor-saving machinery. Thus he says :—

"The Steam Engine is not injurious to the poor, when they can have the benefit of it; and this, on supposition, being *always* the case, instead of being looked upon as a curse, it would be hailed, as a blessing. If, then, it is seen that the steam engine, for example, is likely greatly to impoverish, or destroy the poor, what have they to do, but to lay hold of it, and make it their own? Let them appropriate also, in the same way, the cotton factories, the woolen factories, the iron foundries, the rolling mills, houses, churches, ships, goods, steamboats, fields of agriculture, etc., etc., etc., in manner as proposed in this work, and as is their right; and they will never have occasion any more to consider that as an evil which never deserved that character; which, on the contrary, is all that is good among men; and of which we cannot, under these new circumstances, have too much.''

This is no German Socialism. It is ''pure and simple'' American Socialism formulated and published in New York city by an American, when Karl Marx was eleven years of age and Ferdinand Lassalle was a child of four. And upon the fundamental principles of that early American Socialism, Horace Greeley, Albert Brisbane, Parke Godwin, George Ripley and the Fourierist Socialists stood later, all of whom demanded of society the cure of its economic errors and insisted upon ''the abolition of chattel slavery and of wages slavery.''

There were other works in addition to those named at this early stage of the American Labor Movement, which preceded Greeley's apostleship. One indignant citizen who hid himself under the nom-de-plume of ''A Loaf-Bread Baker,'' in a brochure published in 1827 by ''E. Conrad, 11 Frankfort St., New York,'' indignantly writes :—

''These United States are now in the fifty-first year of their independence, and we might reasonably suppose that during the progress of half a century, experience would have demonstrated the fitness of the *truths* of the Declaration of Independence, and have shown them by this time as a *real state of things*, and in such a manner that every citizen in his calling could certify to the correctness of the dogma—it being exemplified, as in truth it ought to be *in himself.* And are not the boasted truths of that Declaration yet made manifest among all classes and callings of the freemen of America? No indeed—feudal slavery holds a distinctive trait in more than one branch of the division of labor in the city of New York. There corporation restraints are met with at variance with the Dogmas the Declaration indicates. A discrepancy of political rights existing among freemen at this period of time may well challenge enquiry, and demand *why it exists?* *Custom*, steeled and damned custom of European origin still holds her sway through *prejudice.* Through which again she assumes empire, in despite of the solemn truths on which the rights of man are based and fixed *in and by our constitutions.* This is the answer, and the only answer that can be made, *as an excuse*, for the violence and injustice done to the citizens.''

The "Workingmen's Party" found in allies like these great strength. There were, of course, members who rode their immediate personal hobbies, it is true. But even those always had a broad view of the economic situation. One of these was Stephen Simpson, the biographer of Stephen Girard. He was the son of George Simpson, of Philadelphia, who had been cashier of the United States Bank, and who in the War of 1812 had helped the National Government by obtaining loans needed by the United States to carry on the defense of the country against the British invaders. He himself had been a clerk in the United States Bank, but resigning the position, he threw himself heart and soul into the work of the Political Socialists, and it was partly, perhaps, through his influence that

the second demand, "Down with monopolies, especially
the United States Bank," was inserted in the platform.

Stephen Simpson wrote a very important volume *
published at Philadelphia in 1831, the year Horace Greeley
arrived at New York. In this work all the questions
mooted by Socialists are covered by the pen of a master
of English. He tells the wages slaves that the old political
parties supporting feudal laws and customs are to be left
sedulously alone, and that "resisting the seductions of
fanatics on the one hand and demagogues on the other,"
it is their duty to support the "Party of the Workingmen"
and follow with that party "the path of science and
justice, under the banner of *labor the source of wealth, and
industry the arbiter of its distribution.*" He insisted on
public education for the proletariat, notwithstanding that
demand had been met "by the sneer of derision on the
one hand, and the cry of revolution on the other," in order
to make them the mental equals, at least, of the wealthy,
for "the children of toil are as much shunned in society, as
if they were leprous convicts just emerged from loathsome
cells."

Anarchic methods were discountenanced by him and
the use of the ballot eulogized. There are stirring denun-
ciations of then existing evils, such as land monopoly, and
he speaks of the "lord of ten thousand acres tortured on
his sick couch by the agonies of repletion, whilst the laborer
famishes at his gate," and of the conspiracy laws of which

* *The Workingman's Manual:* a New Theory of Political
Economy, on the Principle of Production the Source of Wealth,
including an Enquiry into the Principles of Public Currency, the
Wages of Labor, the Production of Wealth, the Distribution of
Wealth, Consumption of Wealth, Popular Education, and the
Elements of Social Government in General, as they appear open
to the Scrutiny of Common Sense and Philosophy of the Age.
Philadelphia, 1831.

he says : "If mechanics combine to raise their wages the laws punish them as conspirators against the good of society, and the dungeon awaits them as it does the robber. But the laws have made it a just and meritorious act that capitalists shall combine to strip the man of labor of his earnings, and reduce him to a dry crust and a gourd of water."

Ely Moore, whose "Address Delivered before the General Trades' Union of the city of New York, at the Chatham Street Chapel, Monday, December 2, 1833," should be also mentioned. He was President of that Union and was not unlike, in some particulars, the "Pure and Simple Trades Unionists" of our own day. He saw the evils, but evaded the true remedies. Thus he says : "Even in this fair land of freedom, where liberty and equality are guaranteed by all, our written constitutions have so wisely provided limitations to power, and securities for rights, the *twin fiends*, *intolerance* and *aristocracy*, presume to rear their hateful crests. . . . To curb it sufficiently by legislative enactments is impossible. Much *can* be done, however, toward restraining it within proper limits, by unity of purpose and concert of action, on the part of the *producing classes*. . . . Wealth, we all know, constitutes the aristocracy of this country. . . . The greatest danger, therefore, which threatens the stability of our government, and the liberty of the people, is an undue accumulation and distribution of wealth. And I do conceive, that *real danger* is to be apprehended from this source, notwithstanding that tendency to distribution which naturally grows out of the character of our statutes of conveyance, of inheritance, and descent of property ; but by securing to the producing classes a fair, certain, and equitable compensation for their toil and skill, we insure a more just and

equal distribution of wealth than can ever be effected by
statutory law."

Conservative trades unionism of the Moore type occasionally tends to one of two things now-a-days,—Anarchism
on the one hand, or political corruption through association
with the old parties, on the other.   And nothing else can
be expected where egoism rules, without a recognition of
"duty to others," as Horace Greeley pointed out, over and
over again.   This is the great evil of "Pure and Simple
Trades Unionism," which too frequently seems actuated,
although not really so, by a spirit of pure and simple selfishness.   Hence also, during the apathy of the honest rank
and file, who forget that "eternal vigilance is the price of
liberty," we find the development among them of corrupt
leaders, who generally evolute into professional labor
politicians,—vulgarly denominated "political scabs," by
Industrial Socialists.

The "Workingmen's Party" was not, however, confined
to New York.   It did much good work in Massachusetts.
Boston, in February, 1831,—when Greeley was tramping
for work through New England and but rarely finding it,—
saw an assemblage of delegates of the working people
which the following, year culminated into "The New
England Association of Farmers, Mechanics and other
Workingmen."   This body, which received a letter
addressed to the "Workingmen of the United States"
from the "Workingmen of New York," favored "the
organization of the whole laboring population of this
United Republic into an association; the separation of
questions of political morality and economy from the mere
personal and party contests of the day," and the revision
of "our social and political system."   Many reforms were
demanded by these delegates who agreed that it was their

"fixed determination to persevere till our wrongs are redressed, and to imbue the minds of our offspring with a spirit of abhorrence for the usurpations of aristocracy, and of resistance to their oppressions, so invincible, that they shall dedicate their lives to a completion of the work which their ancestors commenced in their struggle for national, and their sires have continued in their contest for personal independence."

Individual wage earners also had their say to their suffering brethren. One of these was Seth Luther, a native American mechanic, who delivered "An Address to the Workingmen of New England on the State of Education, and on the Condition of the Producing Classes in Europe and America," in 1832, throughout Massachusetts, Maine and New Hampshire. His account of the treatment of factory operatives is something awful, and among other facts that he narrates is that of the thrashing of women and children by their employers with cowhides. One little eleven year old girl had her leg broken by a "billet of wood" thrown at her by a wages-slave driver, and a deaf and dumb boy was whipped until, as an eye-witness stated "when he came in (to his home), he lay down on the bed like one without life. . . . . . He was mangled in a shocking manner, from his neck to his feet. He received, I should think, one hundred blows." One boy aged twelve, Seth Luther asserts, committed suicide by drowning, at Mendon, Massachusetts, in order to escape the horrors of New England factory labor.

Another son of Massachusetts, Samuel Whitcomb, Jr., delivered in 1831 "An Address before the Workingmen's Society," at Dedham in that commonwealth, which was afterward printed. His views were identical with those of Stephen Simpson relative to the unjust distribution

among the producers of the products of Labor, the source
of all wealth.

The year previous Edward Everett had thrown his
influence on the side of the workers, as we find from the
title page of the pamphlet: "A Lecture on the Working
Men's Party, first Delivered October Sixth before the
Charlestown Lyceum and Published at their Request. By
Edward Everett. Boston, published by Gray and Bowen,
1830." Everett, who was later Governor of Massachusetts,
United States Minister at the Court of St. James and
President of Harvard University, succeeded Daniel Webster
as Secretary of War in the cabinet of President Zachary
Taylor.

Ralph Waldo Emerson, speaking in his "Historic
Notes," of Edward Everett, remarks: "By a series of
lectures, largely and fashionably attended for two Winters
in Boston, he (Everett) made a beginning of popular
literary and miscellaneous lectures, which in that region, at
least, had important results. These are acquiring greater
importance every day, and becoming a national institution.
I am quite certain that this purely literary influence was
of the first importance to the American mind. . . . .
Germany had created criticism in vain for us until 1820,
when Edward Everett returned from his five years in
Europe, and brought to Cambridge his rich results, which
no one was so fitted by natural grace and the splendor of
his rhetoric to introduce and recommend."

Both Emerson and Everett well knew that "no pent
up" Know-Nothingism should circumscribe the limits of
art or science, even in the domain of politico-economics or
Social Science. Nor did Horace Greeley in the wider ken
of public activity, and he always rebuked, when the
opportunity was favorable, those who favored it. He was

once requested to furnish a toast for a "Know-Nothing" banquet. This is what he forwarded in response to the demand : "The Comrades of Washington. —Let us remember that, while the 'foreigners' Montgomery and Pulaski died gloriously, fighting for our freedom ; while Lafayette, Hamilton, and Steuben proved nobly faithful to the end, the traitor Arnold and the false ingrate Burr were sons of the soil,—facts which only prove that virtue is bounded by no geographical limits, and treachery peculiar neither to the native nor the immigrant." And history is silent as to whether the toast was duly drank or not on some such occasion, as one of those which the poet Fitz-Greene Halleck describes as not unusual with the New York politicians, who were wont to thus enjoy themselves years ago :

> " There's a barrel of porter in Tammany Hall.
> And the Bucktails are swigging it all the night long ;
> In the time of my childhood 'twas pleasant to call
> For a seat and cigar 'mid the jovial throng."

It may be asked, Why mention this in connection with the Socialism of Horace Greeley? And why not? Advocates of Socialism, which he taught fifty years ago, are continually met in these days with the cry that it is "German" and therefore it is "no good" for Americans. Again "German Socialism and German läger" always go together, in fact they are concomitants, in the vulgar mind. They may be there, but are not in fact, any more than "Tammany Democracy and porter" might be in the mind of an investigator of early Nineteenth Century American politics a hundred years hence, who would insist they were,—because Fitz-Greene Halleck so recorded it.

But Socialism is foreign, it is urged. Well, for the sake of argument, suppose it is. If Edward Everett,

lecturing before a fashionable Boston audience, had quoted
Johann Gottlieb Fichte, the German philosopher, on art or
science would there have been any objection? Certainly
not : but if a Socialist public speaker, for instance, were to
take arguments from German literature in favor of Socialism, then fashionable objections would pour in fast and
thick, and no language would be strong enough in the
public press to denounce as demagogism the use of German
arguments.

Yet Fichte in his *Foundation of Natural Right* declared*
it to be "man's inalienable property that he be able to live,
and demanded therefore from the State the right of labor.
The State must see to it that to the right of one part of the
citizens to prepare certain work should correspond the
obligation of the other part to purchase the products of
this labor ; for to him who could not live by his labor
would not be left the enjoyment of his own absolute
property—that is, his life—and he would thenceforth not
be obligated to acknowledge the property of any other
man, since the contract of the State to secure to every one
his own property had been violated. In order, then, that
this insecurity of property through him may not arise, all
must in such case of right and in pursuance of the citizens'
contract give of their own to this man until he should be
able to live.   From the instant at which any one begins to
suffer need, that part of another's property which may be
requisite to rescue him from that need belongs no more to
himself, but to the sufferer. The poor citizen has an
absolute and enforcible right to his support."

It all depends whose "ox is gored." A Socialist
agitator has thus no right, it will be urged, to argue in the

* "Social Democracy in Germany, by Professor Johannes
Huber," in the *International Review*, November–December, 1878.

words of Fichte that the State should "provide a sufficient amount of the necessaries of life, keep up the right relation of production and consumption, and tolerate no idlers." Then let that anti-foreign rule be inexorably put into practice in relation to everything, and what will be found? That the people, principally idlers of the capitalistic class, who "shout" the loudest against alleged Foreign Socialism are those who are pro-foreigners in almost everything else, even to the length, as James W. Gerard states as already quoted, of getting out of the United States as often as possible because "America isn't good enough," for them. And while they are arguing that Socialism from Germany is un-American, the very clothes worn by these male idlers of wealth have been made in England by Poole of London, or some one else there, and the dresses on the backs of their wives and daughters are Worth's of Paris, imported from France.

But economic science should have no such limitations although "American Fashion" may decree otherwise ;— that very "American Fashion" which rules Meissonier the Frenchman, Fortuny the Spaniard, and Munkacsy the Hungarian, to be, with other foreign artists, the producers of paintings alone fit for a plutocrat's walls ; that same "American Fashion" which insists that Salvini the Italian, Irving the Englishman, and Bernhardt the Franco-Israelite, are the only Thespian "stars" fit to be looked at by capitalists ; and that identical "American Fashion" which asserts that Wagner the German, Gounod the Frenchman, and Verdi the Italian, alone composed music able to titillate the ears of a monopolist. And so on in sculpture, in literature, and in almost everything else needed by the owners of our nation's wealth. Foreigners have the preference because it is the modern "American Fashion"

and so "no Americans need apply," including native
American working people, when foreign contract labor
can be imported from Europe.

Yet the finality of economic science,—Socialism,—is
neither American nor foreign absolutely. It is what art
and science should be—International. It developed out of
and belongs to, all Humanity.

But the fact is that Socialism is "quite American,"
both economically and politically. The Grangers are a
product of the West and the Knights of Labor of the East.
The Nationalists are a New England development entirely.
Yet all these are Socialists, as their platforms and declarations of principles will attest.

Modern Political Socialism is discovered to be peculiarly
American in its origin when the facts are investigated as
they have been in this chapter.

We find that in 1776 the Declaration of Independence
of the United States of America presented to the world
through the pens of Thomas Jefferson and Thomas Paine,
becomes the rallying cry of Eighteenth Century "Liberty,
Equality and Fraternity." It is recognized by all lovers of
Humanity as addressed to them individually and collectively, and as a result they come from France, from
Germany, from Poland and elsewhere in Europe to do
battle for America, giving up even their lives if necessary,
for in the Declaration of Independence is found not only
that spirit of rebellion against tyranny which made exiles
of the Pilgrim Fathers, but that new light shed on political
and social economics by the Encyclopedists and their
compatriots.

Then American Liberty and International Fraternity
being triumphant, the French Revolution follows thirteen
years later; and as it expires in the Directory, making way

for Napoleon and the Empire, there happens the martyr-dom of the two Socialists—Babeuf and Darthé.

But, as the "blood of the martyr is the seed of the church," so conjoined to the true Jeffersonian inspiration and the recognition that the Declaration of Indepen-dence has been signed in vain for the bread-winners, American citizens who believe in the Socialist principle and have written thereon, unite with the American proletariat in a political party which shall reaffirm those grand ideas for which the founders of the American republic fought and died, and for which Babeuf and Darthé gave up their lives on the scaffold. And that whole platform of the American Workingmen's Party then endorsed and now recorded in American political history, means in its entirety, divested of all side issues, the abolition of human slavery, white and colored, chattel and wage.

It is taken, as will be shown, from America to England by Robert Owen and accepted, with additions, by the radical wing of the Chartist movement, out of which and through other similar causes, grows the British Social Democracy.

Karl Marx and Frederick Engels, after studying the English Labor Movement, write various economic works, such as that historic document "the Manifesto of the Communist Party," and finally is evolved by the organizing work of Ferdinand Lassalle and other humanitarians, the German Social Democracy.

And American Socialism has all this time been growing and developing, taking within it all the good it can, whether native or foreign, economic or political,—out of which is eventually born the American Socialist Labor Party.

But the link between all these are the teachers of Horace Greeley, the Social Architects, Charles Fourier and Robert Owen.

Before entering into American Fourierist Socialism in the next chapter, and parting with Robert Owen, his position relative to Political English Socialism should be understood. He is wrongfully placed among the Utopian Socialists by some authorities. This is altogether incorrect. After the failure of the New Harmony economic experiment, Robert Owen recognized that human beings must be politically, as well as economically, free—and that economic liberty must be assisted and supplemented by political action.

The founder of Owenite Socialism accordingly aided, for a year or two, his son and his associates in the political movement which was developing in the States of New York, Massachusetts, etc. Then he returned to England. On May 1, 1833, full of his new purpose, he made an address at a great public meeting held at the National Equitable Labor Exchange, Charlotte Street, London, and denounced the "Old System" and announced the "Commencement of the New." On May 13th, 1833, the Owenite Socialists, from the same place, issued a "Manifesto of the Productive Classes of Great Britain and Ireland, to the Governments and People of the Continents of Europe, and of North and South America," winding up with an earnest call to the "Men of the Great Family of Mankind," to unite in these measures :—

"I. To produce a surplus of all kinds of wealth.

"II. To distribute the wealth the most beneficially for all parties (people) in all countries.

"III. To form a superior character for the rising generation, and to improve the adults of the present generation.

"IV. To govern well and wisely for all parties (*i. e.*, peoples).

"V. And to form arrangements to carry these measures into immediate execution, to stop the evident progress making toward a revolution of violence."

At another public meeting held in London on Wednesday, February 12, 1834, ot "the Producers of Wealth and Knowledge," this "Charter of the Rights of Humanity," prepared by Robert Owen, absolutely endorsing political action, was then ratified:—

"The period has arrived when we, the producers of wealth and knowledge, have decided that we will not waste any more of our time or labor on subjects of minor importance, which, if obtained, could effect no permanently beneficial change in our condition; but overlooking the local advantages of class, and considering only the general and permanent interest of Humanity, we will henceforth devote all our energies to the attainment of those superior objects and advantages developed in this our Charter.

"I. A graduated property tax, equal in amount to the full exigencies of government, when wisely administered.

"II. An abolition of all other customs, duties and taxes—national, county and parochial.

"III. Free and protected ingress and egress for all persons into and out of all countries; and the free interchange of all improvements and commodities between all nations.

"IV. Wars to cease; and all differences between nations to be adjusted by an annual congress, to be held in rotation in each of the different States.

"V. Liberty of expression of conscientious opinions, upon all subjects, without limitation.

"VI. No dominant religion to exist, nor any one to be encouraged by any worldly temptations whatever; but all persons to be equally protected in the rights of conscience.

"VII. National, scientific, physical, intellectual and moral education for all, who, from any cause, cannot be otherwise well-trained and cultured in all these respects.

"VIII. National employment for all who cannot otherwise find productive or beneficial occupation, that thereby the greatest amount of wealth may be produced for every individual.

"IX. The children of all classes, without any exception, to be trained and employed, physically or mentally, to produce for society as much as they require from society.

"X. National measures to set the poor and unemployed immediately to beneficial employments, under arrangements which shall reform their feelings and habits, and secure their comfort and happiness.

"XI. National arrangements to distribute the new wealth, created by the national employment of the poor and unemployed, beneficially for them and the nation.

"XII. Unlimited freedom for the production and interchange of all commodities and riches, until more wealth shall be produced than is necessary for the happiness of the population of every country.

"XIII. A change of the vicious and degrading circumstances by which the productive classes are now surrounded, for others possessing a virtuous and superior character.

"XIV. The present property of all individuals, acquired and possessed by the usages and practices of old society, to be held sacred until the possessors shall discover that it can no longer be of any use or exchangeable value, from the facility with which a surplus of wealth will be produced for all ; thus destroying the motive to accumulate individual wealth, as the motive to accumulate water, where it is in abundance, has been destroyed, although it is the most intrinsically valuable of all our wealth.

"XV. The just rights of both sexes to be universally established.

"XVI. The Congress of Nations to determine on some one language, which shall be taught to all the children of each State, in addition to their mother tongue.

"XVII. Arrangements to be adopted, as soon as practicable, to put an end to individual and national competition and contest, now unnecessary, and producing innumerable grievous evils to all classes."

Henry Hetherington, of the *Poor Man's Guardian;* James Bronterre O'Brien, who edited and translated Buonarroti's *History of Babeuf's Conspiracy for Equality;* Thomas Cooper, author of the *Purgatory of Suicides;* Ernest Jones, the poet, and many other Chartists, equally progressive, and most of whom suffered in jail for the cause of human liberty, were friends of Robert Owen, and united with him in the effort for higher political, social and economic freedom, upon the above platform.

The *Legacy of Robert Owen to the Population of the World*, issued by him on March 30, 1834, was a further effort of his in the direction of advising Organized Labor to work both politically and economically for their emancipation and as he urges, "without bloodshed, violence, or evil of any kind." Still later, in 1837, by a joint committee of twelve,—six Members of Parliament, one of whom was Daniel O'Connell, the great Irish "Liberator," and six deputies of the London Workingmen's Association, there was drawn up what was known as the "People's Charter."

But the political inspiration of it all was American and brought back from the United States by Robert Owen, and it has developed in our days into the International Socialist Movement.

Those, therefore, who think that Political Socialism is

German, and not American, are in the same condition as some of the capitalistic idlers, who know it all, and smack their lips over " Chateau-Margaux," believing it to be the best and purest French vintage ; whereas it is ordinary claret, that was raised on the Pacific Slope or in Ohio, was shipped to France, blended there, and re-shipped as the genuine imported article.

Socialism, in a similar manner, was raised in America, exported to Europe, and has been there blended with foreign philosophy and Social Science, much of which was grafted from the American parent trees,—but it is American all the same.

Let those, who have hitherto sustained or may take the contrary position, bear in mind these words of the Ancient Hindu philosopher Narada—

"Never utter these words : 'I do not know there is— therefore it is false.'

"One must study to know, know to understand, understand to judge."

CHAPTER IV.

GREELEY, A SOCIALIST APOSTLE.

JAMES PARTON has told us how Horace Greeley, in view of the various causes which led him to be a Socialist, but more particularly stirred up by the terrible winter of 1838 in New York city, the fearful destitution of the people and the general industrial anarchy, asked—

"Why must these things be?" And Greeley's biographer gives us the response :—"From Paris came soon the calm, emphatic answer, These things NEED NOT be! They are due alone to the short-sightedness and injustice of man! Albert Brisbane brought the message. Horace Greeley heard and believed it. He took it to his heart. It became a part of him."

Greeley had before this, however, felt the inspiration of that noble character, William Ellery Channing, whom Emerson considered "the star of the American church;" but he "left no successor in the pulpit." The founder of the *Tribune* had been deeply moved by the efforts of Channing for the amelioration of the American proletariat. Channing, at the request of industrial organizations in Boston, had delivered two lectures, afterwards printed with the title—"On the Elevation of the Laboring Portion of the Community." By the elevation of the "laboring mass," the eloquent divine did not mean that "they were to be released from labor," or "to force themselves into what are called the upper ranks of society," but that they should have "Elevation of Soul," which should be aided by an "improvement of outward conditions." Greeley appreciated the strength of this argument, because he believed, as did Channing, in an "effectual remedy for the fearful evils of modern civilization ; a system which teaches its members to grasp at everything, and to rise above everybody, as the great aims of life." "Of such a civilization," Channing urged, "the natural fruits are—contempt of others' rights, fraud, oppression, a gambling spirit in trade, reckless adventure, and commercial convulsions, all tending to impoverish the laborer and to render every condition insecure."

Channing, in the preface to the last edition of his works, expressed "his firm belief that our present low civilization, the central idea of which is wealth, cannot last forever ; that the mass of men are not doomed hopelessly and irresistibly to the degradation of mind and heart in which they are now sunk ; that a new comprehension of the true dignity of a social being is to remodel social institutions and manners : that in Christianity, and the powers and principles of human nature, we have the promise of something holier and happier than now exists. It is a privilege to live in this faith and communicate it to others."

Horace Greeley always accepted the Boston divine as one of his spiritual teachers,—as he did later Theodore Parker,—and when Channing died in 1842, in the fullness of his Socialist nobility of heart he wrote :—"Deeply do we deplore his loss, most untimely to the faithless eye of man does it seem—to the cause of truth, of order and of right, and still more deeply do we lament that he has left behind him, in the same department of exertion, so few, in proportion to the number needed, to supply the loss occasioned by his death."

The editor of the *Tribune*, still further to discover the means for the re-organization of society, hunted through the pages of the books on his library shelves, and found there the inspiring truths apprehended by the Utopian Socialists of ages past, in such works as the *Republic* of Plato and the *Utopia* of Sir Thomas More, to which he made allusions later in his lecture on "The Social Architects," where will be found a synopsis of the system of the Socialist Count St. Simon who accompanied Lafayette to this country to help the American colonists in their struggle for liberty against the tyranny of the British monarchy.

Albert Brisbane was, however, the Socialist missionary who converted Greeley, as already alluded to by James Parton, who proves how this enthusiast "brought the message" for the redemption of the masses from industrial bondage.

Horace Greeley in his *Recollections* tells us how he pondered over the scenes of misery in New York during the winter of 1838, where, as he asserts :—

"I saw extreme destitution more closely than I had ever before observed it, and was enabled to scan its repulsive features intelligently. I saw two families, including six or eight children, burrowing in one cellar under a stable,—a prey to famine on the one hand, and to vermin and cutaneous maladies on the other, with sickness adding its horrors to those of a polluted atmosphere and a wintry temperature. I saw men who each, somehow, supported his family on an income of $5 per week or less, yet who cheerfully gave something to mitigate the sufferings of those who were *really* poor. I saw three widows, with as many children, living in an attic on the profits of an apple-stand, which yielded less than $3 per week, and the landlord came in for a full third of that. But worst to bear of all was the pitiful plea of stout, resolute, single young men and young women: 'We do not want alms; we are not beggars; we hate to sit here day by day idle and useless; help us to work,—we want no other help; why is it that we can have nothing to do?'"

Such scenes as these, Greeley goes on to state, impelled him—"to write for the *New Yorker*,—I think in the winter of 1839–1840,—a series of articles entitled 'What shall be done for the laborer?' I believe these attracted the attention of Mr. Albert Brisbane, a young man of liberal education and varied culture, a native of Batavia, N. Y., which he still regarded as his home, but who had traveled widely and observed thoughtfully; making the acquaintance in Paris of the school of Socialists called (after their founder) St. Simonians; and that also of Charles Fourier, the founder of a different school, which had been distinguished by his name. Robert Owen, by his experiments at New Lanark and his *New View of Society*, was the first in this century to win public attention to Socialism, though (I believe) Fourier had not only speculated, but written, before either of his co-laborers. But Owen was an extensive and successful manufacturer; St. Simon was a soldier, and the heir of a noble family; while Fourier was a poor clerk, reserved and taciturn, whose hard, dogmatic, algebraic style seemed expressly calculated to discourage readers and repel adherents; so that his disciples were few indeed, down to the date of his death in 1837. Mr. Brisbane, returning not long afterward from Europe, prepared and published his first work—which was an exposition and commendation of Fourier's industrial system—in 1840. My acquaintance with the author and his work commenced soon afterward."

James Parton adds some further information. He says:

"Albert Brisbane was a young gentleman of liberal education, the son of wealthy parents. His European tour included, of course, a residence at Paris, where the fascinating dreams of Fourier were the subject of conversation. He procured the works of that amiable and noble-minded man, read them with eager interest, and became completely convinced that his captivating theories were capable of speedy realization—not, perhaps, in slow and conservative Europe, but in progressive and unshackled America. He returned home a Fourierite, and devoted himself with a zeal and disinterestedness that are rare in the class to which he belonged, and that in any class cannot be too highly praised, to the dissemination of the doctrines in which he believed. He wrote essays and pamphlets. He expounded Fourierism in conversation. He started a magazine called the *Future*, devoted to the explanation of Fourier's plans, published by Greeley and Co. He delivered lectures. In short, he did all that a man could do to make known to his fellow men what he believed it became them to know. He made a few converts, but only a few, till the starting of the *Tribune* gave him access to the public ear."

Fourierist Socialism is first referred to in the columns of the *Tribune* on October 21, 1841, in a notice of one of Mr. Brisbane's lectures, as follows :—"Mr. A. Brisbane delivered a lecture at the Stuyvesant Institute last evening, upon the Genius of Christianity considered in its bearing on the Social Institutions and Terrestrial Destiny of the Human Race. He contended that the mission of Christianity upon earth has hitherto been imperfectly understood, and that the doctrines of Christ, carried into practical effect, would free the world of Want, Misery, Temptation and Crime. This, Mr. B. believes, will be effected by a system of Association, or the binding up of individual and family interests in Social and Industrial Communities, wherein all faculties may be developed, all energies usefully employed, all legitimate desires satisfied, and idleness, want, temptation and crime be annihilated. In such Associations, individual property will be maintained, the family be held sacred, and every inducement held out to a proper ambition. Mr. B. will lecture hereafter on the practical details of the system of FOURIER, of whom he is a zealous disciple, and we shall then endeavor to give a more clear and full account of his doctrines."

The *London Times*, a month later, made a snarling and captious attack on the Fourierist movement, which was then demanding considerable attention in France. Greeley threw himself into the breach and answered the British "Thunderer" in the following remarks in the editorial columns of the New York *Tribune* in November, 1841 :—

"We have written something, and shall yet write much more, in illustration and advocacy of the Great Social Revolution which our age is destined to commence, in rendering all useful Labor at once attractive and honorable, and banishing Want and all consequent degradation from the globe. The germ of this revolution is developed in the writings of Charles Fourier, a philanthropic and observing Frenchman, who died in 1837, after devoting thirty years of a studious and unobtrusive life to inquiries, at once patient and profound, into the causes of the great mass of Social evils which overwhelm Humanity, and the true means of removing them. These means he proves to be a system of Industrial and Household Association, on the principle of Joint Stock Investment, whereby Labor will be ennobled and rendered attractive and universal, Capital be offered a secure and lucrative investment, and Talent and Industry find appropriate, constant employment, and ade-

quate reward, while Plenty, Comfort, and the best means
of Intellectual and Moral Improvement is guaranteed to
all, regardless of former acquirements or condition. This
grand, benignant plan is fully developed in the various
works of M. Fourier, which are abridged in the single
volume on *The Social Destiny of Man*, by Mr. A. Brisbane,
of this State. Some fifteen or sixteen other works in
illustration and defense of the system have been given to
the world, by Considérant, Chevalier, Paget, and other
French writers, and by Hugh Doherty, Dr. H. McCormack,
and others in English. A tri-weekly journal (*La Phalange*)
devoted to the system, is published by M. Victor Considérant in Paris, and another (the *London Phalanx*) by Hugh
Doherty, in London, each ably edited.''

Horace Greeley later accepted the gospel of Socialism
according to Fourier, and expressed thus his conversion to
a belief therein :—

"Here, then, is the basis of our demand for the integral
and all pervading reform in the circumstances and conditions of human existence which we term ASSOCIATION, and
in which rests my hope of a better day at hand for the
down-trodden millions. Association affirms that every
child born into the world has a rightful claim upon the
community around him for subsistence, until able to earn
for himself an education, which shall enable him to earn
efficiently, as well as rightly to improve and enjoy ; and
for opportunity to earn at all times, by honest industry,
steadily employed and justly remunerated. These it affirms
as the Common Rights of Humanity, denied or subverted
as to many by our present social arrangements, but which
Society ought to be and must be so recast as to establish
and secure. To short-sighted human impatience, it now
seems deplorable that Philanthropy and Christianity do

not instantly rally the influential and the affluent to our
aid, and enable us to demonstrate the feasibility of a vast
and beneficent Social Reform forthwith, but I doubt not
that those who shall ultimately reap where we shall have
sown will clearly perceive, that the Providential direction
was far wiser than our haste, and that our rebuffs and
disappointments were a part of the necessary agencies
whereby their success was rendered perfect and enduring.''

Four years before his death in 1872, Greeley summed
up the three empirical systems of Socialism formulated by
Owen, St. Simon and Fourier as follows :—

"OWEN.—Place human beings in proper relations,
under favoring circumstances (among which I include Education and Intelligence), and they will do right rather than
wrong. Hitherto, the heritage of the great majority has
been filth, squalor, famine, ignorance, superstition ; and
these have impelled many to indolence and vice, if not to
crime. Make their external conditions what they should
be, and these will give place to industry, sobriety, and
virtue.

"ST. SIMON.—' Love is the fulfilling of the law ;' secure
to every one opportunity ; let each do whatever he can do
best; and the highest good of the whole will be achieved
and perpetuated.

"FOURIER.—Society, as we find it, is organized rapacity. Half of its force is spent in repressing or resisting the
jealousies and rogueries of its members. We need to
organize Universal Justice based on Science. The true Eden
lies before, not behind us. We may so provide that Labor,
now repulsive, shall be attractive; while its efficiency
in production shall be increased by the improvement of
machinery and the extended use of natural forces, so as to
secure abundance, education and elegant luxury to all.

What is needed is to provide all with homes, employment, instruction, good living, the most effective implements, machinery, etc., securing to each the fair and full recompense of his achievement ; and this can best be attained through the association of some four to five hundred families in a common household (phalanstery), and in the ownership and cultivation of a common domain, say of 2,000 acres, or about one acre to each person living thereon.''

Parton writes :—''Horace Greeley made no secret of his conversion to Fourierism. On the contrary, he avowed it constantly in private, and occasionally in public print, though never in his own paper till toward the end of the *Tribune's* first year. His native sagacity taught him that before Fourierism could be realized, a complete revolution in public sentiment must be effected ; a revolution which would require many years of patient effort on the part of its advocates.'' The same author further says :—'' Early in 1842, a number of gentlemen associated themselves together for the purpose of bringing the schemes of Fourier fully and prominently before the public ; and to this end, they purchased the right to occupy one column daily on the first page of the *Tribune* with an article, or articles, on the subject, from the pen of Mr. Brisbane. The first of these articles appeared on the first of March, 1842, and they continued, with some interruptions, at first daily, afterwards three times a week, till about the middle of 1844, when Mr. Brisbane went again to Europe. The articles were signed with the letter B., and were known to be communicated. They were calm in tone, clear in exposition. At first, they seem to have attracted little attention, and less opposition. They were regarded (as far as my youthful recollection serves) in the light of articles to be skipped, and by most of the city readers of the *Tribune*, I presume, they were skipped with the utmost regularity, and quite as a matter of course. Occasionally, however, the subject was alluded to editorially, and every such allusion was of a nature to be read. Gradually, Fourierism became one of the topics of the time. Gradually, certain editors discovered that Fourierism was un-Christian. Gradually, the cry of Mad Dog arose. Meanwhile, the articles of Mr. Brisbane were having their effect upon the People."

Ralph Waldo Emerson was also about this time quite deeply attracted by Socialism as expounded by Albert Brisbane. The "Sage of Concord," over forty years afterwards, in 1883, recorded, in a good humored, but slightly satiric spirit of raillery, some of his mental experiences with Fourierism, and in his *Historic Notes* among other things said :—" We had an opportunity of learning something of these Socialists and their theory from the indefatigable apostle of the sect in New York, Albert Brisbane. Mr. Brisbane pushed his doctrine with all the force of memory, talent, honest faith and importunacy. As we listened to his exposition, it appeared to us the sublime of mechanical philosophy ; for the system was the perfection of arrangement and contrivance. The force of arrangement could no further go. The merit of the plan was that it was a system ; that it has not the partiality and hint-and-fragment character of most popular schemes, but was coherent and comprehensive of facts to a wonderful degree. It was not daunted by distance, or magnitude, or remoteness of any sort, but strode about nature with a giant's step, and skipped no fact, but wove its large Ptolemaic web of cycle and epicycle, of phalanx and phalanstery, with laudable assiduity. . . . . Genius hitherto has been shamefully misapplied, a mere trifler. It must now set itself to raise the social condition of man. . . . . . Society, concert, coöperation, is the secret of the coming Paradise. By reason of the isolation of men at the present day, all work is drudgery. By concert and the allowing each laborer to choose his own work, it becomes pleasure. 'Attractive Industry' would speedily subdue, by adventurous, scientific and persistent tillage, the pestilential tracts; would equalize temperature, give health to the globe, and cause the earth to yield, 'healthy, imponderable fluids,' to the solar system, as it now yields noxious fluids. . . . . Poverty shall be abolished; deformity, stupidity and crime shall be no more. Genius, grace, art, shall abound.''

"Certainly," continues Emerson, "we listened with great pleasure to such magnificent pictures. The ability and earnestness of the advocate and his friends, the comprehensiveness of their theory, its apparent directness of proceeding to the end they would secure, the indignation they felt and uttered in the presence of so much social misery, commanded our attention and respect. It contained so much truth, and promised in the attempts that shall be made to realize it so much valuable instruction, that we are engaged to observe every step of its progress. . . . . The value of Fourier's system is that it is a statement of such an order externized, or carried outward into its correspondence in facts. The mistake is that this particular order and series is to be imposed, by force or preaching and votes, on all men, and carried into rigid execution. But what is true and good must not only be begun by life, but must be conducted to its issues by life. Could not the conceiver of this design have also believed that a similar model lay in every mind, and that the method of each associate might be trusted, as well as that of his particular Committee and General Office, No. 200 Broadway? Nay, that

it would be better to say, Let us be lovers and servants of
that which is just, and straightway every man becomes a
center of a holy and beneficent republic, which he sees to
include all men in its law, like that of Plato and of Christ?
Before such a man the whole world becomes Fourierized,
or Christized, or Humanized, and in obedience to his most
private being he finds himself, according to his presenti-
ment, though against all sensuous probability, acting in
strict concert with all others who followed their private
light.   Yet in a day of small, sour and fierce schemes, one
is admonished and cheered by a project of such friendly
aims and of such bold and generous proportion; there is an
intellectual courage and strength in it, which is superior
and commanding; it certifies the presence of so much
truth in the theory, and in so far is destined to be fact.''

Emerson also remarked :—''I regard these philanthropists as themselves the effects of the age in which we live,
and, in common with so many other good facts, the efflor-
escence of the period, and predicting a good fruit that
ripens.   They were not the creators they believed themselves, but they were unconscious prophets of a true state
of society; one which the tendencies of nature lead unto,—
one which always establishes itself for the same soul, though
not in that manner in which they paint it; but they were
describers of that which is really being done.   The large
cities are phalansteries; and the theorists drew all their
argument from facts already taking place in our experience.
The cheap way is to make every man do what he was born
for.   One merchant, to whom I described the Fourier project, thought it must not only succeed, but that agricultural association must presently fix the price of bread, and
drive single farmers into association in self-defense, as the
great commercial and manufacturing companies had done.

Society in England and America is trying the experiment again in small pieces, in coöperative associations, in cheap eating-houses, as well as in the economies of club-houses."

Charles Fourier himself was far from being as idealistic or transcendental as Emerson might lead one to believe in some of his criticisms on the system. Thus, in his *Theory of the Four Movements*, published in 1808, he gives a very practical view of the "mercantile spirit" which, he claimed, "has opened new paths to crime; at each war it extends its ravages upon both hemispheres, and carries, even into the bosom of savage regions, the scandal of civilized cupidity; our vessels make the circuit of the world only to associate the barbarians and savages in our vices and our madness*; yes, civilization becomes more odious as it draws near its fall; the earth presents only a horrible political chaos; it calls for the arm of another Hercules to purge it from the social monstrosities which dishonor it."

The founder of Fourerism believed that what Society now calls civilization is "a false and imperfect condition, with poverty, crime, ignorance, idleness, repugnant toil, disease, wasting wars, general antagonism, oppression and misery. He believed that Association (*i. e.*, Socialism) would produce general riches, honesty, attractive and varied industry, health, peace and universal happiness, and held that 'attractions are proportional to destinies,' or that the desires or passions of men, their aptitudes and inclinations, if they could have free scope, would infallibly produce the highest condition and greatest happiness of which they are capable. He (Fourier) believed in a universal harmony and that there is, therefore, a principle of 'universal analogy.' Seeing that all things, from suns and planets to atoms

---

* Is not this happening now in Africa and Polynesia?

range themselves in groups and series, according to certain fixed laws of attraction and repulsion, he labored to discover the kind of human society that must eventually form itself in obedience to those laws.''

The practical outcome of Fourier's Socialistic system,—which modern Sociocrats should ever recognize as of the highest importance in organization, was "the Association or Phalanstery, which is to consist of 400 families or 1,800 persons, which number he found included the whole circle of human capacities. These should live in one immense edifice, in the center of a large and highly cultivated domain, and furnished with workshops, studios and all the appliances of industry and art as well as all the sources of amusement and pleasure. When the earth is covered with PALACES of ATTRACTIVE INDUSTRY, the associations will also unite in groups and series under a UNITARY GOVERNMENT. There will be but one language and one Government, and the only armies will be the great industrial armies. The property of the Association is to be held in shares, and the whole product of the industrial and artistic groups is to be divided into twelve parts, of which five parts are due to labor, four to capital, and three to talent. The apartments are to be of various prices, and the styles of living to vary in luxury and cost; but the poorest person in the Association is not only to be secure of comfort, but his minimum of enjoyments will be greater than the present social arrangements can give to princes and millionaires; while these will have opened to them pleasures of which they can now scarcely have a conception. The economics of the large scale in the Phalanstery reduce by two-thirds the expenses of living, while an attractive and scientific industry would quadruple the products of civilization.''

Albert Brisbane, the great American expounder of Fourier's Socialist theories, in his volume *Social Destiny of Man: or Association and Reorganization of Industry*, published by C. F. Stollmeyer, of Philadelphia, in 1840, presents the whole system in its best and most practical character, and proves that—

"There can exist but two methods in the exercise of Industry, to wit: the incoherent order, or cultivation carried on by isolated families as we now see it; or the combined order, cultivation by large assemblages, with fixed laws as respects an equitable distribution of profits to each individual, according to the three following qualifications, Labor, Capital, Talent. . . . . Individual incoherent labor causes the predominance of all scourges opposed to the principles of Divinity—indigence, fraud, oppression, carnage. And, inasmuch as the system of incoherent labor, the basis of barbarian and civilized societies, perpetuates these calamities in spite of all the efforts of science, it is self evident that they are an abyss of error, the antipodes of the views of God, 'portæ inferi,' from which man can only escape by the invention and organization of association and combined industry."

Taken in conjunction with the present aspect of the Labor Movement, although not an infallible guide by any means, Brisbane's writings are a storehouse of argument for present Socialist agitators and future legislators on the lines of Scientific Socialism. They are particularly so in explaining the history of labor's crucifixion in past ages, its present development and future evolution when its emancipation will be progressing to gradual and peaceful accomplishment, as so earnestly advocated by Horace Greeley, who hated war, capital punishment and similar anachronisms of alleged civilization, as do the American State Socialists.

Brisbane records ably and tersely "the changes that have taken place in the condition of the laboring classes since the commencement of societies, (and which) have only been so many varieties of one general tyranny; at one epoch we see them Parias, at another Slaves, at another Serfs, and now they are the Working Classes, (for) Individual Slavery, as it universally existed in antiquity, has been changed and replaced by the Collective Servitude of the mass in modern times."

The author of the *Social Destiny of Man* will be found also of service in arguments against what he called that "tolerated fraud" of society, Commerce, and which he insisted, to use his own words, "is permitted to commit a great variety of frauds, which have become legalized by custom, and are practiced as a kind of right, while they ought, according to a true standard of equity, to be punished as crimes. We will explain this by an example. Society punishes the obtaining of goods under false pretenses as a variety of swindling, that is, as a crime; but it takes no notice of, and does not punish the thousand swindles of commerce; they are nevertheless as much swindles in principle as the one above cited. Take the adulteration of products as an example; it is a means of obtaining the money of the consumer under false pretenses, and attacks, in addition to the purse, his health. The sale of products under false brands and trade-marks, which are means of deceiving as to quality, are in fact swindles. Commerce resorts in innumerable ways, to such false pretenses to increase its profits, and obtain that for which it gives no equivalent. Fraud, we may truly say, has become legalized, and is tolerated by public opinion in the commercial operations of Civilization."

Albert Brisbane,—and Horace Greeley accepted his

position and endorsed it,—demanded that "the veil of prejudice be torn away. We assert," he wrote, "that the evil, misery and injustice, now predominant on the earth, have not their foundation in political and administrational errors, in the defects of this or that institution, in the imperfection of human nature, or in the depravity of the passions; but in the FALSE ORGANIZATION OF SOCIETY ALONE. We assert that the present social mechanism is not ADAPTED to the nature of man and to his passions; that its laws are in flagrant opposition to those which regulate or govern their action; that it perverts, misdirects and develops them subversively, and that the selfishness, oppression, fraud, injustice and crime, which mark the course of his societies, are attributable to that artificial or social misdirection and perversion, and not to any inborn, inherent depravity in the human being himself."

Then Brisbane tells the alleged statesmen of that period, that is, when Martin Van Buren was President of the United States :—

"In good faith, politicians, if you thought it were possible to harmonize the passions, instinct and characters, would not Association (Socialism) and combination in all branches of industry, directing appropriately the labor, capital and talent of society to the best advantage, be a magnificent scheme? Is it not an object of a far superior order to the questions agitated by the various political parties, which have appeared upon, and disappeared from the scene of action? How miserably slow, how contested on all sides, and of what piecemeal application are the improvements and ameliorations of civilization, when compared with the gigantic and unanimous ameliorations which could, with unity of action, be effected in Association !"

Following this line of argument Brisbane led it to the

Socialist conclusion :—"But if Industry be organized, if populations have a true foundation to stand upon, if combination and unity of interests unite them, as the conflict of these interests now divide them, important reforms and ameliorations can easily be affected. Hence the importance of first giving a true organization to Industry, and of introducing into the FOUNDATION OF THE SOCIAL COMPACT, order, equilibrium and unity of interests. WHEN A TRUE BASIS IS LAID, we may hope to organize a true POLITICAL SYSTEM, in which the majority will not be plundered by a small minority, and the weaker interest sacrificed to the stronger. We may even hope more,—we may hope to establish a society in which the misery and injustice which now exist under a thousand forms, and which we falsely believe to be inherent in human nature, will be effectually done away with."

But, Albert Brisbane was not the only teacher of Fourierism that Greeley looked up to, when a Disciple, and later followed mentally, when an Apostle of Socialism.

Parke Godwin, of whom we have already spoken, and who wrote a *Life of Charles Fourier*, was one of his principal mentors, although an associate. That author's little pamphlet of fifty pages entitled *Democracy, Pacific and Constructive*, written in 1844, was one of Greeley's text books, and few more valuable literary auxiliaries to Socialist propaganda have ever been written. It is an appeal of an American to Americans, and suggested the introduction of the work of the Socialism of Fourierism into the practical work of the township in a "peaceful and positive" manner; thus fulfilling all the duties and answering all the ends of society, which he regarded, as now existing, as actually a "Social Hell," and the eleventh chapter of his brochure is so headed. He asserted, nigh upon fifty years ago, that :—

"Blind competition tends to the formation of gigantic monopolies in every branch of labor; that it depreciates the wages of the working classes; that it excites an endless warfare between human arms, and machinery and capital— a war in which the weak succumbs; that it renders the recurrence of failures, bankruptcies, and commercial crises a sort of endemic disease; and that it reduces the middling and lower classes to a precarious and miserable existence. We have stated, on the authority of authentic documents, that while the few rich are becoming more and more rich, the unnumbered many are becoming poorer. Is anything further necessary to prove that our modern world of industry is a veritable Hell, where disorder, discord, and wretchedness reign, and in which the most cruel fables of the old mythology are more than realized? The masses— naked and destitute, yet surrounded by a prodigality of wealth; seeing on all sides heaps of gold, which by a fatal decree they cannot reach; stunned by the noise of gilded equipages, or dazzled by the brilliance of splendid draperies and dresses; their appetites excited by the magnificence of heaped up luxuries of every climate and all arts; provoked by all that can gratify desire, yet unable to catch one jot or tittle of it—offer a terrible exemplification of Tantalus, tormented by an eternal hunger and thirst after fruits and water, always within his reach, yet perpetually eluding his grasp. Was the penalty of Sisyphus, condemned to roll his stone to a summit, from which it was forever falling, more poignant than that of many fathers of families, among the poorer classes, who, after laboring to exhaustion during their whole lives, to amass somewhat for their old age or for their children, see it swallowed up in one of those periodical crises of failure and ruin which are the inevitable attendants of our methods of loose competition? Or the story of the Danaides, compelled incessantly to draw water in vessels from which it incessantly escaped, does it not with a fearful fidelity symbolize the implacable fate of nearly two-thirds of our modern societies, who draw from the bosom of the earth and the workshops of production, by unrelaxing toil, floods of wealth, that always slip through their hands, to be collected in the vast reservoirs of a moneyed aristocracy?

"Walk through the streets of any of our crowded cities," Parke Godwin urged. "See how within stone's throw of each other stand the most marked and frightful contrasts! Here, look at this marble palace reared in a pure atmosphere and in the neighborhood of pleasing prospects. Its interior is adorned with every refinement that the accumulated skill of sixty centuries has been able to invent; velvet carpets, downy cushions, gorgeous tapestries, stoves, musical instruments, pictures, statues and books. For the gratification and development of its owner and family, industry, science and art have been tasked to their utmost capacity of production. They bathe in all the delights, sensuous and intellectual, that human existence at this period of its career can furnish. They feel no cares; they know no interruption to the unceasing round of their enjoyments.

"Look you again, to that not far distant alley, where some diseased, destitute and depraved families are nestled under the same rickety and tumbling roof;* no fire is

---

* This allusion to a "tumbling roof" calls the author's recollection to the "horrible holocaust," a few brief months ago, when nearly a hundred human beings, mostly proletarians, were crushed to death in Park Place, New York, through the negligence for nearly twenty years of the Building Inspectors of that city, men who were paid by the people's money to protect the wages slaves from such possibilities. But what could have been expected, when the

there to warm them; no clothes to cover their bodies; a pool of filth sends up its nauseousness, perhaps in the very midst of their dwelling; the rain and keen hail fall on their almost defenseless heads; the pestilence is forever hovering over their door-posts; their minds are blacker than night with the black mists of ignorance; and their hearts are torn with fierce lusts and passions; the very sunlight blotted from the firmament and life itself turned into a protracted and bitter curse! Look you, at this, we say, and think that unless something better than what we now see is done, it will all grow worse! Oh, heaven; it is an oppressive and heart rending thought!"

Parke Godwin, however, was no mere grumbler, who developed into a ruthless iconoclast or a brutal Anarchist, like too many reformers, who forget that "to destroy, you must replace." He was a State Socialist at heart, a constructive of constructives, and presented in the course of his essay, the following eight points:—

"I. That there is, in civilized society, a rapid increase of population, without any due provision by society for its employment or support.

"II. That the working classes, who are a majority everywhere, by the present system of blind competition, are picking each other's pockets and cutting each other's throats.

"III. That, according to the admission of nearly all the distinguished political economists, the condition of laborers is rapidly deteriorating.

"IV. That the continued invention of labor-saving

---

building belonged to the family of a prominent politician of the corrupt, dominant faction which holds all the offices; he has since been "whitewashed" by complaisant brother officeholders and a specially selected Grand Jury of the capitalistic class?

machinery is still further tending to the reduction of all laborers for the sake of the capitalists.

"V. That Capital is more and more concentrated in the hands of the few, who are thus forming an oppressive Money-Feudalism.

"VI. That no political party has as yet proposed any measure that in the remotest degree touches the root of these evils.

"VII. That some plan for the unity of the material interests of men is the only one that can prevent our downward tendencies.

"VIII. That this plan is presented in the doctrine of Association (Socialism), on the basis of Attractive Industry."

Fervently believing, as Horace Greeley and Parke Godwin did, the progressive principles of Fourierism, we cannot wonder that their faith was so strong that they too believed "The Future is Ours," and that Godwin confessed his faith therein, like a good Socialist. As Socialists say now, he said then, assured of final triumph.—

"We are confident of victory. Already the white light of the rising sun is caught upon the mountain tops—already we see the streaks of the coming day. Whence the present unusual ferment of the public mind? Why are the deepest religious feelings of the soul, the oldest religious institutions, undergoing such sifting and earnest controversy? Is it not that the world is travailing in the birth-throes of a mighty and better Future? Even the ephemera of literature are seized with the common sympathy and become unconscious prophets of the days about to be. . . . Why tingles the blood? . . . . It is because you know in your hearts that all is wrong with your miserable death-struck Societies, and that you inwardly long for the Better Time.

It is because you would like to join in some practicable and generous movement for the extirpation of pauperism and crime. That movement is at hand: the field of battle is before you; but oh! how different the weapons and objects from those of former warfares. Our weapons are truth, justice and religion. Our objects, universal conciliation and universal love. Unity and Peace are the banner-words of our host."

Horace Greeley never wavered in the Socialist cause, as he accepted it. As an Apostle he always appealed in such striking language, as for instance, in the following dedication:—"To the Generous, the Hopeful, the Loving, who, firmly and joyfully believing in the impartial and boundless goodness of Our Father, trust, that the errors, the crimes, and the miseries which have long rendered earth a Hell, shall yet be swallowed up and forgotten, in a far exceeding and unmeasured reign of Truth, Purity, and Bliss."

He was, however, forced to be ever on the defensive. In 1842, some of his brother editors on rival papers were particularly bitter with him, for having attacked "vested rights." Here is one answer made to the yelps of some of these journalistic creatures of capitalism:—"The kindness of our friends of the New York *Express*, Rochester *Evening Post*, and sundry other journals which appear inclined to wage a personal controversy with us respecting Fourierism, (the *Express* without knowing how to spell the word,) is duly appreciated. Had we time and room for disputation on that subject, we would prefer opponents who would not be compelled to confess frankly or betray clearly their utter ignorance of the matter, whatever might be their manifestations of personal pique or malevolence, in unfair representations of the little they *do* understand. We counsel our too belligerent friends to possess their souls in patience, and not be too eager to rival the fortune of him whose essay proving that steamships could *not* cross the Atlantic happened to reach us in the first steamship that *did* cross it. 'The proof of the pudding' is not found in wrangling about it."

That he had opposition and a considerable quantity of it too, there is no question. Thus after acting as first Vice-President at a Fourierist Socialist Convention held at New York City in 1844, in answer to the toast at a banquet on Fourier's birthday, when lauded as the one man of all, who had "created the cause on this continent," Greeley responded :—"When I took up this cause, I knew that I went in the teeth of many of my patrons, in the teeth of prejudices of the great mass, in the teeth of religious prejudices, for I confess I had a great many more clergymen on my list before than I have now, as I am sorry to say, for had they kept on, I think I could have done them a little good. [Laughter.] But in the face of all this, in the face of constant advice, 'Don't have any thing more to do with that Mr. Brisbane,' I went on. 'Oh!' said many of my friends, 'consider your position—consider your influence.' 'Well,' said I, 'I shall endeavor to do so, but I must try to do some good in the meantime, or else what is the use of the influence.' [Cheers.] And thus I have gone on, pursuing a manly and at the same time a circumspect course, treading wantonly on no man's prejudice, saying on the contrary, 'Universal man, I will defer to your prejudices, as far as I can consistently with duty ; but when duty leads me, you must excuse my stepping on your corn if it be in the way.' [Cheers.]"

But Horace Greeley rarely allowed himself to do his Socialist preaching at the dinner table à la Chauncey Depew. He never indulged in a logomachy of frothy nonsense. On the contrary, he went among the people and talked directly to them. We have the record of his first lecture in New York, which was announced January 3, 1843, as follows:—"Horace Greeley will lecture before the New York Lyceum at the Tabernacle, this evening. Subject, 'Human Life.' The lecture will commence at half past 7, precisely. If those who care to hear it will sit near the desk, they will favor the lecturer's weak and husky voice."

Occasionally he spoke to small meetings outside of New York and in very primitive places much in the style of our present Socialist agitators, who are obliged in the face of the deadliest opposition frequently to go,—being wofully misreported by some tyro of a scribe afterwards,* —among the "publicans and sinners," when their own people harden their hearts against them. Here is a paragraph from the *Tribune* in the direction of humble work in a humble way:—"T. W. Whitley and H. Greeley will address such citizens of Newark as choose to hear them on the subject of 'Association' at 7:30 o'clock this evening at the Relief Hall, rear of J. M. Quimby's Repository."

---

* The author does not believe journalists as a rule want to be unfair to Socialists, but the trouble is that a great many newspaper men, neither understanding the philosophy of the progressive movement, nor even its aims, much less the difference between opposing factions, unintentionally misrepresent. Another thing is that as sensationalism rules the press, reporters are always on the *qui vive* for kaleidoscopic effects, so to say, and when Socialist public speakers have indulged in irresponsible oratorical pyrotechnics, neither warranted by facts, nor in the true line of the agitation for the Coöperative Commonwealth, they have been very quickly snapped up by the "knights of the pencil" and a "big story" made out of their unscientific advocacy of the industrial movement. A workingman may be a splendid mechanic with his hands, but a mighty bad agitator with his tongue, for the simple reason that he is neither a politician by profession nor a "jaw-smith" by trade.

Horace Greeley forced the Socialist issues upon the American people. Speaking of the propaganda work done by him and his associates, he said :—"By persevering effort, the subject was thrust, as it were, on public attention ; a few zealous converts made to the new ideas, and probably more vehement adversaries aroused ; while the far greater number could not be induced to read or consider, but regarded all Socialist theories with stubborn indifference. Those who were in good circumstances, or hoped yet to be, wished no such change as was contemplated by the new theories ; the ignorant, stolid many, who endure lives of destitution and squalid misery, were utterly devoid of faith or hope, receiving with profound incredulity and distrust any proposal to improve their condition. My observation justifies the belief, that the most *conservative* of mankind, when not under the influence of some great, convulsive uprising like the French Revolution, are those who have nothing to lose."

Out of the really. marvelous agitation of the Fourierist movement much good however came, as will be shown later. It was regularly organized from the inception of the first attempts to realize, practically what the French Social economist had presented in theory, and in 1848 the directing body of the "American Union of Associationists" had printed on the cover of Pellarin's *Life of Charles Fourier*, published by "William H. Graham, Tribune Buildings" the following :—

"AMERICAN UNION OF ASSOCIATIONISTS. The purpose of this Society is the popular diffusion of the principles of Associative Science, as discovered by CHARLES FOURIER, with a view to their ultimate realization by the establishment of Phalanxes. It is highly desirable that all persons, friendly to the object, should connect themselves with one of the Local Unions, which are now established in many of the principal cities and villages of the United States, or should take immediate measures to form one in their own vicinity. The operations of the American Union depend on funds contributed by the members of Local Unions, or forwarded directly to the Treasurer of the Parent Society. The office of the Union is at No. 9 Spruce Street, New York, where all its business is transacted, and where its weekly organ, *The Harbinger*, is published. A full assortment of French and English Association Works are for sale at the same place.

"*President*, HORACE GREELEY, New York.

"*Domestic Corresponding Secretary*, GEORGE RIPLEY, New York.

"*Foreign Corresponding Secretary*, PARKE GODWIN, New York.

"*Recording Secretary*, EDWARD GILES, New York.

"*Treasurer*, EDWARD TWEEDY, New York."

Horace Greeley published in 1850 a volume, *Hints Toward Reforms*, consisting principally of lectures and addresses, which show that in the work of propaganda done by him on the platform, he always spoke, as William Morris* the English Poet-Socialist does to-day, in terse and vigorous phraseology. He was a popular Socialist agitator, coming down to the level of those he was addressing, and never permitted himself to become that despair of working people "a scientific doctrinaire," neither using polysyllabic words undiscoverable in Webster or Worcester; nor scholastic argumentation suitable only for those who have passed the ordeal of a university.

---

* *William Morris, Poet, Artist, Socialist.* A Selection from his Writings together with a Sketch of the Man. Edited by Francis Watts Lee." New York, Humboldt Publishing Co., 1891.

The subject of all Greeley's oratory was "one alone," wrote James Parton, who knew him well, and when both were living his biographer said :—

Horace Greeley's "subject is ever the same ; the object of his public life is single. It is the 'EMANCIPATION OF LABOR ;' its emancipation from ignorance, vice, servitude, insecurity, poverty. This is his chosen, *only* theme, whether he speaks from the platform, or writes for the *Tribune.* If slavery is the subject of discourse, the Dishonor which Slavery does to *Labor* is the light in which he prefers to present it. If protection—he demands it in the name and for the good of American *workingmen*, that their minds may be quickened by diversified employment, their position secured by abundant employment, the farmers enriched by markets near at hand. If Learning—he laments the unnatural divorce between Learning and *Labor*, and advocates their re-union in manual-labor schools. If 'Human Life'—he cannot refrain from reminding his hearers, that 'the deep want of the time is, that the vast resources and capacities of Mind, the far-stretching powers of Genius and of Science, be brought to bear practically and intimately on Agriculture, the Mechanic Arts, and all the now rude and simple processes of Day-Labor, and not merely that these processes may be perfected and accelerated, but that the benefits of the improvement may accrue in at least equal measure to those whose accustomed means of livelihood—scanty at best—are interfered with and overturned by the change.' If the 'Formation of Character'— he calls upon men who aspire to possess characters equal to the demands of the time, to 'question with firm speech all institutions, observances, customs, that they may determine by what mischance or illusion thriftless Pretense and Knavery shall seem to batten on a brave Prosperity, while

Labor vainly begs employment, Skill lacks recompense, and Worth pines for bread.' If Popular Education—he reminds us, that 'the narrow, dingy, squalid tenement, calculated to repel any visitor but the cold and the rain, is hardly fitted to foster lofty ideas of Life, its Duties and its Aims. And he who is constrained to ask each morning, 'Where shall I find food for the day?' is at best unlikely often to ask, 'By what good deed shall the day be signalized?'"

Greeley, who was the greatest American editor, as well as the foremost economic advocate and public controversialist of his time, could never escape from the overpowering presence of Human Slavery. He was in that respect like Horace Mann, who ever insisted that "there is no evil as great as slavery." Greeley's writings teem with anti-slavery arguments. Consequently, in the words of Lawson, when standing by the dead Socialist's graveside, "the *Tribune* was the very lexicon of liberty. Its great battle against slavery was the fiercest struggle which has ever been fought, and triumph was its reward ; for while Abraham Lincoln, who, without the editor of the *Tribune* could not have been President of the United States, wrote with his own hand the Decree of Emancipation, it is to Horace Greeley that history will assign the credit of having extinguished the institution of slavery on this hemisphere."

Like the rest of the Socialists of his period, the principal portion of Greeley's efforts was devoted, it is true, to the Abolition movement, but never in the spirit of too many anti-slavery agitators, who regarded "slavery," simply as negro slavery alone. He always insisted that the wages slavery system was as bad as the human chattel system, that the victims of both were equally in bondage and both must be freed. Greeley was requested once, in 1845, to attend an anti-slavery convention. This is what he responded, and his views on "Human Slavery" could hardly have been misunderstood by those who had invited him :—

"NEW YORK, June 3, 1845.

"DEAR SIR :—I received, weeks since, your letter inviting me to be present at a general convention of opponents of Human Slavery, irrespective of past differences and party organizations. I have delayed to the last moment my answer, hoping I might this season indulge a long-cherished desire and purpose by visiting your section and city, in which case I should certainly have attended your Convention. Being now reluctantly compelled to forego or indefinitely postpone that visit, I have no recourse but to acknowledge your courtesy in a letter.

"In saying that I should have attended your Convention had I been able to visit Cincinnati this month, I would by no means be understood as implying that I should have chosen to share in its deliberations ; still less that I should have been likely to unite in the course of action to which those deliberations will probably tend. Whether there 'can true reconcilement grow' between those opponents of Slavery whom the Presidential Election arrayed against each other in desperate conflict, I do not venture to predict. Most surely, that large portion of them with whom *I* acted and still act, have been confirmed in our previous convictions of duty by the result of that election, and by the momentous consequences which it has drawn after it, not merely with regard to this question of Slavery, but to all questions. I have by that result been warned against pledging myself to any special and isolated Reform in such manner as to interfere with and fetter my freedom and ability to act decisively and effectively upon more general and immediately practical considerations of National interest and of Human well-being. You and yours, I understand, have been confirmed in an opposite conviction. Time must decide on which side is the right.

"But, while I cannot hope that I should have been able to unite with you upon any definite course of action to be henceforth pursued by *all* opponents of Slavery, irrespective of past or present differences, I should have gladly met you, conferred with you, compared opinions, and agreed to act together so far as joint action is not forbidden by conflicting opinions. Animated by this spirit, I shall venture to set before you, and ask the Convention to consider, some views which I deem essential, as bearing on the present condition and ultimate success of the Anti-Slavery movement.

" *What is Slavery ?* You will probably answer, 'The 'legal subjection of one human being to the will and power 'of another.' But this definition appears to me inaccurate on both sides—too broad, and at the same time too narrow. It is too broad, in that it includes the subjection founded in other necessities, not less stringent than those imposed by statute. We must seek some truer definition.

" *I understand by Slavery, that condition in which one human being exists mainly as a convenience for other human beings*—in which the time, the exertions, the faculties of a part of the Human Family are made to subserve, not their own development, physical, intellectual and moral, but the comfort, advantage or caprices of others. In short, wherever service is rendered from one human being to another, on a footing of one-sided and not of mutual obligation— where the relation between the servant and the served is one not of affection and reciprocal good offices, but of authority, social ascendency and power over subsistence on the one hand, and of necessity, servility and degradation, on the other—there, in my view, is Slavery.

"You will readily understand, therefore, that, if I regard your enterprise with less absorbing interest than you do, it is not that I deem Slavery a less, but a greater evil. If I am less troubled concerning the Slavery prevalent in Charleston or New Orleans, it is because I see so much Slavery in New York, which appears to claim my first efforts. I rejoice in believing that there is less of it in your several communities and neighborhoods ; but that it does exist there, I am compelled to believe. In esteeming it my duty to preach Reform first to my own neighbors and kindred, I would by no means attempt to censure those whose consciences prescribe a different course. Still less would I undertake to say that the Slavery of the South is not more hideous in kind and degree than that which prevails at the North. The fact that it *is* more flagrant and palpable renders opposition to it comparatively easy and its speedy downfall certain. But how can I devote myself to a crusade against distant servitude, when I discern its essence pervading my immediate community and neighborhood? nay, when I have not yet succeeded in banishing it even from my own humble household? Wherever may lie the sphere of duty of others, is not mine obviously *here ?*

"Let me state what I conceive to be the essential characteristics of Human Slavery :

"1. Wherever certain human beings devote their time and thoughts mainly to obeying and serving other human beings, and this not because they choose to do so but because they *must*, there (I think) is Slavery.

"2. Wherever human beings exist in such relations that a part, because of the position they occupy and the functions they perform, are generally considered an inferior class to those who perform other functions, or none, there (I think) is Slavery.

" 3. Wherever the ownership of the Soil is so engrossed by a small part of the community that the far larger number are compelled to pay whatever the few may see fit to exact for the privilege of occupying and cultivating the earth, there is something very like Slavery.

"4. Wherever Opportunity to Labor is obtained with difficulty, and is so deficient that the Employing class may virtually prescribe their own terms and pay the Laborer only such share as they choose of the product, there is a very strong tendency to Slavery.

"5. Wherever it is deemed more reputable to live without Labor than by Labor, so that 'a gentleman' would be rather ashamed of his descent from a blacksmith than from an idler or mere pleasure-seeker, there is a community not very far from Slavery. And—

"6. Wherever one human being deems it honorable and right to have other human beings mainly devoted to his or her convenience or comfort, and thus to live, diverting the labor of these persons from all productive or general usefulness to his or her own special uses, while he or she is rendering or has rendered no corresponding service to the cause of human well-being, there exists the spirit which originated and still sustains Human Slavery.

"I might multiply these illustrations indefinitely, but I dare not so trespass on your patience. Rather allow me to apply the principles here evolved in illustration of what I deem the duties and policy of Abolitionists in reference to their cause. And here I would advise:

" 1. *Oppose Slavery in* ALL *its forms.* Be at least as careful not to *be* a slaveholder as not to *vote* for one. Be as tenacious that your own wives, children, hired men and women, tenants, etc., enjoy the blessings of rational Liberty, as that the slaves of South Carolina do.

"2. *Be at least as ardent in opposing the* NEAR *as the* DISTANT *forms of Oppression.*—It was by beginning at home that Charity was enabled to perform such long journeys, even before the construction of railroads. And it does seem clear to my mind that if the advocates of Emancipation would unite in well-directed, persistent efforts to improve the condition of the Colored Race in their own States and neighborhoods respectively, they could hardly fail to advance their cause more rapidly and surely than by any other course. Suppose, for example, they were to resolve in each State to devote their political energies in the first place to a removal of the shameful, atrocious civil disabilities and degradations under which the African Race now generally labor, and to this end were to vote systematically for such candidates, whom their votes could probably elect, (if such there were,) as were known to favor the removal of those disabilities : Would not their success be sure and speedy? But,

"3. *Look well to the Moral and Social condition of the Blacks in the Free States.* Here is the refuge of the conscientious slaveholder. He declines emancipating, because he can not perceive that emancipation has thus far conduced to the benefit of the liberated. If the mass of the Blacks are to remain ignorant, destitute, unprincipled, degraded (as he is told the Free Blacks are) he thinks it better that his should remain Slaves.

"I know that the degradation of the Blacks is exaggerated. I know that so much of it as exists is mainly owing to their past and present wrongs. But I feel also that the process of overcoming this debasement must be slow and dubious, while its causes continue to exist. I entreat, therefore, that those who have the ear of these children of Africa and of their philanthropic friends, shall consider the propriety of providing for them cities of refuge, townships— communities, I would say—wherein they may dwell apart from the mass of our people, in a social atmosphere of their own, not poisoned by the universal conviction of their inferiority, at least until they shall have had a chance to show whether they are or are not necessarily idle, thriftless, vicious and content with degradation. I most earnestly believe the popular assumptions on these points erroneous; I ask that the Blacks have a fair chance to prove them so. A single township in each Free State mainly peopled by them, with churches, schools, seminaries for scientific and classical education, and all Social influences untainted by the sense of African humiliation, would do more (if success- ful, as I doubt not it would be) to pave the way for Universal Freedom, than reams of angry vituperation against slaveholders. These are in good part men of integrity and conscience; they see the wrong almost as clearly as you do; it is the *right* which they should see and can not; will you enable them to see it?

"Yours respectfully,

"HORACE GREELEY."

The founder of the *Tribune* notwithstanding all his efforts to have his broad, generous views on Human Slavery understood by the world, found all his attempts were utterly useless, just the same as were those to awaken the conscience of the people to the iniquity of both chattel slavery and wages serfdom. But even this misunderstanding gave him splendid opportunities for Socialist propaganda. Thus when he was in London in the year 1851 he made a

speech at Exeter Hall, under the following circumstances
narrated by Parton :—"Three colored gentleman and an
M. P. had extolled Britain as the land of *true* freedom and
equality, had urged Britons to refuse recognition to 'pro-
slavery clergymen,' to avoid using the products of slave-
labor, and to assist the free-colored people to educate their
children. One of the colored orators had observed the
entrance of Horace Greeley, and named him commendingly
to the audience; whereupon he was invited to take a seat
upon the platform, and afterwards to address the meeting;
both of which invitations were promptly accepted. He
spoke fifteen minutes. He began by stating the fact, that
American Slavery justifies itself mainly on the ground, that
the class who live by manual toil are everywhere, but
particularly in England, degraded and ill-requited. Therefore, he urged upon English Abolitionists, first, to use
systematic exertions to increase the reward of Labor and
the comfort and consideration of the depressed Laboring
Class *at home;* and to diffuse and cherish respect for Man
as Man, without regard to class, color or vocation.
Secondly, to put forth determined efforts for the eradication
of those Social evils and miseries *in England* which are
appealed to and relied on by slaveholders and their cham-
pions everywhere as justifying the continuance of Slavery;
and thirdly, to colonize our Slave States by thousands of
intelligent, moral, industrious Free Laborers, who will
silently and practically dispel the wide-spread delusion
which affirms that the Southern States must be cultivated
and their great staples produced by Slave Labor, or not
at all."

The Apostleship of Greeley and the results of his
work, as a Christian Socialist, as a Farmer Socialist, and
an Industrial Socialist will be treated in separate chapters.

But his position on the slavery question is the one matter of all others in which the public were most interested while he was living, as they are now. They have never, it seems to the writer, been able to understand the true meaning of his philanthropy, much less his position politically. With Greeley, it was unswerving devotion to a high principle :— the Abolition of all Human Slavery—that of the colored people first, politically, and concurrently with it economically, that of the white wages slaves by "association," through their own industrial organizations then in existence or to be formed, aided by the people through legislation.

Horace Greeley had been politically a Whig in his early manhood because the Whigs had opposed the extension of chattel slavery, but when the "Compromise Measures of 1850" took place and fructified, he sympathized with the "Free Soil Movement," which endorsed "Free Soil, Free Speech, Free Labor and Free Men," holding that Congress could not constitutionally establish slavery in States and Territories. In 1852, when Gen. Winfield Scott ran for the Presidency, although Greeley, as he put it, "spat upon the Whig platform," he thought it was better to help its candidate in the *Tribune*, though he knew that he could not be elected, than "risk the success of the Democrats" and the Slave-holding Capitalists. He was an anti-slavery Whig and was one of the founders of the old Republican party,—not the present spoils hunting party of demagogues and corruptionists,—which was brought into existence in 1854 by anti-slavery advocates belonging to different parties who "could act without the embarrassment of a pro-slavery Whig."

These pro-slavery Whigs had become in 1850, as a party, as bad in Greeley's eyes through truckling for "offices only," to chattel slave Capitalists by the "Slavery Compromise Measures" during Zachary Taylor's administration, as he had thought the Democratic Party was seven years before. Then in his burning wrath he had written :

"When American Citizens used to gather by hundreds to sing and dance around Hickory Poles, with barrels of whisky rolled out and heads of Beer-Casks stove in—when right here, in the heart of this enlightened emporium, men were seen, after a cask of beer had been poured into the hole where the Pole was to be set in front of Tammany Hall, to lie down and drink it from the ground like hogs—the Kinderhooker saw nothing 'disreputable' then. When American Citizens have been swept away from the polls of our city with clubs, by bands of misguided and excited immigrants, half civilized and maddened with liquor furnished them by party liberality, we had no hint from Mr. Van Buren that such scenes were 'disreputable' or calculated to impair 'the confidence of mankind in our fitness for free institutions.' When men who felt it their duty to bear testimony against Slavery were mobbed and bludgeoned for peacefully so doing, and the owner of a free press was shot down in his own tenement for guarding his press from destruction by a band of ruffians who chose to suspect that it *would be* used against Slavery, this demagogue could see in it nothing calculated to shake confidence in our fitness for free institutions, but coolly remarked in his Inaugural that a 'reckless disregard of the consequences of their conduct has exposed individuals to popular indignation.' "

But Horace Greeley, who was opposed to capital punishment and war, both of which he inveighed against with all the power of his rhetoric, was, except in "defense, not defiance," utterly antagonistic to the Civil War, when it was brought on later by the Southern Capitalists. Thus even when the strife was raging, the famous *Tribune* editorial of July 1-4, 1861, was not inserted by his consent :—

"THE NATION'S WAR-CRY! *Forward to Richmond! Forward to Richmond! The Rebel Congress must not be allowed to meet there on the 20th of July!* BY THAT DATE THE PLACE MUST BE HELD BY THE NATIONAL ARMY."

As James Parton says, it was the work of "some of the more ardent spirits in the office impatient of delay," and when the defeat of Bull Run followed in consequence, Greeley was stricken down with brain fever and hovered between life and death for weeks.

The war over, however, he recognized that it was impossible to do otherwise than "expect human nature such as it is, to give away, or to put away, $4,000,000,000 worth of property, even though we have grossly exaggerated our estimate of its value," without there being extenuating circumstances to be considered even for the ex-slaveholders ; and then his daily watchwords were "Universal Amnesty —Impartial Suffage." It was "in accordance with this humane policy that he prevented the trial of Jefferson Davis for treason by going on his bail for one hundred thousand dollars, (by which) magnanimous act was saved the barbarous spectacle of making bloody reprisals among the chieftains of the Confederacy ; and this was the keynote to Horace Greeley's entire life from the time when Lee surrendered his sword to Grant at Appomattox till the great editor was borne to his tomb. For him the fight was over, the battle had been won, and fraternal love was the doctrine which he preached should thenceforth reign between the sections."

Yet it was hardly possible, however, for Horace Greeley to be absolutely forgetful when he saw the old chattel slaveholding power, attempting to raise its crushed head and endeavoring to strike and poison anew the nation. Thus on February 6, 1868, he wrote in defense of the colored people :—

"In those dark years when the slaveholder ruled from Boston to New Orleans, the Democratic party cheerfully wore his collar, and when he fell from power it still howled and barked at the heels of the nation throughout the long and agonizing struggle for life. This virtue at least it had— the fidelity with which an ill-treated cur sometimes follows a brutal master, and it is faithful yet. The slaveholder is dead, but over his grave the Democratic party whines and raves in the hope that some miracle may yet work his resurrection. Loving the dead master so well, it hates the liberated slave. Look for the purpose which controls its action, and it may be found only in its mad, unreasoning, inhuman hatred of the negro. Take this away, and the party falls to pieces. Without the inspiration of hate, Democracy becomes no more than a disorganized faction, a superannuated rioter, and a sturdy beggar for office. If the colored race in this country had ever given cause for hatred, some excuse, however slight, might be made for their persecutors. But they have committed no offense. In Slavery they carried the virtue of patience to an excess which made it almost a crime. Aliens and outcasts and pariahs, Christians who were forbidden to read the Bible, forbidden to marry, yet condemned to see their women held in concubinage by their masters; counted as men and sold as beasts—this people mutely endured unparalleled oppression for generations, without striking a blow. Here, in the North, the colored race has always been law-abiding and orderly; it is only in the large cities that they become corrupted to any great extent, and even in New York there is no case known in which they hung Democrats upon lamp posts, or burned down asylums for Democratic orphans. Patience and fortitude and forgiveness greater than theirs the world has never seen, and in a Christian nation there has never been a meaner spectacle than their persecution. Pitiful, indeed, is the political party whose solitary great principle is hatred of the negro, and whose chief aim is to keep him in ignorance and bondage."

Horace Greeley was a statesman and no politician in the present sense of the word, yet he once felt constrained to write :—"If the designation of politician is a discreditable one, I trust I have done nothing toward making it so. If to consider not only what is desirable, but what is possible as well,—if to consider in what order desirable ends can be attained, and attempt them in that order,—if to seek to do one good so as not to undo another,—if either or all of these constitute one a politician, I do not shrink from the appellation." He twice held political office. But on both occasions he acted with a laudable purpose in view.

When Brigadier-General Charles G. Halpine, that brave songster, better known as "Private Miles O'Reilly," died in 1868, he was Register of the city and county of New York. Greeley was offered the appointment, accepted it and discharged the duties gratuitously, handing over the salary to the widow of his old friend and predecessor in the office.

Horace Greeley's only other political office was a ninety days' seat in Congress. He was elected in 1848 by two classes—"working men and thinking men," and by a majority of 3,177, the whole number of votes cast being 5,985. When the result was known, he wrote one of his characteristic screeds in the form of a "Card of Thanksgiving," and which commenced as follows :

"The undersigned, late a candidate for Congress, respectfully returns his thanks—first, to his political opponents for the uniform kindness and consideration with which he was treated by them throughout the canvass, and the unsolicited suffrages with which he was honored by many of them; secondly, to the great mass of his political brethren, for the ardent, enthusiastic and effective support which they rendered him; and, lastly, to that small portion of the Whig electors who saw fit to withhold from him their votes, thereby nearly or quite neutralizing the support he received from the opposite party. Claiming for himself the right to vote for or against any candidate of his party as his own sense of right and duty shall dictate, he very freely accords to all others the same liberty, without offense or inquisition.

"During the late canvass I have not, according to my best recollection, spoken of myself, and have not replied in any way to any sort of attack or imputation. I have in no manner sought to deprecate the objections, nor to soothe the terrors of that large and most influential class who deem my advocacy of Land Reform and Social Re-organization synonymous with Infidelity and systematic Robbery. . . ."

One of Greeley's main desires in going to Congress was to help real Land Reform,—no mere re-assessment for real estate taxation,—and through his advocacy was passed the Homestead Bill. He also worked and spoke against Human Slavery, but his day had not come. He achieved one of his principal objects, and that was to strike a blow at political corruption. Greeley had attacked in the *Tribune* the "mileage swindle" by which congressmen regularly robbed the Nation of money that was not due them. The editor of the paper which had shown this up, being a member of the House of Representatives, the issue of defense was forced upon those charged with obtaining moneys by false pretenses. A whitewashing committee was appointed "with instruction to inquire into and report whether said publication does not amount, in sub-

stance, to an allegation of fraud against most of the members
of this House in this matter of their mileage; and if, in the
judgment of the Committee, it does amount to an allegation of fraud, then to inquire into it, and report whether
that allegation is true or false." Nothing came of it however. The matter was quashed and the same condition of
things in the way of "mileage" has been continued until
these days, but not so flagrantly.

James Parton, summing up Greeley's three months in
Congress, said:—"No man ever served his country more
faithfully. No man ever received less reward. One would
have supposed that such a manly and brave endeavor to
economize the public money and the public time, such
singular devotion to the public interests in the face of
opposition, obloquy and insult, would have elicited from
the whole country, or at least from many parts of it, cordial
expressions of approval. It did not, however. With no
applauding shouts was Horace Greeley welcomed on his
return from the Seat of Corruption. No enthusiastic
mass-meetings of his constituents passed a series of resolutions, approving his course. He has not been named for
re-election. Do the people, then, generally feel that an
Honest Man is out of place in the Congress of the United
States?

"Only from the little town of North Fairfield, Ohio,
came a hearty cry of WELL DONE! A meeting of the
citizens of that place was held for the purpose of expressing
their sense of his gallant and honorable conduct. He
responded to their applauding resolutions in a characteristic letter. 'Let me beg of you,' said he, 'to think little of
Persons, in this connection, and much of *Measures*. Should
any see fit to tell you that I am dishonest, or ambitious, or
hollow-hearted in this matter, don't stop to contradict or

confute him, but press on his attention the main question respecting the honesty of these crooked charges. It is with these the public is concerned, and not this or that man's motives. Calling me a hypocrite or demagogue cannot make a charge of $1,664 for coming to Congress from Illinois and going back again an honest one.' "

Horace Greeley did not appear in active politics again for many years, except through the editorial columns of his newspaper. What he had to say directly to his country-men was spoken from the lecture platform. In 1861, he was a candidate to represent the State of New York in the United States Senate, but the corruptionists, lobbyists and wire-pullers did not want a Socialist Reformer there, so he was defeated. Greeley, in 1872, was the nominee for the Presidency of the United States of the Liberal Republican Party, which had then assumed a national organization. Its members had split off principally from the Republican Party, which under Grant's administration became synonymous with the term corruption. Rings to rob the country had been brought into existence and were stealing the people's money by wholesale. Scandals, such as the Navy frauds, the Belknap affair, the Freedmen's Bank swindle, and the District of Columbia Ring,—developed out of the general laxity of political morals, and they were the order of the day. And they were not peculiar to one party, for if there was a Republican "Boss" Shepherd Ring in Washington, there was a Democratic "Boss" Tweed Ring in New York, both engaged—and successfully—in embezzling millions of dollars out of the public treasuries.

Again, these Liberal Republicans deeply resented the conduct of the Grant administration to Charles Sumner, who was really a great statesman, and to America's best historian John Lothrop Motley. They also antagonized

the Grant scheme to annex San Domingo and opposed
the thievery and methods of the carpet-bag state governments down South. Greeley represented this sentiment
through the columns of the *Tribune* and was chosen the
standard bearer of this hostility to the dominant faction of
the Republicans and their truly infamous ways. Besides
this, no one living was considered so fitting to take the
country politically away from that "slough of despond," to
which Horace Mann called the attention of the people of
the United States in 1842 when, in his Fourth of July
Oration before the civic authorities of Boston, he had
said :—

"Fellow-Citizens, there is one strongly developed tendency in our political affairs which I cannot pass by, on an
occasion like this, without an admonitory word. Though
less obvious, yet it is of more evil portent, than any in the
dark catalogue I have exhibited. It leads by swift steps
to proximate ruin. I refer to the practice of the different
political parties, into which we are unhappily divided, of
seizing upon some specious aspect of every event, giving
it an exaggerated and factitious importance, and perverting
it to factitious profit. In common and expressive phrase,
this is called *making political capital* out of a thing ; and
the art of making this *capital* seems now to be incorporated
into the regular tactics of party leaders. But it is forged
capital, and in the end, it must bring forger and accom-
plices to judgment and condemnation, as well as all their
dupes to political and moral insolvency. In law, such
practices, or rather mal-practices, are called *chicanery ;*
and they justly subject to infamy the practitioner who is
corrupted with them. But law deals with private interests,
—politics with the vaster interests of the whole community.
And why should not the trick and knavery which strike a

man's name from the roll of the court, strike it also from the red-book of the nation !

"Look at it Fellow-Citizens :—A great question arises in the Legislative Halls of the State or Nation, or springs up in any part of our country ; and immediately the party leaders and the party press reflect before the eyes of all the people,—not segments or fragments, even,—but distorted and discolored images of all the truths, facts and principles, pertaining to that question, so distorted and discolored that no impartiality or patience can reproduce any likeness to the original. So extensive has this practice become, that an honest inquirer into the merits of men or measures, in reading accounts of the same individuals or transactions, in the rival newspapers of the day, would suppose them to relate to wholly different men and different measures, were it not for the occasional identity of the proper names which are used. Must it not follow that the vast majority of the people will get mutilated and false views ; and come, habitually, to decide the real question by looking at the counterfeited, until the mind itself is as perverted as the lights which shine on it. Immense responsibilities attach here to all who influence public opinion, whether they sit in the presidential, or gubernatorial, or editorial chair. The habit of ascribing, to trivial and fleeting considerations, the prominence and inviolability of eternal laws ; the habit of discarding at every political crisis, the great principles which lie under the whole length of existence, and are the only possible basis of our well-being, in order to gain some temporary end ; the habit, at our oft-recurring elections, of risking all future consequences, to secure present success, is high treason against the sovereignty of truth, and must be the harbinger of a speedy destruction. We can conceive of no power in the universe, that could uphold its throne under so fatal a policy.

"I do not advert to this prominent feature of our times, —worthy of far more extended consideration,—in order that one party may look into the conduct of its adversaries, to find cause of accusation ; but that each may look upon its own course, and in view of it, demand and effect a speedy amendment."

Horace Greeley, accordingly, was the nominee of the Liberal Republicans and in his response to the action of the National Convention accepted, as he said, "with the distinct understanding, that, if elected, I shall be the President, not of a party, but of the whole people. I accept your nomination in the confident trust that the masses of our countrymen, North and South, are eager to clasp hands across the bloody chasm which has too long divided them, forgetting that they have been enemies in the joyful consciousness that they are, and must henceforth remain, brethren."

But, apparently, as if to hurt Greeley's chances of election, the Democratic Party endorsed him and then through "a side-show" nominated Charles O'Conor as a third candidate. Naturally, Grant was reëlected, but at the price of Greeley's life. The strain upon his naturally weak frame had been too great and he died of nervous exhaustion and inflammation of the brain, which were superinduced as much by his own heartrending sorrow on the death of his revered wife during his presidential campaign, as by the effect upon him of the vile caricatures and shameful libels attacking him, distributed by his corrupt political enemies—both Republican and Democrat alike.

Had Horace Greeley been elected President, much, doubtless, would have been done by him for the cause of

Socialism and against the capitalist successors of those
"dangerous classes" referred to by the poet Henry
Wadsworth Longfellow, when he wrote Charles Sumner:

"In every country the 'dangerous classes' are those
who do not work. For instance, the nobility in Europe
and the slaveholders here. It is evident the world needs a
new nobility—not of the blood that is blue, because it
stagnates—but of the new arterial blood that circulates
and has a heart in it, and life and labor."

But Greeley's whole life was a fight for Socialism,—not,
perhaps, as comprehensive or as scientific as that urged by
modern Socialists, but Socialism all the same. As Alchemy
had to precede Chemistry, so the Utopians of Owenism
and Fourierism were the St. John Baptists of the full
development of Social Democracy—and no one recognized
such a fulfillment better than Horace Greeley as far back
as 1845, when he stated :—

"It has been urged as an objection to the *Tribune,* that
it proposed to 'give hospitality to every *new* thought.' To
that profession we shall be constant, at whatever sacrifice.
Full of error, and suffering as the world yet is, we cannot
afford to reject unexamined any idea which proposes to
improve the Moral, Intellectual, or Social condition of
mankind. Better incur the trouble of testing and explod-
ing a thousand fallacies than, by rejecting, stifle a single
beneficent truth. Especially on the vast theme of an
Improved Organization of Industry, so as to secure constant
opportunity and a just recompense to every human being
able and willing to labor, we are not and cannot be indifferent. Although we cannot devote much space to this or
any abstract purpose, yet we shall endeavor to keep our
readers apprised of whatever is suggested and whatever
shall be done tending to improve the Social condition of

the toiling millions of mankind. No subject can be more important than this; no improvement more certain of attainment. The plans hitherto suggested may all prove abortive; the experiments hitherto set on foot may all come to nought (as many of them doubtless will); yet these mistakes shall serve to indicate the true means of improvement, and these experiments shall bring nearer and nearer the grand consummation which they contemplate. The securing of thorough Education, Opportunity, and just Reward to all, cannot be beyond the reach of the Nineteenth Century."

It should never be forgotten that with Horace Greeley the Abolition of Human Chattel Slavery was simply the first political step toward Socialistic growth, economic development and final evolution. His argument was that the distasteful labor of the world, such as mining, should receive higher recompense under the future system than those easier tasks which might fall to the lot of a select few. This, he apprehended, would lead, under wonderfully different conditions, to that true individualism, now stifled, which would recognize the noblest good in working for or considering others.

Horace Greeley wished to make all industry "attractive," believed in its accomplishment and presaged its triumph. Thus he writes:

"As yet, the Great Reform which shall abolish all Slavery, as it only *can* be effectually, really abolished, by leaving none coveting the position of a master, none possessing the soul of a slave, is in its infancy, silently and slowly but surely progressing to matured energy and vigor. ATTRACTIVE INDUSTRY, the dream of the past age, the aspiration of the present, shall be the fruition and joy of the next. The reunion of Desire and Duty, divorced and

warring since the Fall, restores Man at once to the
unchanging, uncloying bliss of Eden. That this is a Moral
renovation is, indeed, most true, but false is the deduction
that it is wrought or endures, regardless of Physical conditions. Idly do the lips of the widow murmur expressions
of contentment and thankfulness when her children pine
for bread and have no prospect of procuring it; vainly
does the forlorn wretch essay to thank that Providence
whose ways he cannot fathom, but whose present results
are to him famine, disease, and utter, hopeless destitution.
Here and there the keen eye of Faith may pierce the
deepest gloom of the Present, and rest exultingly on the
compensating glories of the Future; but such are exceptions to the general law which renders present privation
and anguish an Aaron's rod, swallowing up all thought,
overclouding all hope, of future bliss. We must know
what happiness is, ere we can rightly appreciate the prospect of it; we must have exemption from pressing wants
of the body, ere we can duly heed and be faithful to the
loftiest promptings of the soul. The individual engrossed
in a constant and arduous struggle for daily bread, makes
slow and capricious progress on the path to Heaven.
Those who cannot obey the Divine precept, 'Take no
[anxious] thought for the morrow,' can hardly hope to
obey any precept relating to their own spiritual growth and
elevation. Not till the pressing demands of our outward
and bodily nature shall have been provided for, may we
rationally look for a general conformity of our Actual State
to the Ideal of sentient, intelligent being.

"That the Physical conditions of a calmer and nobler
existence for the great mass of mankind are slowly but
surely preparing, I recognize with gladness; I will not
doubt that the Moral elements are also commingling. In

all the forms and shows of present and threatening Evil, I discern the shadows of approaching Good. The age now dawning shall reap in gladness the fields tearfully sown in defiance of tempests of contumely and reproach. It will have its Statesmen, who may continue to serve their Nations without stooping to flatter their worst and most dangerous passions; orators, whose trumpet-tones shall be employed to chasten and rebuke whatever is selfish in the thronging multitudes they address, rather than impel them to envy and hate their fellows; teachers of religion, meek, earnest followers of the carpenter's son of Bethlehem and Paul the tent-maker, who, living, or at all times ready to live, if need be, by the labor of their own hands, shall minister to God in houses unpartitioned to men, asking of a prospective field of labor, not what salary is to be paid, but what sin is to be cured, and setting forth the duties and reproving the delinquencies of Wealth, as few or none have dared to do since He, who had not where to lay His head."

Before the Emancipation of the Chattel Slave was accomplished, Greeley kept exhorting the working people to use all the political means at their command to help it along by their votes, and that in order to advance their own Emancipation later. On the other hand he tried his utmost to keep them from issues that would sidetrack the great movement. And in this he was only following in the footsteps of that great teacher, William Ellery Channing, who over half a century ago told the American proletariat:—

"Many of you busy yourselves with other questions, such as the probable result of the next election of President, or the prospects of this or that party. But these are insignificant, compared with the great question, Whether the laboring classes here are destined to the ignorance and depression of the lower ranks of Europe, or whether they can secure to themselves the means of intellectual and moral progress. You are cheated, you are false to yourselves, when you suffer politicians to absorb you in their selfish purposes, and to draw you away from this great question.''

Socialist friends of the author of these pages, have questioned whether Horace Greeley could be considered a Social Democrat, a State Socialist, from their doctrinal position, which, by-the-by, is necessary now-a-days for the purposes of party discipline. He was in a measured degree, a State Socialist. But those who suggested this criticism did not remember the comparative failure of any legislation in this country and Europe for industrial reform up to the time of his death.

The English translation of Karl Marx's wonderful work *Capital*,* recognized by thousands as the economic ''Bible of Socialism,'' † was not issued and edited by Frederick Engels, till fifteen years after Greeley's death. It was only first published in German five years before that event. Now there are editions so cheap that the poorest workingman can obtain the work. Again, Ferdinand Lassalle's

---

* *Capital: A Critical Analysis of Capitalistic Production*, by Karl Marx. Translated by Samuel Moore and Edward Aveling, and edited by Frederick Engels. New York, Humboldt Publishing Co.

† Prof. Richard T. Ely, in *The Labor Movement in America*, states that objection has been raised to his denominating *Das Kapital*, ''the Bible of the Socialists.'' He says : '' Recently one of their papers, the *New Yorker Volkszeitung*, protested against this epithet as applied to the work of Marx, as it was not desired that any book should be regarded in the light of an infallible guide. It was feared that this would hinder progress. Yet the term describes better than anything else the actual feeling toward *Das Kapital*, and among the more ignorant Socialists reverence for a great leader has ere this approached idolatry.'' The writer has known a great many poor Socialists, some who were very poor indeed, yet speaking three languages fluently, but not one who was ''ignorant.''

agitation among the German proletarians had only begun to develop European Socialism in its modern phases toward the last year or two of Greeley's life.

Horace Greeley thoroughly believed in Economic Association or Coöperative Socialism all his life, but not to the exclusion of political means for the success of the movement. That he would have appreciated and worked in harmony with Modern American Socialism, had he lived, is unquestionable from these "foreign" allusions written by him in 1868 :—

"I do not believe men naturally lazy ; but I judge that they prefer to receive the fair recompense of their labor,— to work for themselves and those dear to them, rather than for hundreds, if not for thousands, whom they scarcely know by sight. I believe in Association, or Coöperation, or whatever name may be given to the combination of many heads and hands to achieve a beneficent result, which is beyond the means of one or a few of them ; for I perceive that vast economies, and vastly increased efficiency, may thus be secured ; I reject Communism as at war with one of the strongest and most universal instincts,—that which impels each worker to produce and save far himself,— his own. Yet Religion often makes practicable that which were else impossible, and Divine Love triumphs where Human Science is baffled. Thus I interpret the past successes and failures of Socialism.

"Coöperation—the combination of some hundreds of producers to dispose of their labor or its fruits, or of consumers in like manner to supply their common wants of food, etc., more economically and satisfactorily than by individual purchases from markets, stalls, or stores—is one-sided, fragmentary Association. Its advantages are signal, obvious, immediate ; its chief peril is the rascality of the agent, treasurer, or manager, whom it is obliged to trust. As it involves no decided, radical change of habits and usages, it is destined to achieve an early success, and thus to pioneer further and more beneficent reforms. It has already won signal triumphs in sober, practical England ; it is winning the intellectual assent of earnest, meditative Germany.* I shall be sorely disappointed if this Nineteenth Century does not witness its very general adoption as a means of reducing the cost and increasing the comfort of the poor man's living. It ought to add twenty-five per cent. to the average income of the thriftier half of the laboring class ; while its advantages are free to all with whom economy is an object. And even above its direct advantages I prize the habits of calculation, of foresight, of saving which it is calculated to foster and promote among those who accept its principles and enjoy its most material blessings.''

---

* The New York *Tribune* even now at times allows a little "progressive light '' to be shed on its at present capitalist columns. Thus on October 18, 1890, American Socialists were amazed to discover this editorial paragraph,—which might have been written by Horace Greeley himself,—illuminating the surrounding darkness : '' Although there was a general disposition to question the policy of Emperor William when in defiance of Prince Bismarck's protests he declared himself opposed to any renewal of the Anti-Socialist laws, yet it must now be admitted that he has acted with great foresight and sagacity in dealing with the matter. For it is obviously absurd to attempt to extinguish by means of mere repressive legislation a party which, at the general election last spring, cast a vote of 1,427,000 out of a total vote of 7,031,000. Moreover, according to the figures issued by the Socialist Congress, which is now in session at Halle, the leaders of the movement own no less than 104 trade organs, and possess the controlling influence of a large number more. The Congress, which is of an International nature, is attended by delegates from Paris, London, Copenhagen, Stockholm, Warsaw, Vienna, The Hague, Brussels, Rome and Barcelona, and seems to fulfill the prediction of Karl Marx to the effect that the proletarians of all countries would eventually unite to accomplish 'the liberation of suffering humanity.' ''

Greeley knew many of the difficulties of Economic
Socialism just as clearly as do the present political agitators
and organizers of the movement. Thus, twenty-three years
ago he wrote : "A serious obstacle to the success of any
Socialist experiment must always be confronted. I allude
to the kind of persons who are naturally attracted to it.
Along with many noble and lofty souls, whose impulses are
purely philanthropic, and who are willing to labor and suffer
reproach for any cause that promises to benefit mankind,
there throng many of whom the world is too full,—the conceited, the crochety, the selfish, the headstrong, the pugna-
cious, the unappreciated, the played-out, the idle, and the
good-for-nothing generally ; who, finding themselves utterly out of place and at a discount in the world as it is, rash-
ly conclude that they are exactly fitted for the world as it
ought to be. These may have failed again and again, and
been protested at every bank to which they have been presented ; yet they are sure to jump into any new movement,
as if they had been born expressly to superintend and direct
it, though they are morally certain to ruin whatever they
lay their hands on. Destitute of means, of practical ability,
of prudence, tact, and common sense, they have such a
wealth of assurance and self-confidence that they clutch the
responsible positions, which the capable and worthy modestly shrink from ; so responsibilities, that would tax the
ablest, are mistakenly devolved on the blindest and least fit.
Many an experiment is thus wrecked, when, engineered by
its best members, it might have succeeded. I judge not
what may be done and borne by a mature, thoroughly organized Association ; but a pioneer, half-fledged experiment—
lacking means, experience, edifices, everything—can bear
no extra weight, but needs to be composed of, and directed
by, most efficient, devoted, self-sacrificing men and
women."

There is no question that early in his Socialistic career, when he was full of Fourierism alone, Greeley did not believe in over interfering by statutory law with the purely industrial movement; nevertheless, although depending overmuch on "Association," he was willing that experiments should be carried out by statutes in "sister States side by side" and the results watched. Later he broadened out and in 1850 we find him answering some of those he styled the "do-nothing, stand-still, anti-social school" in these words :—

"We believe that Government, like every other intelligent agency, is bound to do good to the extent of its ability—that it ought actively to promote and increase the general well-being—that it should encourage and foster Industry, Science, Invention, Intellectual, Social and Physical Progress, as well as provide Prosecuting Attorneys, Constables and Executioners. Such is our idea of the sphere of Government."

James Parton recognized Greeley's State Socialism thoroughly in his biography, first published in 1855. Thus in the chapter "On the Platform—Hints toward Reform," he said: "Mr. Greeley does not attempt to refute the arguments of the prosperous conservative. He dwells for a moment upon the fact, that while life is a battle in which men fight, not *for*, but *against* each other, the victors must *necessarily* be few and ever fewer, the victims numberless and ever more hopeless. Resting his argument upon the evident fact that the majority of mankind are poor, unsafe, and uninstructed, he endeavors to show how the condition of the masses can be alleviated by Legislation, and how by their own Coöperative exertions. The State, he contends, should ordain—and the law should be fundamental—that no man may own more than a certain very limited extent of land ; that the State should fix a definition to the phrase, 'a day's work ;' that the State should see to it, that no child grows up in ignorance ; that the State is bound to prevent the selling of alcoholic beverages ;" etc.

Horace Greeley thought "that with more wise Prevention, there may be less Punishment," and expatiates thereupon in his lecture on the "Organization of Labor." He necessarily cordially detested the "do-nothing, anti-social school," of political economists, and warned them and their capitalist supporters that the "right of Eminent Domain" resides "in the State itself :" and this most certainly was as State Socialist an argument as State Socialist can be. Here are some of his criticisms on this type of publicists taken from his *Labor's Political Economy :*

"'*Laissez faire*'—'Let us alone.' That those who are profiting, amassing wealth and rolling in luxury, from the proceeds of some craft or vocation gainful to them but perilous and fraught with evil to the common weal, should strive to lift this maxim from the mire of selfishness and heartless indifference to others' woes to the dignity of Statesmanship, is not remarkable ; but that any one seriously claiming to think and labor for National or Social well-being should propound and defend it, this is as amazing as lamentable. Regarded in the light of Morality, it cannot stand a moment : it is identical in spirit with the sullen insolence of Cain—'Am I my brother's keeper?' If it be, indeed, a sound maxim, and the self-interest of each individual—himself being the judge—be necessarily identical with the common interest, then it is difficult to determine why Governments should exist at all—why constraint should in any case be put on the action of any rational being. But it needs not that this doctrine of '*Laissez faire*' should be traced to its ultimate results, to show that it is inconsistent with any true idea of the interests of Society or the duties of Government. The Genius of the Nineteenth Century—the expanding Benevolence and all-embracing Sympathy of our age—emphatically repudiate and condemn it. Everywhere is Man awaking to a truer and deeper regard for the welfare and worth of his brother. Everywhere is it beginning to be felt that a bare *opportunity* to live ·nmolested if he can find and appropriate the means of subsistence—as some savages are reported to cast their new-born children into the water, that they may save alive the sturdy who can swim, and leave the weak to perish—is not all that the community owes to its feebler and less fortunate members. It cannot have needed the horrible deductions of Malthus, who, admiringly following out the doctrine of '*Laissez faire*' to its natural result, declares that the earth cannot afford an adequate subsistence to all her human offspring, and that those who cannot find food without the aid of the community should be left to starve! —to convince this generation of the radical unsoundness of the premises from which such revolting conclusions can be drawn.

"Our standard Political Economists may theorize in this direction as dogmatically as they will, modestly pronouncing their own views liberal and enlightened, and all others narrow and absurd; but though they appear to win the suffrage of the subtle Intellect, the great Heart of Humanity refuses to be thus guided—nay, insists on impelling the entire Social Machinery in an exactly opposite direction. The wide and wider diffusion of a public provision for General Education and for the support of the destitute Poor—inefficient as each may thus far have been— is of itself a striking instance of the triumph of a more benignant principle over that of '*Laissez faire.*' The inquiries, so vigorously and beneficently prosecuted in our day, into the Moral and Physical, Intellectual and Social condition of the depressed Laboring Classes, of Great Britain especially—of her Factory Operatives, Colliers, Miners, Silk-Weavers, etc., etc., and the beneficent results which have followed them, abundantly prove that, for Governments no less than Communities, any consistent following of the 'Let us alone' principle, is not merely a criminal dereliction of duty—it is henceforth utterly impossible.

"Governments must be impelled by a profound and wakeful regard for the common interests of the People over whom they exercise authority, or they will not be tolerated. It is not enough that they repress violence and outrage as speedily as they can; this affords no real security, even to those exposed to wrong-doing: they must search out the *causes* of evil, the influences which impel to its perpetration, and labor zealously to effect their removal. They might reënact the bloody code of Draco, and cover the whole land with fruitful gibbets, yet, with a People destitute of Morality and Bread—nay, destitute of the former alone—they could not prevent the iteration of every crime which a depraved imagination might suggest. That theory of Government which affirms the power to punish, yet in effect denies the right to prevent evil, will be found as defective in its Economical inculcations as in its relations to the Moral and Intellectual wants of Mankind.

"The great principle that the Laborer has a RIGHT OF PROPERTY in that which constitutes his only means of subsistence, is one which cannot be too broadly affirmed nor too earnestly insisted on. 'A man's trade is his estate;' and with what justice shall one-fourth of the community be deprived of their means of subsistence in order that the

larger number may fare a little more sumptuously or obtain
what they buy a little more advantageously? The cavil at
the abuse of this principle to obstruct the adoption of all
labor-saving machinery, etc., does not touch the vitality of
the principle itself. All Property, in a justly constituted
State, is held subject to the right of Eminent Domain
residing in the State itself;—when the public good requires
that it should be taken for public uses, the individual right
must give way."

Greeley, on his return from the Great Exhibition of
London in 1851, published in the second edition of his
Hints Toward Reforms, his lecture on the "Crystal Palace
and Its Lessons." What he had seen in Europe and what
was brought to his attention by the first World's Show,
forty years ago, made him recognize the future effect of
machinery and other causes that would help to place the
wage-earners in worse slavery, than they were then. And it
made him see the duties of "Society, the State, the
Commonwealth" more clearly than ever before. Under
this influence he wrote:—

"Why roam this haggard legion from day to day, from
week to week, from month to month, idle, anxious, famished,
tattered, miserable, and despairing? Do you answer that
they lack Industrial training, and thence Productive efficiency? Then, I tell you, the greater shame to us, practical
workers, or in some sense capitalists, who, realizing their
defect, and how it crushes them to the earth—realizing, at
least, that they must live somehow, and that, so long as
they may remain idle, their sustenance must come out of
our earnings or our hoards—still look vacantly, stupidly
on, and see them flounder ever in this tantalizing and
ultimately devouring whirlpool, without stretching forth a
hand to rescue and save them. As individuals, the few can

do little or nothing; but as the State, the whole might do much—everything—for these poor, perishing strugglers. As I look out upon their ill-directed, incoherent, ineffective efforts to find work and bread, they picture themselves on my mind's eye as disjointed fragments and wrecks of Humanity—mere heads, or trunks, or limbs—oftener 'hands'—torn apart by some inscrutable Providence, and anxiously, dumbly awaiting the creative word, the electric flash, which can alone recombine and restore them to their proper integrity and practical efficiency. That word no individual has power to speak; but Society, the State, the COMMONWEALTH, may readily pronounce it. Let the State but decree, 'There shall be work for every one who will do it; but no subsistence in pauper idleness for any save the incapable of working'—and all will be transformed. Take the orphan from the cellar, the beggar from the street, the petty filcher from the crowded wharves, and place them all where they must earn their bread, and in earning it acquire the capacity to labor efficiently for themselves—this is a primary dictate of Public Economy, no less than of enlightened Philanthropy. Palaces vaster and more commodious than Paxton ever dreamed of might be built and furnished by the Labor which now wears itself out in vain attempts to find employment, by the application of faculties now undeveloped or perverted to evil ends. Only let Society recognize and accept its duty to find work for all who can find none for themselves, and the realm of Misery and Despair will be three-fourths conquered at a blow by Industry, Thrift, and Content.''

The meaning of Greeley's work as an Apostle of Socialism cannot be more plainly defined than by his own language in the above extract. But well he knew, as do most of his successors to-day, that to rouse his countrymen from

their Rip Van Winkle apathy was a Herculean task and
worse than that because, as he said in 1837, and it is true
now, that : —

"Beneath the thin veil of a democracy more free than
that of Athens in her glory, we cloak a despotism more
pernicious and revolting than that of Turkey or China.
It is the despotism of Opinion.   Whoever ventures to
propound opinions strikingly at variance with those of the
majority, must be content to brave obloquy, contempt and
persecution.   If political, they exclude him from public
employment and trust; if religious, from social intercourse
and general regard, if not from absolute rights.   However
moderately heretical in his political views, he cannot be a
justice of the peace, an officer of the customs, or a lamp-
lighter."

Then it was that Greeley saw his way very clear before
him, and in his poem on *The Faded Stars* printed in 1840
he told the world that—

> ". . . . a stern high duty
> Now nerves my arm and fires my brain;
> Perish the dream of shapes of beauty,
> So that *this* strife be not in vain ;
> To war on Fraud entrenched with Power—
> On smooth Pretense and specious Wrong—
> This task be mine, though Fortune lower;
> For this be banished sky and song."

Horace Greeley was more or less of an Idealist in his
views, but he was, nevertheless, very practical.   From his
lecture on "Human Life," this passage is taken, which
shows how he made use of what is supposed to be the
most impossible of Christ's teachings and applied it
"literally" to the subject of future Socialistic National
Industry :

"Shall we never be able to obey the Divine injunction to 'take no thought for the morrow?'

"And here is the root of that demand for a Social Reform, which, springing up simultaneously in so many earnest hearts, is beginning at length to make itself heard and felt. The thoughtless Million may scoff, as their prototypes in all ages have scoffed, at ideas which look beyond the sensual wants of the individual and the hour; but the observing understand that these do not even comprehend the evil which is resisted—the change which is desired. It is not merely that the widow and the orphan lack food under our present Social Order—it is not merely the contemplation of the yawning abysses of degradation, misery and crime, into which millions after millions are constantly driven by our Society's harsh denial to them of any honest means of earning their needful bread—though this and its train of consequences are enough to drown a nation in tears of blood—but the cry for a truer Social basis has yet a deeper source than this. It is the Soul's indignant protest against its own perpetual involvement in a system of heartlessness and war—of chaffering and struggling for daily bread, when its healthful existence demands an atmosphere of serenity and love. It willingly proffers physical powers to obtain physical ends—the hands to plant and to build, to fashion and produce; but the surrender of itself to a perpetual round of ignoble anxieties and petty, yet exacting collisions, is felt to be too much. The desolate and crushed heart that lives but on one cherished though saddening memory, is willing, nay, eager, to give faithful daily labor for the plainest daily bread; it is the constant, haunting dread that even that hard exchange will not long be attainable—the exposure to rude rebuffs and wounding suspicions in obeying the frequently recurring necessity to seek anew the privilege of giving much toil for little recompense—it is *this* which gnaws and kills.   It is the conviction that Society—that of Christendom at least —ought to be a condition, not of war, but of peace—not of jarring rivalry, but of generous emulation in good deeds— not calculated to develop and aggravate, but to chasten and correct whatever in man is selfish and unsympathizing —it is this which underlies and impels the great Social Movement, not now prominent to the careless eye, but which is destined to render our age memorable in the History of Man.   Let those who think slightingly of this idea of a pervading Reform—a Reform which shall embosom almost every other—ponder the following words of a great man lately departed—the philanthropic yet cautious, high-souled and far-seeing Channing :

"'Our present civilization is characterized and tainted by a devouring greediness of wealth.   The passion for gain is everywhere sapping pure, generous feeling, and raising up bitter foes against any reform which may threaten to turn aside the stream of wealth.   I sometimes feel as if a great reform were necessary to break up our present mercenary civilization, in order that Christianity, now repelled by the universal worldliness, may come into nearer contact with the soul, and reconstruct Society after its own pure and disinterested principles.'

"Such thoughts as these are already familiar to many generous hearts, and the number is daily increasing.   Let us not fear that they will long remain unacted.

"Let none accuse me of the enthusiast's common error —the presumption that the world is to be transformed in a day.   I know well how great the interval which ever divides the perception of a noble idea by a few earnest minds from its hearty acceptance, its practical realization, by the great mass of mankind. I know how any such idea must ever suffer from the errors or imperfections of its Apostles, from the faithlessness of the selfish and undiscerning, from its perversion and corruption by many on whom it makes an impression. But, on the other hand, I will not close my eyes to the decided progress which Society has made during the last two centuries, nor to the *direction* of that progress. When I perceive that UNITY OF EFFORT, resting on Community of interest, has checkered Christendom with roads, bridges, canals, railroads, and before unimagined facilities for the interchange of products and of thought; when I see Universal Education, so recently regarded as a benevolent chimera, now admitted in theory to be essential and attainable, though but distantly approached in practice; when I find the right of the destitute to a support at the public expense admitted and acted upon—blindly, imperfectly, if you please, but still at so serious a cost and with such a uniformity, both in time and space, as to forbid the idea that it rests on any other foundation than that of acknowledged and imperative duty; when I consider that so few generations have passed since the ignorant and the destitute were left to live in darkness and die by unheeded famine, no man questioning its rightfulness, and the learned, the affluent, the noble,—blasphemously pronouncing all this the order of Providence!—I will not doubt that all these meliorations of the hard lot of the unfortunate are but slight precursors of the Vast Reform which is yet to embosom all other Reforms—which is to secure Education and Bread even to the deepest poverty and darkest misfortune, by simply making the sinews, the exertions, of any intelligent child of Adam worth the cost of his instruction and subsistence—which shall replace all our miserable and too often pernicious public and private alms to the vigorous, by a system of undegrading and self-sustaining GENERAL INDUSTRY, in which a place shall be open to every one who needs or asks it."

The "Loftier Ideal," meaning "perfect manhood," Greeley portrays in chaste language in his lecture on "Life—the Actual and the Ideal." He says among other ennobling thoughts that :—

"We need a Loftier Ideal to nerve us for heroic lives. Only on forgetfulness of Self, or rather on a consciousness that we are all but motes in the beam whose sun is God, drops in the rivulet whose ocean is Humanity, can our souls be molded into conformity with the loftiest ideal of our race. To know and feel our nothingness without regretting it; to deem fame, riches, personal happiness, but shadows of which Human Good is the substance—to welcome Pain, Privation, Ignominy, so that the sphere of Human Knowledge, the Empire of Virtue, be thereby extended—such is the soul's temper in which the Heroes of the Coming Age shall be cast. To realize profoundly that the individual is nothing, the universal everything—to feel nothing a calamity whereby the sum of human virtue or happiness is increased, this is the truest wisdom. When the stately monuments of mightiest conquerors shall have become shapeless and forgotten ruins, the humble graves of Earth's Howards and Frys shall still be freshened by the tears of fondly admiring millions, and the proudest epitaph shall be the simple entreaty,

"'Write me as one who *loved* his fellow-men.'

"Say not that I thus condemn and would annihilate Ambition. The love of approbation, of esteem, of true glory, is a noble incentive, and should be cherished to the end. But the ambition which points the way to fame over torn limbs and bleeding hearts—which joys in the Tartarean smoke of the battle-field and the desolating tramp of the war-horse *that* ambition is worthy only of 'archangel ruined.' To make one conqueror's reputation, at least one hundred thousand bounding, joyous, sentient beings must be transformed into writhing and hideous fragments —must perish untimely by death of agony and horror, leaving half a million widows and orphans to bewail their loss in anguish and destitution. This is too mighty, too awful a price to be paid for the fame of any hero, from Nimrod to Wellington. True fame demands no such sacrifices of others; it requires us to be reckless of the outward well-being of but one. It exacts no hecatomb of victims for each triumphal pile; for the more who covet and seek it, the easier and more abundant is the success of each and all. With souls of the celestial temper, each human life might be a triumph, which angels would lean from the skies delighted to witness and admire.

"And, beyond doubt, the loftiest ambition possible to us finds its fruition in perfect, simple Manhood. A robber may be a great warrior; a pirate an admiral; a dunce a king; a slimy intriguer a President; but to be a thorough and true Man, that is an aspiration which repels all accident or seeming. And let us not fear that such are too common to be distinguished or famous. Could there appear among us a realization of the full idea of Manhood—no mere general, nor statesman, nor devotee, but a complete and genuine Man—he need not walk naked or in fantastic garb to gather all eyes upon him. The very office-seekers would forget for a moment their fawning, and prowling, their coaxing and slandering, to gather eagerly, though awed, around him to inquire from what planet he had descended. No merman, nor centaur, nor chimpanzee,

nor mastodon, nor megalosaurus, ever excited half the
curiosity which would be awakened and requited by the
presence among us of a whole and complete Man.   And
to form this character, inadequate as have been all past
approaches to it by unaided human energy, the elements
are visibly preparing.   Men are becoming slowly but
sensibly averse to whatever erects barriers between them
and cuts them into fragments and particles of Manhood.
The priest in his surplice, the *militaire* in his regimentals,
the duke under his coronet, all begin to feel rather uneasy
and shame-faced, if confronted with a throng of irreverent
citizens, hurrying to and fro, intent on their various errands.
Among a corps, a bevy of his own order, the farce may
still be played by each with decorous propriety, but apart
from these it palls and becomes a heaviness.   Day by day
it is more and more clearly felt that the world is outgrowing
the dolls and rattles of its childhood, and more and more
disdains to be treated childishly.   Direct, earnest speech,
with useful deeds evincing lofty purpose—these are more
and more insisted on, and whatever lacks them is quietly
left to perish.   An undeserved popularity, a sham celebrity,
may still be got up by due incantations; but frailer than
the spider's gossamer, the first breath resolves them into
their essential nothingness.   Gas to gas, they mingle with
the blue surrounding ether, and neither its serenity nor its
purity is visibly affected by the infusion.

"Yes, a brighter day dawns for us, sinning and suffering children of Adam.   Wiser in its very follies, less cruel
and wanton even in its crimes, our Race visibly progresses
toward a nobler and happier realization of its capacities
and powers.   Compared century with century, this progress
is not so palpable, since what is an age to individuals, is
but a moment in the lifetime of the Race; but, viewed on
a large scale, the advance becomes cheeringly evident."

Horace Greeley's Socialist Apostleship has been but superficially, treated in this chapter. But no words can do full justice to his forty years of disinterested and altruistic labor. He looked forward with eyes of faith to the future "Humanity," of whom he thus spoke with words of wisdom :—

"THE watchword of the Nineteenth Century is BROTHERHOOD. Rapid and wonderful as is the progress of Physical Science—valuable to Man as are the Steamboat, the Railroad, the Magnetic Telegraph—mighty as are the results attained, mightier the hopes excited and justified, by the march of discovery and invention—the great discovery being made, and to be made, by the children of men, is that of their Community of origin, of interests, of aspirations. 'God hath made of one blood all people,' is its essence, proclaimed many years ago ; the new truth is but the old realized and made practical. Humanity refuses longer to be separated and arrayed against itself. Whoever oppresses or injures any human being, however abject or culpable, wrongs and tramples all men, himself included.

"A grave, momentous truth—let it be heard and heeded. Hear it, grim and ruthless warrior ! eager to rush over myriads of gashed and writhing bodies to coveted fame and power ! These thou wouldst so readily trample into the earth are not really enemies, not merely victims— not something which may be separated from thee and thine : they are thy fellows, kinsmen, brethren—with thee, 'members of one another !' and of Humanity. The sword which hews them down, maims thee : the hoof that tramples them, wounds thee. No armor ever devised by cunning or selfishness can prevent this : no walls of stone or living men can ward off the blow. As surely as the verdant tree must mark its shadow in the sunshine—as surely as the stone projected upward will not rest in mid-air, but descend —so surely falls the evil on him by whom evil is done or meditated.

"Miser! heaping up fresh hoards of yellow dross! thou art starving, not others only, but thyself! Bread may fill thy garners, and thy vaults be stored with ruddy wines; but Plenty cannot come where dwells the insatiable thirst for more; and baleful are the possessions which contract the brow and harden the heart; speedy and sure is the judgment which avenges the woes of thy pale, hollow-cheeked victims!

"Libertine! believe not that the anguish thou so reck-lessly invokest on others shall leave thee unscathed! The contrary is written in the law whose date is Eternity, whose sphere the Universe. Fleeting and hollow are the guilty joys thou seekest, while the crimes by which they are compassed shall darken thy soul and embitter thy thoughts for ever!

"And thou humble, self-denying votary of the highest good—the good of thy brethren, thy fellow-beings—vainly shalt thou strive to sacrifice thy own happiness to brighten the dark pathway of the needy, the wretched: the kindly fates will not permit it; Heaven will persist in promptly repaying thee more and better than thou hast given. Give all thou hast to lighten the burdens of others to-day, and the bounteous reward will not wait for to-morrow's sun. It will insist on making thee richer, in thy hunger and nakedness, than the king amid his pomp, the banker amid his treasures. Thy riches are safe from every device of villainy, from every access of calamity; they cannot be separated from nor made unavailable to thee. While thou art, they shall be to thee a chastened gladness, a tranquil rapture for ever!

"And thou, saintly devotee, and shrine of all virtues ! look not down in loathing, but in pity, on the ruined votary of vice and crime. He is here to teach thee not pride, but humility. The corrupt, revolting thing he is, tells thee what thou mightest easily have been, had not Divine Goodness, for its own high ends, not *thine*, willed otherwise. The drunkard's maudlin leer—the lecher's marred and hideous visage—the thief's cat-like tread and greedy eyes—even the murderer's stony heart and reeking hand— all these, rightly viewed, are but indications of the possibilities of thy own nature, commanding gratitude to God, and compassion for all human errors.

"Ay, 'we are members together of one body' of Humanity. Whether blackened by the fervid sun of tropical deserts, or bleached by the fogs of a colder clime —whether worshiping God or the Grand Lama, erecting Christian altars in the savage wilderness or falling in frenzy beneath the wheels of Juggernaut—whether acting the part of a Washington or a Nicholas, a Howard or a Thug—the same red current courses through all our veins—the same essential nature reveals itself through all. The slave in his coffle, the overseer brandishing his whip, the Abolitionist denouncing oppression—who shall say that any one of these might not have been trained to do the deeds and think the thoughts of any other? Who shall say that the red-handed savage of the wilds might not have been the meek, benign village pastor, blessing and blest by all around him, if his lot had been cast in Vermont instead of Oregon? Who shall say how far his crimes are treasured up against him in the great account, and how far they are charged to the perverting, darkening force of Christian rapacity and fraud, or esteemed the result of a Christian indifference and lethargy only less culpable?

"Away, then, from human sight with the hideous implements of human butchery and destruction! Break the sword in its scabbard, bury the cannon in the earth, sink the bombs in the ocean! What business have these to disturb by their hateful presence the visible harmony of God's universe? How dare men go out into the balmy air and bright sunshine, and there, in the full view of Heaven, essay to maim and massacre each other? How would their wretched babblement of National interests or National honor sound, if addressed directly to the All-Ruling, as an apology for wholesale slaughter? Who would dare be their mouth-piece in proffering an excuse so pitiful? And do not the abettors of War realize that their vile appeals to the baser passions of our nature resound in the ears of the Recording Angel?

"But not War alone, the grossest form of human antagonism, but every form, is destined to a speedy extinction. The celestial voice that asked of old the terrific question, 'Where is thy brother Abel?' shall yet be heard and responded to by every one who would win profit or enjoyment from that which oppresses or degrades a single human being. The oppressor, the dram-seller, the gamester, are already beginning to listen, perforce, to its searching appeal —listen, at first, perhaps, with frowns, and sneers, and curses? but even these are symptoms of the inward convulsion—first mutterings of the mighty earthquake at hand.

"In the day of light now dawning, no relation so palpably vicious as theirs can possibly abide. But theirs are the rude, salient outworks, which cover, while they stand, the smoother, ampler, sturdier citadel of error. That all-pervading selfishness, which forgets or disregards the general well-being, is yet to be tracked to its most secret recesses, and extirpated.

"The avocations of Life, the usages and structure of Society, the relations of Power to Humility, of Wealth to Poverty, of served and servant, must all be fused in the crucible of Human Brotherhood, and whatever abides not the test, rejected. Vainly will any seek to avert or escape the ordeal—idly will any hope to preserve from it some darling lust or pampered luxury or vanity. Onward, upward, irresistibly, shall move the Spirit of Reform, abasing the proud, exalting the lowly, until Sloth and Selfishness, Tyranny and Slavery, Waste and Want, Ignorance and Corruption, shall be swept from the face of the earth, and a golden age of Knowledge, of Virtue, of Plenty, and Happiness, shall dawn upon our sinning and suffering Race. Heaven speed its glorious coming and prepare us to welcome and enjoy it!"

CHAPTER V.

THE GREELEY-RAYMOND SOCIALISTIC DISCUSSION.

HORACE GREELEY discovered by bitter experience that the way of the Socialist Reformer, like that of the transgressor, is most assuredly hard. Many of his "esteemed contemporaries" virulently attacked him, the general public did not understand his progressive ideas, and only a few cultured people—like Ralph Waldo Emerson, Nathaniel Hawthorne, Parke Godwin, Theodore Parker, George Ripley, William Henry Channing, Margaret Fuller, George W. Curtis, Charles A. Dana, Henry D. Thoreau, Amos Bronson Alcott, and others of that type, who were either Socialists themselves or were favorably disposed toward Fourierism,—supported him in his faith. One editor even went so far as to call Greeley an infidel, compared him with Thomas Paine,—going at length into the life of the author of the *Age of Reason*,—and forced out of the Founder of the *Tribune* the following response:

"As to poor Tom Paine, since I have never heard that he was an Associationist, nor even a Land Reformer, I am unable to account for the bitterness of vituperation with which you assail him. That to him, more than to any other man, this country is indebted for the impulse to its Independence from Great Britain; that its separation from the Mother Country was more ably and cogently advocated and justified by him than by any other writer; that his voice cheered the discomfited defenders of our Liberties, as they tracked with blood the frozen soil of New Jersey,

on their retreat before the overwhelming numbers of the
enemy in the Winter of 1776, and reanimated the People
to make the efforts and sacrifices necessary to secure our
Freedom, I confess, seem to me to entitle him to some
measure of kindly regard at the hands of every American
citizen. I trust these are not among the incitements to the
vindictive hatred with which you pursue and blacken his
memory."

We will now come to the famous "Socialistic Discussion" which took place between November 20, 1846, and
May 20, 1847, in the columns of the New York *Tribune*
and the New York *Courier and Enquirer*, in which the
opponents were Horace Greeley and Henry J. Raymond,
who had been associated together previously on the *Tribune*.
Greeley put on record his opinion of Raymond, relatively
to their journalistic connection, forty years after this Socialistic tournament was over. He says : "On the intellectual
side, my venture' (the *Tribune*) was not so rash as it
seemed. My own fifteen years' devotion to newspaper-
making, in all its phases, was worth far more than will be
generally supposed ; and I had already secured a first
assistant in Mr. Henry J. Raymond, who—having for two
years, while in college at Burlington, Vt., been a valued
contributor to the literary side of *The New Yorker*—had
hied to the city directly upon graduating, late in 1840, and
gladly accepted my offer to hire him at eight dollars per
week until he could do better. I had not much for him
to do till the *Tribune* was started : then I had enough :
and I never found another person, barely of age and just
from his studies, who evinced so signal and such versatile
ability in journalism as he did. Abler and stronger men
I may have met ; a cleverer, readier, more generally
efficient journalist, I never saw. He remained with me

nearly eight years, if my memory serves, and is the only
assistant with whom I ever felt required to remonstrate, for
doing more work than any human brain and frame could
be expected long to endure. His salary was of course
gradually increased from time to time; but his services
were more valuable in proportion to their cost than those
of any one else, who ever aided me on the *Tribune*."

But as the best of friends must part, so Greeley and
Raymond severed company on the *Tribune*. Later Raymond, the whilom "Fantome" of Greeley's *New Yorker*,
became the founder of the New York *Times*, with which
he is most popularly associated in the recollection of the
public, in consequence of his support of Abraham Lincoln
and of the war against the Confederacy. He died on June
18, 1869, then being in his fiftieth year. James Parton
gave a brief but admirable comparison of the two men in
1854, relative to the Discussion. He said: "Mr. Raymond
had left the *Tribune*, and joined the *Courier and Enquirer*,
at the solicitation of Col. Webb, the editor of the latter.
It was a pity the *Tribune* let him go, for he is a born journalist, and could have helped the *Tribune* to attain the
position of the great, only, undisputed Metropolitan Journal,
many years sooner than it will. Horace Greeley is not a
born journalist. He is too much in earnest to be a perfect
editor. He has too many opinions and preferences. He
is a BORN LEGISLATOR, a Deviser of Remedies, a Suggester
of Expedients, a Framer of Measures. The most successful
editor is he, whose great endeavor it is to tell the public
all it wants to know, and whose comments on passing events
best express the *feeling of the country* with regard to them.
Mr. Raymond is not a man of first-rate talent—great talent
would be in his way—he is most interesting when he
attacks; and of the varieties of composition, polished

vituperation is not the most difficult. But he has the right *notion* of editing a daily paper, and when the *Tribune* lost him, it lost more than it had the slightest idea of—as events have since shown. However, Horace Greeley and Henry J. Raymond, the one naturally liberal, the other naturally conservative—the one a Universalist, the other a Presbyterian—the one regarding the world as a place to be made better by living in it, the other regarding it as an oyster to be opened, and bent on opening it—would have found it hard to work together on equal terms. They separated amicably, and each went his way."

Parton described how it happened that the Greeley-Raymond Socialistic Discussion arose, as follows: "Mr. Brisbane, on his return from Europe, renewed the agitation of his subject (Fourierism). The *Tribune* of August 19th, 1846, contained a letter by him, addressed to the editors of the *Courier and Enquirer*, proposing several questions, to which answers were requested, respecting Social Reform. The *Courier* replied. The *Tribune* rejoined editorially, and was answered in turn by the *Courier*. Mr. Brisbane addressed a second letter to the *Courier*, and sent it direct to the editor of that paper, in manuscript. The *Courier* agreed to publish it, if the *Tribune* would give place to its reply. The *Tribune* declined doing so, but challenged the editor of the *Courier* to a public discussion of the whole subject."

Horace Greeley personally took the matter up, editorially saying—"Though we cannot now open our columns to a set discussion by others, of social questions (which may or may not refer mainly to points deemed relevant by us), we readily close with the *spirit* of the *Courier's* proposition. . . . As soon as the State election is fairly over—say Nov. 10th—we will publish an entire article, filling a column of the *Tribune*, very nearly, in favor of Association as we understand it, and, upon the *Courier* copying this and replying, we will give place to its reply, and respond; and so on, till each party shall have published twelve articles on its own side, and twelve on the other, which shall fulfill the terms of this agreement. All the twelve articles of each party shall be published without abridgment or variation in the Daily, Weekly, and Semi-weekly editions of both papers. Afterward each party will, of course, be at liberty to comment at pleasure in his own columns. In order that neither paper shall be crowded with this discussion, one article per week, only, on either side, shall be published, unless the *Courier* shall prefer greater dispatch. Is not this a fair proposition? What says the *Courier?* It has, of course, the advantage of the defensive position and of the last word.''

Greeley's biographer proceeded: ''The *Courier* said, after much toying and dallying, and a preliminary skirmish of paragraphs, COME ON! and, on the 20th of November, the *Tribune* came on. The debate lasted six months. It was conducted on both sides with spirit and ability, and it attracted much attention. The twenty-four articles, of which it consisted, were afterwards published by the Harpers in a pamphlet of eighty-three closely-printed, double-columned pages, which had a considerable sale, and has long been out of print. On one side we see earnestness and sincerity; on the other tact and skill. One strove to convince, the other to triumph. The thread of argument is often lost in a maze of irrelevancy. The subject, indeed, was peculiarly ill calculated for a public discussion. When men converse on a scheme which has for its object the good of mankind, let them confer in awful whispers—apart, like conspirators, not distract themselves in dispute in the hearing of a nation; for they who would benefit mankind must do it either by stealth or by violence."

Horace Greeley opened the Discussion on November 20, 1846, with an essay headed "The Right to Labor," which is here reprinted in full. Those separate articles succeeding, which are considerably abridged, in the form of a conversation, are, by the kindness of the late James Parton, printed in these pages from his abstract of the Discussion. A week before his recent death, he gave this permission to the author of this volume, who was Secretary of the New York Liberal Club, while James Parton was President, Horace Greeley being his predecessor.

HORACE GREELEY, Nov. 20th. "'In the beginning God created the heaven and the earth.' The earth, the air, the waters, the sunshine, with their natural products, were divinely intended and appointed for the use and sustenance of Man (Gen. i. 26, 28)—not for a part only, but for the whole Human Family.

"Civilized Society, as it exists in our day, has divested the larger portion of mankind of the unimpeded, unpurchased enjoyment of their natural rights. That larger portion may be perishing with cold, yet have no legally recognized right to a stick of decaying fuel in the most unfrequented morass, or may be famishing, yet have no legal right to pluck and eat the bitterest acorn in the depths of the remotest wilderness. The defeasance or confiscation of Man's natural right to use any portion of the Earth's surface not actually in use by another, is an important fact, to be kept in view in every consideration of the duty of the affluent and comfortable to the poor and unfortunate.

"It is not essential in this place to determine that the divestment of the larger number of any recognized right to the Soil and its Products, save by the purchased permission of others, was or was not politic and necessary. All who reflect must certainly admit that many of the grants of land by hundreds of square miles to this or that favorite of the power which assumed to make them, were made thoughtlessly or recklessly, and would not have been so large, or so unaccompanied with stipulations in behalf of the future occupants and cultivators, if a reasonable foresight and a decent regard for the General Good had been cherished and evinced by the granting power. Suffice it here, however, that the granting of the Soil—of the State of New York, for example—by the supreme authority, representing the whole, to a minor portion of the whole is a 'fixed fact.' By a Law of Nature, every person born in the State of New York had (unless forfeited by crime), a perfect right to *be* here, and to his equal share of the Soil, the woods, the waters, and all the natural products thereof. By the law of Society, all but the possessors of title-deeds exist here only by the purchased permission of the land-owning class, and were intruders and trespassers on the soil of their nativity, without that permission. By law, the landless have no inherent right to stand on a single square foot of the State of New York, except in the highways.

"The only solid ground on which this surrender of the original property of the whole to a minor portion can be justified, is that of Public Good—the good, not of a part, but of the whole. The people of a past generation, through their rulers, claimed and exercised the right of divesting, not themselves merely, but the majority of all future generations, of their original and inherent right to possess and cultivate any unimproved portion of the soil of our State, for their sustenance and benefit. To render this assumption of power valid to the fearful extent to which it was exercised, it is essential that it be demonstrated that the good of the whole was promoted by such exercise.

"Is this rationally demonstrable now? Can the widow, whose children pine and shiver in some bleak, miserable garret, on the fifteen or twenty cents, which is all she can earn by unremitted toil, be made to realize that she and her babes are benefited by or in consequence of the granting to a part an exclusive right to use the earth and enjoy its fruits? Can the poor man who, day after day, paces the streets of a city in search of any employment at any price, (as thousands are now doing here,) be made to realize it on his part? Are there not thousands on thousands—natives of our State who never willfully violated her laws—who are to-day far worse off than they would have been if Nature's rule of allowing no man to appropriate to himself any more of the earth than he can cultivate and improve, had been recognized and respected by Society? These questions admit of but one answer. And one inevitable consequence of the prevailing system is that, as Population increases and Arts are perfected, the income of the wealthy owner of land increases, while the recompense of the hired or leasehold cultivator is steadily diminishing. The labor of Great Britain is twice as effective now as it was a century ago, but the laborer is worse paid, fed and lodged than he then was, while the incomes of the landlord class have been enormously increased. The same fundamental causes exist here, and tend to the same results. They have been modified, thus far, by the existence, within or near our State, of large tracts of unimproved land, which the owners were anxious to improve or dispose of, on almost any terms. These are growing scarcer and more remote; they form no part of the system we are considering, but something which exists in opposition to it, which modifies it, but is absolutely sure to be ultimately absorbed and conquered by it. The notorious fact that they do serve to mitigate the exactions to which the landless mass, even in our long and densely settled towns and cities, are subject, serves to show, that the condition of the great mass must inevitably be far worse than at present, when the natural consummation of land-selling is reached, and all the soil of the Union has become the property of a minor part of the People of the Union.

"The past cannot be recalled. What has been rightfully (however mistakenly) done by the authorized agents of the State or Nation, can only be retracted upon urgent public necessity, and upon due satisfaction to all whose private rights are thereby invaded. But those who have been divested of an important, a vital natural right, are also entitled to compensation. THE RIGHT TO LABOR, secured to them in the creation of the earth, taken away in the granting of the Soil to a minor portion of them, must be restored. Labor, essential to all, is the inexorable condition of the honest, independent subsistence of the Poor. It must be fully guaranteed to all, so that each may know that he can never starve or be forced to beg while able and willing to work. Our public provision for Pauperism is but a halting and wretched substitute for this. Society exercises no paternal guardianship over the poor man, until he has surrendered to despair. He may spend a whole year and his little all in vainly seeking employment, and all this time Society does nothing, cares nothing for him ; but when his last dollar is exhausted, and his capacities very probably prostrated by the intoxicating draughts to which he is driven to escape the horrors of reflection, *then* he becomes a subject of public charity, and is often maintained in idleness for the rest of his days at a cost of thousands, when a few dollars' worth of foresight and timely aid might have preserved him from this fate, and in a position of independent usefulness for his whole after-life.

"But the Right to Labor—that is, to constant Employment with a just and full Recompense—cannot be guaranteed to all without a radical change in our Social Economy. I, for one, am very willing, nay, most anxious, to do my full share toward securing to every man, woman, and child, full employment and a just recompense for all time to come. I feel sure this can be accomplished. But I cannot, as the world goes, give employment at any time to all who ask it of me, nor the hundredth part of them. 'Work, work! give us something to do!—anything that will secure us honest bread,' is at this moment (1846) the prayer of not less than Thirty Thousand human beings within sound of our City Hall bell. They would gladly be producers of wealth, yet remain from week to week mere consumers of bread which somebody has to earn. Here is an enormous waste and loss. We must devise a remedy. It is the duty, and not less the palpable interest, of the wealthy, the thrifty, the tax-paying, to do so. The ultimate and thorough remedy, I believe is found in ASSOCIATION."

H. J. RAYMOND, Nov. 23d. "Heavens! Here we have one of the leading Whig presses of New York advocating the doctrine that *no man can rightfully own land!* Fanny Wright was of that opinion. The doctrine is erroneous and *dangerous*. If a man cannot rightfully own land, he cannot rightfully own anything which the land produces; that is, he cannot rightfully own anything at all. The blessed institution of property, the basis of the social fabric, from which arts, agriculture, commerce, civilization spring, and without which they could not exist, is threatened with destruction, and by a leading Whig paper, too. Conservative Powers, preserve us!"

HORACE GREELEY, Nov. 26th. "Fudge! What I
said was this : Society, having divested the majority of any
right to the soil, is bound to compensate them by guaran-
teeing to each an opportunity of earning a subsistence by
Labor. Your vulgar, clap-trap allusion to Fanny Wright
does not surprise me. I shall neither desert nor deny a
truth because she, or any one else has proclaimed it. But
to proceed. By Association I mean a Social Order, which
shall take the place of the present Township, to be composed of some hundreds or some thousands of persons,
who shall be united together in interest and industry for
the purpose of securing to each individual the following
things : 1, an elegant and commodious house ; 2, an education, complete and thorough ; 3, a secure subsistence ; 4,
opportunity to labor; 5, fair wages ; 6, agreeable social
relations ; 7, progress in knowledge and skill. As society
is at present organized, these are the portion of a very
small minority. But by Association of capital and industry,
they might become the lot of all ; inasmuch as Association
tends to *Economy* in all departments, economy in lands,
fences, fuel, household labor, tools, education, medicine,
legal advice, and commercial exchanges. My opponent
will please observe that his article is three times as long as
mine, and devoted in good part to telling the public that
the *Tribune* is an exceedingly mischievous paper; which is
an imposition."

H. J. RAYMOND, Nov. 30th. "A home, fair wages,
education, etc., are very desirable, we admit ; and it is the
unceasing aim of all good men in society, as it now exists,
to place those blessings within the reach of all. The
Tribune's claim that it can be accomplished only by
Association is only a claim. Substantiate it. Give us

proof of its efficacy. Tell us in whom the property is to be vested, how labor is to be remunerated, what share capital is to have in the concern, by what device men are to be induced to labor, how moral offences are to be excluded or punished. Then we may be able to discuss the subject. Nothing was stipulated about the length of the articles; and we *do* think the *Tribune* a mischievous paper.''

HORACE GREELEY, Dec. 1st. ''The property of an Association will be vested in those who contributed the capital to establish it, represented by shares of stock, just as the property of a bank, factory, or railroad now is. Labor, skill and talent, will be remunerated by a fixed proportion of their product, or of its proceeds, if sold. Men will be induced to labor by a knowledge that its rewards will be a certain and major proportion of the product, which of course will be less or more, according to the skill and industry of each individual. The slave has no motive to diligence, except fear; the hireling is tempted to eye-service; the solitary worker for himself is apt to become disheartened; but men working for themselves, in groups, will find labor not less attractive than profitable. Moral offences will be punished by legal enactment, and they will be rendered unfrequent by plenty and education.''

H. J. RAYMOND, Dec. 8th. ''Oh—then the men of capital are to own the land, are they? Let us see. A man with money enough may buy an entire domain of five thousand acres; men without money will cultivate it on condition of receiving a fixed proportion of its products; the major part, says the *Tribune*; suppose we say *three-fourths*. Then the contract is simply this:—One rich man (or company) owns five thousand acres of land, which he leases forever to two thousand poor men at the yearly rent of one-fourth of its products. It is an affair of landlord and tenant—the lease perpetual, payment in kind; and the landlord to own the cattle, tools, and furniture of the tenant, as well as the land. Association, then, is merely a plan for extending the relation of landlord and tenant over the whole arable surface of the earth."

HORACE GREELEY, Dec. 10th. "By no means. The capital of a mature association would be, perhaps, half a million of dollars; of an infant association, fifty thousand dollars; and this increase of value would be both created and *owned* by Labor. In an ordinary township, however, the increase, though all created by Labor, is chiefly owned by Capital. The majority of the inhabitants remain poor; while a few—merchants, land-owners, mill-owners, and manufacturers—are enriched. That this is the fact in recently-settled townships, is undeniable. That it would not be the fact in a township settled and cultivated on the principle of Association, seems to me equally so."

H. J. RAYMOND, Dec. 14th. "But not to me. Suppose fifty men furnish fifty thousand dollars for an Association upon which a hundred and fifty others are to labor and to live. With that sum they buy the land, build the houses, and procure everything needful for the start. The capitalists, bear in mind, are the absolute owners of the entire property of the Association. In twenty years, that property may be worth half a million, and it still remains the property of the capitalists, the laborers having annually drawn their share of the products. They may have saved a portion of their annual share, and thus have accumulated property; but they have no more title to the *domain* than they had at first. If the concern should not prosper, the laborers could not buy shares; if it should, the capitalists would not sell except at their increased value. What advantage, then, does Association offer for the poor man's acquiring property superior to that afforded by the present state of things? None, that we can see. On the contrary, the more rapidly the domain of an Association should increase in value, the more difficult it would be for the laboring man to rise to the class of proprietors; and this would simply be an *aggravation* of the worst features of the Social System. And how you Associationists *would* quarrel! The skillful would be ever grumbling at the awkward, and the lazy would shirk their share of the work, but clamor for their share of the product. There would be ten occasions for bickerings where now there is one. The fancies of the Associationist, in fact, are as baseless, though not as beautiful, as More's Utopia, or the Happy Valley of Rasselas.''

HORACE GREELEY, Dec. 16th. ''No, *Sir!* In Association, those who furnish the original capital are the owners merely, of *so much stock* in the concern—not of all the land and other property, as you represent. Suppose that capital to be fifty thousand dollars. At the end of the first year it is found that twenty-five thousand dollars have been added to the value of the property by Labor. For this amount *new stock* is issued, which is apportioned to Capital, Labor and Skill as impartial justice shall dictate—to the non-resident capitalist a certain proportion; to the working capitalist the same proportion, plus the excess of his earnings over his expenses; to the laborer that excess only. The apportionment is repeated every year; and the propor-

tion of the new stock assigned to Capital is such that when
the property of the Association is worth half a million,
Capital will own about one-fifth of it. With regard to the
practical working of the Association, I point you to the fact
that Association and Civilization are one. They advance
and recede together. In this age we have large steamboats, monster hotels, insurance, partnerships, joint stock
companies, public schools, libraries, police, Odd Fellow-
ship—all of which are exemplifications of the *idea* upon
which Association is based; all of which work well as
institutions, and are productive of incalculable benefits to
mankind.''

H. J. RAYMOND, Dec. 24th. "Of course;—but Association assumes to shape and govern the details of *social life,*
which is a very different affair. One *'group,'* it appears,
is to do all the cooking, another the gardening, another
the plowing. But suppose that some who want to be
cooks are enrolled in the gardening group. They will
naturally sneer at the dishes cooked by their rivals, perhaps
form a party for the expulsion of the cooks, and so bring
about a kitchen war. Then, who will consent to be a
member of the boot-blacking, ditch-digging and sink-
cleaning groups? Such labors must be done, and groups
must be detailed to do them. Then, who is to settle the
wages question? Who is to determine upon the *comparative* efficiency of each laborer, and settle the comparative
value of his work? There is the religious difficulty too,
and the educational difficulty, the medical difficulty, and
numberless other difficulties, arising from differences of
opinion, so radical and so earnestly entertained as to
preclude the *possibility* of a large number of persons
living together in the intimate relation contemplated by
Association.''

Horace Greeley, Dec. 28th. "Not so fast. After the first steamship had crossed the Atlantic all the demonstrations of the impossibility of that fact fell to the ground. Now, with regard to Associations, *the first steamship has crossed!* The communities of Zoar and Rapp have existed from twenty to forty years, and several Associations of the kind advocated by me have survived from two to five years, not only without being broken up by the difficulties alluded to, but without their presenting themselves in the light of *difficulties* at all. No inter-kitchen war has disturbed their peace, no religious differences have marred their harmony, and men have been found willing to perform ungrateful offices, required by the general good. Passing over your objections, therefore, I beg you to consider the enormous difficulties, the wrongs, the waste, the misery, occasioned by and inseparable from society as it is now organized. For example, the coming on of winter contracts business and throws thousands out of employment. They and their families suffer, the dealers who supply them are losers in custom, the alms-house is crowded, private charity is taxed to the extreme, many die of diseases induced by destitution, some are driven by despair to intoxication; and all this, while every ox and horse is well fed and cared for, while there is inaccessible plenty all around, while Capital is luxuriating on the products of the very Labor which is now palsied and suffering. Under the present system, Capital is everything, Man nothing, except as a means of accumulating capital. Capital founds a factory, and for the *single* purpose of increasing capital, taking no thought of the human beings by whom it is increased. The fundamental idea of Association, on the other hand, is to effect a just *distribution* of products among Capital, Talent and Labor."

H. J. RAYMOND, Jan. 6th.   "The *idea* may be good
enough; but the means are impracticable; the details are
absurd, if not inhuman and impious.   The *Tribune's*
admission, that an Association of indolent or covetous
persons could not endure *without a moral transformation
of its members*, seems to us fatal to the whole theory of
Association.   It implies that *individual* reform must precede
social reform, which is precisely our position.   But how is
individual reform to be effected?   *By Association*, says the
Tribune.   That is, the motion of the water-wheel is to
produce the water by which alone it can be *set* in motion—
the action of the watch is to produce the main-spring
without which it cannot move.   Absurd."

HORACE GREELEY, Jan. 13th.   "Incorrigible mis-stater
of my positions!   I am as well aware as you are that the
mass of the ignorant and destitute are, at present, incapable
of so much as understanding the Social Order I propose,
much less of becoming efficient members of an association.
What I say is, let those who *are* capable of understanding
and promoting it, *begin* the work, found associations, and
show the rest of mankind how to live and thrive in Harmonious Industry.   You tell me that the sole efficient agency
of Social Reform is Christianity.   I answer that Association
is Christianity; and the dislocation *now* existing between
Capital and Labor, between the capitalist and the laborer,
is as Atheistic as it is inhuman."

H. J. RAYMOND, Jan 20th.   "Stop a moment.   The
test of true benevolence is practice, not preaching; and
we have no hesitation in saying that the members of any
one of our city churches do more every year for the practical relief of poverty and suffering than any phalanx that

ever existed.   There are in our midst hundreds of female sewing societies, each of which clothes more nakedness and feeds more hunger, than any 'Association' that ever was formed.   There is a single individual in this city whom the *Tribune* has vilified as a selfish, grasping despiser of the poor, who has expended more money in providing the poor with food, clothing, education, sound instruction in morals and religion, than all the advocates of Association in half a century.   While Association has been *theorizing* about starvation, Christianity has been *preventing* it. Associationists tell us, that giving to the poor deepens the evil which it aims to relieve, and that the bounty of the benevolent, as society is now organized, is very often abused.   We assure them, it is not the Social System which abuses the bounty of the benevolent; it is simply the dishonesty and indolence of individuals, and they would do the same under any system, and especially in Association."

HORACE GREELEY, Jan. 29th.   "Private benevolence is good and necessary; the *Tribune* has ever been its cordial and earnest advocate.   But benevolence relieves only the *effects* of poverty, while Association proposes to reach and finally eradicate its *causes*.   The charitable are doing nobly this winter for the relief of the destitute; but will there be in this city *next* winter fewer objects of charity than there are now?   And let me tell you, sir, if you do not know it already, that the advocates of Association, in proportion to their number, and their means, are, at least, *as* active and *as* ready in feeding the hungry and clothing the naked, as any class in the community.   Make the examination as close as you please, bring it as near home as you like, and you will find the fact to be as I have asserted."

H. J. RAYMOND, Feb. 10th. "You overlook one main objection. Association aims, not merely to re-organize Labor, but to revolutionize Society, to change radically Laws, Government, Manners and Religion. It pretends to be a new Social Science, *discovered* by Fourier. In our next article we shall show what its principles are, and point out their inevitable tendency."

HORACE GREELEY, Feb. 17th. "Do so. Meanwhile let me remind you, that there is *need* of a new Social System, when the old one works so villainously and wastefully. There is Ireland, with three hundred thousand able-bodied men, willing to work, yet unemployed. Their labor is worth forty-five millions of dollars a year, which they need, and Ireland needs, but which the present Social System dooms to waste. There is work enough in Ireland to do, and men enough willing to do it; but the spell of a vicious Social System broods over the island, and keeps the workmen and the work apart. Four centuries ago the English laborer could earn by his labor a good and sufficient subsistence for his family.* Since that time Labor and Talent have made England rich 'beyond the dreams of avarice;' and, at this day, the Laborer, as a rule, cannot, by unremitting toil, fully supply the necessities of his family. His bread is coarse, his clothing scanty, his home a hovel, his children uninstructed, his life cheerless. He lives from hand to mouth, in abject terror of the poor-house, where, he shudders to think, he must end his days. Precisely

---

* There is no better authority extant on this subject than—*Six Centuries of Work and Wages*, a History of English Labor, by James E. Thorold Rogers, M. P., late Professor of Political Economy in the University of Oxford. An American edition with charts and appendix by Rev. W. D. P. Bliss has been published in the Social Science Library. (Humboldt Publishing Co.)

the same causes are in operation here, and, in due time, will produce precisely the same effects. There is NEED of a Social Re-formation.''

H. J. RAYMOND, March 3d. ''You are mistaken. The statement that the laborers of the present day are worse off than those of former ages, has been exploded. They are *not.* On the contrary, their condition is *better* in every respect. Evils under the present Social System exist, great evils—evils, for the removal of which the most constant and zealous efforts ought to be made; yet they are very far from being *as* great or as *general* as the Associationists assert. The fact is indisputable, that, as a rule throughout the country, no honest man, able and willing to work, need stand idle from lack of opportunity. The exceptions to this rule are comparatively few, and arise from temporary and local causes. But we proceed to examine the fundamental principle of the Social System proposed to be substituted for that now established. In one word, that principle is *Self-Indulgence!* 'Reason and Passion,' writes Parke Godwin, the author of one of the clearest expositions of Socialism yet published, 'will be in perfect accord: duty and pleasure will have the same meaning; without inconvenience or calculation, *man will follow his bent:* hearing only of Attraction, he will never act from necessity, and *never curb himself by restraints.'* What becomes of the *self-denial* so expressly, so frequently, so emphatically enjoined by the New Testament? Fourierism and Christianity, Fourierism and Morality, Fourierism and Conjugal Constancy are in palpable hostility! We are told, that if a man has a passion for a dozen kinds of work, he joins a dozen *groups;* if for a dozen kinds of study, he joins a dozen *groups;* and, if for a dozen women, the System requires that there must be a dozen different *groups* for his full gratification ! For man will follow his *bent*, and never curb himself by *restraints !*"

HORACE GREELEY, March 12th. "Not so. I re-assert what I before proved, that the English laborers of to-day are worse off than those of former centuries; and I deny with disgust and indignation that there is in Socialism, as American Socialists understand and teach it, any provision or license for the gratification of criminal passions or unlawful desires. Why not quote Mr. Godwin fully and fairly. Why suppress his remark, that 'so long as the Passions may bring forth Disorder—*so long as Inclination may be in opposition to Duty*—we reprobate as strongly as any class of men all indulgence of the inclinations and feelings; and where Reason is unable to guide them, have no objection to other means?' Socialists know nothing of Groups, organized, or to be organized, for the perpetration of crimes, or the practice of vices."

H. J. RAYMOND, March 19th. "Perhaps not. But *I* know, from the writings of leading Socialists, that the law of Passional Attraction, *i. e.*, Self-Indulgence, is the essential and fundamental principle of Association; and that, while Christianity pronounces the free and full gratification of the passions a *crime*, Socialism extols it as a *virtue*."

HORACE GREELEY, March 26th. "Impertinent. Your articles are all entitled 'The Socialism of the *Tribune* examined'; and the *Tribune* has never contained a line to justify your unfair inferences from garbled quotations from the writings of Godwin and Fourier. What the *Tribune* advocates is, simply and solely, such an Organization of

Society as will secure to every man the opportunity of uninterrupted and profitable labor, and to every child nourishment and culture. These things, it is undeniable, the present Social System does not secure; and hence the necessity of a new and better organization. So no more of your 'Passional Attraction.'"

H. J. RAYMOND, April 16th. "I tell you the scheme of Fourier is essentially and fundamentally *irreligious!* by which I mean that it does not follow my Catechism, and apparently ignores the Thirty-Nine Articles. Shocking."

HORACE GREELEY, April 28th. "Humph!"

H. J. RAYMOND, May 20th. "The *Tribune* is doing a great deal of harm. The editor does not know it—but it *is*."

This Discussion fairly exhibited the Economics of Fourierist Socialism and, says Parton, familiarized "the public mind with the idea of Association—an idea susceptible of a thousand applications, and capable, in a thousand ways, of alleviating and preventing human woes. We see its perfect triumph in Insurance, whereby a loss which would crush an individual falls upon the whole company of insurers, lightly and unperceived. Future ages will witness its successful application to most of the affairs of life."

Horace Greeley made what may be considered a supplementary argument to this Discussion in 1868. Showing, as it does, the position he took in later years relative to Fourierist Socialism, it should be studied with interest. It is herewith presented:—

"I accept unreservedly the views of no man, dead or

living. 'The master has said it' was never conclusive with
me. Even though I have found him right nine times, I do
not take his tenth proposition on trust. Unless that also be
proved sound and rational, I reject it. But I am convinced
after much study and reflection, that the Social Reformers
are right on many points, even when clearly wrong on
others; and I deem Fourier—though in many respects
erratic, mistaken, visionary—the most suggestive and
practical among them. I accept nothing on his authority;
for I find many of his speculations fantastic, erroneous, and
(in my view) pernicious; but on many points he commands
my unreserved concurrence. Yet I prefer to set forth my
own SOCIAL CREED rather than his, even wherein mine was
borrowed from his teachings; and mine is, briefly, as
follows :—

"I. I believe that there need be, and should be, no
paupers who are not infantile, idiotic, or disabled; and that
civilized society pays more for the support of able-bodied
pauperism than the necessary cost of its extirpation.

"II. I believe that they babble idly and libel Providence
who talk of surplus Labor, or the inadequacy of Capital to
supply employment to all who need it. Labor is often
most required and best paid where Capital is scarcest (as
was shown in California in 1849–50); and there is always
—even in China—far more work than hands, provided the
ability to devise and direct be not wanting. Where Labor
stands idle, save in the presence of some great public
calamity, there is a demonstrated deficiency, not of Capital,
but of brains.

"III. I believe that the efficiency of human effort is
enormously, ruinously diminished by what I term Social
Anarchy. That is to say: We spend half our energies in
building fences and providing safeguards against each

other's roguery, while our Labor is rendered inefficient and inadequately productive by bad management, imperfect implements, a deficency of power (animal or steam), and the inability of our producers to command and wield the most effective machinery. It is quite within the truth to estimate the annual product of our National Industry at less than one-half what it might be if better applied and directed.

"IV. Inefficiency in production is paralleled by waste in consumption. Insects and vermin devour at least one-fourth of the farmer's harvests, which inadequate fertilizing and unskillful cultivation have already reduced far below the proper aggregate. A thousand cooks are required, and a thousand fires maintained, to prepare badly the food of a township; when a dozen fires and a hundred cooks might do it far better, and with a vast saving in quantity as well as improvement in quality. [I judge that the cooks of Paris would subsist One Million persons on the food consumed or wasted by Six Hundred Thousand in this city; feeding them better than they are now fed, and prolonging their lives by an average of five years.]

"V. Youth should be a season of instruction in Industry and the Useful Arts, as well as in Letters and the Sciences mastered by their aid. Each child should be trained to skill and efficiency in Productive Labor. The hours of children should be alternately devoted to Labor, Study, and Recreation,—say, two hours to each before, and a like allotment after dinner each secular day. Thus each child would grow up an adept, not merely in letters, but in arts, a skillful worker as well as a proficient in the lessons of the school-room,—able to do well, not one thing only, but many things,—familiar with mechanical as well as agricultural processes, and acquainted with the use of steam and the direction of machinery.   Not till one has achieved the fullest command, the most varied use, of *all* his faculties and powers, can he be properly said to be educated.

"VI. Isolation is at war with efficiency and with progress. As 'iron sharpeneth iron,' so are man's intellectual and inventive faculties stimulated by contact with his fellow-men. A nation of herdsmen, dwelling in movable tents, invents little or nothing, and makes no progress, or next to none.   Serfdom was the general condition of the laboring class in Europe, until aggregation in cities and manufactories, diffusing intelligence, and nourishing aspiration, wrought its downfall.

"VII. The poor work at perpetual disadvantage in isolation, because of the inadequacy of their means.   Let us suppose that four or five hundred heads of families propose to embark in Agriculture.   Each buys his little farm, his furniture, his implements, animals, seeds, fertilizers, etc., etc., and—though he has purchased nothing that he does not urgently need—he finds his means utterly exhausted, and his farm and future exertions heavily burdened by debt.   He hopes and labors to clear off the mortgage ; but flood and drouth, frost and fire, work against him ; his poverty compels him to do without many implements, and to plow or team with inadequate force ; he runs up an account at the store, and pays twenty per cent. extra for his goods, because others, who buy on credit, fail to pay at all ; and so he struggles on, till his strength fails, and he dies oppressed with debt.   Such is the common lot.

"VIII. Association would have these unite to purchase, inhabit, and cultivate a common domain,—say, of two thousand acres,—whereby these advantages over the isolated system would be realized :

"1. One-fourth (at most) of the land required under the old system would be found abundant.

"2. It could be far better allotted and appropriated to Grain, Grass, Fruits, Forest, Garden, etc.

"3. The draught animals that were far too few, when dispersed among five hundred owners, on so many different farms, would be amply sufficient for a common domain.

"4. Steam or water power could now be economically employed for a hundred purposes—cutting and sawing timber, threshing and grinding grain, plowing the soil, and for many household uses—where the small farmer could not think of employing it.

"5. Industry would find new and powerful incentives in the observation and praise or censure of the entire community; uniforms, banners and music, with the rivalry of bands of competing workers, would provoke emulation and lighten labor; while such recreations as dramas, concerts, readings, etc.,—now utterly beyond the reach of rural workers,—would give a new zest to life. At present, our youth escape from rural industry when they can,—not that they really hate work,—but that they find their leisure hours even duller and less endurable than those they give to rugged toil."

Horace Greeley knew no other systems of Socialism, than those based on the empirical and semi-capitalistic theories of Owen, St. Simon and Fourier, except perhaps those of Byllesby, Skidmore, Simpson, Brisbane and Godwin, which were immature and American improvements, developed in the first half of this century from the works of the earlier Social Architects. A Socialist Pioneer, like each of those mentioned, he formulated a Social Creed, imperfect in itself, but presaging future possibilities for the human race, when taken into consideration with the whole of his other social, political and economic writings and labors.

Greeley's arguments in the Discussion with Henry J. Raymond were based alone on the crude writings of the Socialists named, conjoined to a personal knowledge of the Shaker, Harmonist, Separatist and Owenite Communities.

His efforts to carry out the "abolition of chattel slavery and of wages slavery" are shown in these pages, and what he accomplished should give him a place among the philanthropists of Humanity. Had he commenced his life work a generation or two later, in our time, and been able to pursue the study of Social Science with the exact philosophy, positive evidence and scientific methods of the New School of Socialism, Greeley would have seen the light and hailed it, as emanating from the true political and economic gospels.

But he saw and followed the Truth as he had it delivered to himself in his own time, and he has to be honored and remembered in future ages, by those who will come after us, as—

Horace Greeley, a Pioneer American Socialist.

CHAPTER VI.

GREELEY'S CHRISTIAN SOCIALISM.

HORACE GREELEY was a devoted Christian Socialist. By that, however, is not meant that he accepted the Socialistic Communism of the Christian Church to such an extent as to devote himself to a conventual life, or to become a brother in any such organization as the Shakers,* or Harmonists or Separatists, whose economic methods he has put himself on record as accepting as a higher and better life than that carried out by those who think our present civilization does not need changing.

His theological creed was that of the Universalists, who developed as a distinct religious sect in the United States about 1770. This is not the place to enter into such questions as what Bossuet called the "Variations," but those who desire information on the subject are referred to Hosea Ballou's *Ancient History of Universalism* and Thomas Whittemore's *Modern History* of the same.

What Greeley's belief actually was, he describes in his *Recollections* as follows: "With the great body of the Universalists of our day (who herein differ from the earlier pioneers in America of our faith), I believe that ' our God is *one* Lord,'—that 'though there be that are called gods,

---

* William Dean Howells resided for a time with the Shakers, and in his *Undiscovered Country* after referring to their "placidity," eulogizes "their truth, charity, and purity of life, and that scarcely less lovable quaintness, to which no realism could do perfect justice."

as there be gods many and lords many, to us there is but one God, the Father, *of* whom are all things, one Lord Jesus Christ, *by* whom are all things;' and I find the relation between the Father and the Saviour of mankind most fully and clearly set forth in that majestic first chapter of Hebrews, which I cannot see how any Trinitarian can ever have intently read, without perceiving that its whole tenor and burden are directly at war with his conception of 'three persons in one God.' Nor can I see how Paul's express assertion, 'when all things shall be subdued unto him, then shall the Son himself also be subject to Him that put all things under him, that God may be all in all,' is to be reconciled with the more popular creed. However, I war not upon others' convictions, but rest satisfied with a simple statement of my own."

Horace Greeley's Socialism was over and over again confounded in the public mind with Infidelity, and he was always indignant when such a preposterous charge was made against him. Thus, when the New York *Express* twitted him with being an Infidel, he retorted: "The editor of the *Tribune* has never been anything else than a believer in the Christian Religion, and has for many years been a member of a Christian Church. He never wrote or uttered a syllable in favor of Infidelity. But truth is lost on the *Express*, which can never forgive us the 'Infidelity' of circulating a good many more copies, Daily and Weekly, than are taken of that paper."

He always antagonized anything approaching Atheism, and upon one occasion discussing Communism, he said: "Even the followers of Comte, the swallowers of his Pantheistic fog, will yet be banded or melted into Communities, and will endeavor to realize the exaltation of Work into Worship, with a degree of success to be measured by the individual character of the associates." On another occasion he wrote: "Mere recognition of God as an Architect is not sufficient: still less is belief in Him as a blind Power— like the Destiny of the Greek Drama or the Fatalism which challenges the Turk's submission. Worse still is the vulgar idea of him as an African Mumbo-Jumbo, to be placated by flattery or won over by servile compliances in place of practical and hearty obedience. Whoever truly knows Him as He is, knows that no act or thought, whether good or evil, can possibly fail of its due recompense, and that all attempts to evade this by finesse or formula are at once preposterous and audacious. That His mercy to the erring and the penitent never faileth, is a glorious, cheering truth ; but vainly shall any hope for Vice, penitent on its deathbed, the rewards of enduring Virtue. Were He but known as He is, we should have more lives of active beneficence and fewer death-beds of abject repentance when too late to be of any earthly use. No Louis XV. worn out with fifty years of debauchery and tyranny, would think of 'making the *amende honorable* to God' by mumbling a wafer and a prayer in his death-throes, but all would realize that 'Whatsoever a man soweth that shall he also reap,' and that the Virtue which holds its even way through life, realizing that God governs and judges here as well as elsewhere, is alone deserving of his favor or calculated to secure it, and that hardly to Heaven itself is it possible to efface utterly from the soul the stains of a career of guilt and shame, save through the purifying fires of a righteous and fearful retribution."

Greeley took the position that most American Industrial Socialists do, whatever their particular form of belief or disbelief may be. He believed in the Humanitarian teachings of Jesus of Nazareth, finding therein, as do the

religious orders of the Roman Catholic Church, the highest
incentives to the ideal life of Humanity.   The Sermon on
the Mount was to him the very acme of metaphysical philosophy spiritualized.   The denunciation of the rich and
mighty and the exaltation of the poor and lowly, uttered by
the "Carpenter's Son," were ever present in Greeley's
mind, and he always carried as far as he could into practice,
what he believed in theory.   The texts which, preaching to
millionaires, relative to the rich and poor, fashionable divines
gloss over and recommend as not to be taken literally, were
to him absolute truths, divine orders to be carried out in
every day life as the actual foundations of a True Civilization.
Thus he wrote :—

" It seems evident that a radical reform in the popular
apprehension of religious teaching, if not in the teaching
itself, is here needed.   Since the earthly pilgrimage of the
Divine 'Man of Sorrows,' we have had few preachers who
said frankly and pointedly, 'How hardly shall they that
have riches enter into the Kingdom of God !'—'Sell all
that thou hast and give to the poor ; *then* come and follow
me,' and so forth.   Do we realize that these were not the
exaggerations of petulance or asceticism, but the simple,
natural conditions of spiritual health, illumination and progress?   What He required was but the disencumbering of
the soul of clogs which impeded and bore it heavily earth-
ward.   What Christ said of wealth, its influences and proper
uses, had no mere local or transitory significance.   It is as
true in New England as it was in Palestine,—as true in 1846
as it was in the year one."

But Horace Greeley recognized that his Socialism should
not be allowed to interfere with other people's religion, or
with the family relation, and American Socialists take the
same position and consider these matters as appertaining to

the individual's sacred rights, with which it is the duty of the State not to interfere, unless called upon by those immediately and personally concerned.

Why should American Industrial Socialists enter into them? They are not in their Platform or Demands, for Socialism is essentially an Industrial Movement, insisting, through its newspapers and agitators, that whatever reforms it advocates shall be carried into effect politically through Legislation, or economically through Organized Labor. In fact so conservative, yet so broad are its views, that its political and social demands must be carried through, if opposed to the Constitution of the United States, by amendments endorsed by the whole people, under Article V. of that Constitution. This is in accordance with the views of the Social Democracy, where constitutional methods prevail,—yet even in despotic Russia its main industrial demands could be safely carried into effect under the Czar, without hurting the prerogatives of the State, but on the contrary, simply enlarging them.

Were not Bismarck and Napoleon III. considered the greatest State Socialists in Europe? They ruled where Church and State were united. But in America, where they are separate, the extension of the Socialistic principle in every domain of activity associated with labor could be carried into effect, as the Nation has already the Post Office, the State, the Inspection of Factories, and the Municipality, Education,—all of which, at one time, were functions looked after by private individuals and not by the Collectivity.

American Socialism proposes that American Citizens should, in a law-abiding spirit, carry to a logical sequence, in fact, extend the principle, by which these functions have been undertaken by the Nation, State or County, and which principle is a fundamental of government in the United States.

American Socialists, like Greeley, say, therefore, with Christ, "Render unto Cæsar, the things that are Cæsar's," with the limitation however, that the people shall decide, living in a Democratic Republic, what appertains to Cæsar, —that is the people themselves through the ballot box, statute or amendment, and administration.

Fortunate it is that American Christianity has had within its clerical ranks men like Horace Greeley's spiritual adviser William Ellery Channing, who said in 1841 :—

"The present civilization of the Christian world presents much to awaken doubt and apprehension. It stands in direct hostility to the great ideas of Christianity. It is selfish, mercenary, sensual. Such a civilization cannot, must not endure forever. How it is to be supplanted, I know not. I hope, however, that it is not doomed, like the old Roman civilization, to be quenched in blood. I trust that the works of ages are not to be laid low by violence, rapine and the all-devouring sword. I trust that the existing Social State contains in its bosom something better than it has yet unfolded. I trust that a brighter future is to come, not from the desolation, but from gradual, meliorating changes of the present. Among the changes to which I look for the salvation of the Modern World, one of the chief is the intellectual and moral elevation of the laboring class. The impulses which are to reform and quicken Society are probably to come, not from its more conspicuous, but from its obscurer divisions ; and among these, I see with joy new wants, principles and aspirations beginning to unfold themselves. Let what is already won, give us courage."

And, supplementary to these words of hope, can be

added the lines of Henry Ware, the New England divine and religious poet :—

> "Hasten the day, just Heaven!
>   Accomplish thy design,
> And let the blessings Thou hast freely given
>   Freely on all men shine;
> Till Equal Rights be equally enjoyed,
> And human power for human good employed;
> Till Law, and not the Sovereign, rule sustain,
> And Peace and Virtue undisputed reign."

All of the Protestant Clergy did not regard Greeley's Christian Socialism as did, in later years, Theodore Parker, who was a Socialist himself. The ministers of the churches in the aristocratic neighborhoods of New York city, forty years ago, denounced to their capitalistic congregations, the editor and reformer who preached the Coöperative Commonwealth, and who asserted in the *Tribune* that :—

"This thing Association (Socialism), as I hold and advocate it, is a matter of Practice altogether—the simple actualization of the truth of the Universal Human Brotherhood. Christ's Law of Love is palpably outraged and contemned in a world of palaces and mud hovels—of famished toil and pampered uselessness—of boundless wealth, uselessly hoarded, and helpless infancy dying in bitter agony and supplication for 'only three grains of corn.' Let us redress the palpable wrongs before us by prompt action, and we will consider theories and speculations at our leisure. Fourier's idea, that God governs the Universe throughout by attraction—that this is the law of life and health for all intelligent beings—is a grand and inspiring one—it may possess great practical value, when we come fully to understand and apply it."

One well-salaried parson with the appropriate name of

Hawks, "in the usual style of well-fed thoughtlessness,"
denounced Greeley and "the Socialists" from his pulpit.
The *Tribune* a day or two afterwards answered him in these
caustic words :—

"If 'the Socialists' as a¯ body were called upon to
pronounce upon the propriety of taking the property of
certain doctors of divinity and dividing it among the
mechanics and laborers, to whom they have run recklessly
and heavily in debt,* we have no doubt they would vote
very generally and heartily in the affirmative."

Another clergyman with the euphonious cognomen of
Potts, the pastor of the Presbyterian Church at the corner
of University Place and Tenth Street, New York city,
charged the *Tribune* and its editor with being Socialists,
Agrarians, Anti-Renters and the like, and his sermon was
reported in the columns of the *Courier and Enquirer*.
Greeley paid his satiric respects to both the journal and
the dominie.   The *Tribune* editor first referred to his
newspaper rivals :—

"We do not find, in the *Courier's* report of this sermon,
any censures upon that very large and popularly respectable
class of journals, which regularly hire out their columns,
editorial and advertising, for the enticement of their
readers to visit groggeries, theaters, horse-races, as we sometimes have thoughtlessly done, but hope never, unless
through deplored inadvertence, to do again.   The difficulty
of entirely resisting all temptations to these lucrative vices
is so great, and the temptations themselves so incessant,

---

* Horace Greeley here refers indirectly to the fact that, in 1849,
a subscription of $15,000 had to be raised in New York city to
relieve the impecunious Protestant-Episcopal minister, the Rev. Dr.
Francis Lister Hawks from "pecuniary embarrassment," and to
assist him in paying the workmen and others, the money that he
owed them, in consequence of his various building speculations,
including the erection of St. Thomas's Hall, Flushing, Long Island.

while the moral mischief thence accruing is so vast and palpable, that we can hardly think the Rev. Dr. slurred over the point, while we can very well imagine that his respected disciple and reporter did so. At this moment, when the great battle of Temperance against Liquid Poison and its horrible sorceries, is convulsing our State, and its issue trembles in the balance, it seems truly incredible that a Doctor of Divinity, lecturing on the iniquities of the Press, can have altogether overlooked this topic. Cannot the *Courier* from its reporter's notes supply the omission?''

Then Greeley replied to Rev. Dr. Potts, saying :—

''It is quite probable that we have some readers among the pew-holders of a church so wealthy and fashionable as the Dr.'s, though few, we presume, among divines as well salaried as he is. We will only ask those of our patrons, who may obey his command, to read for their next Scripture lesson the xxvth Chapter of Leviticus, and reflect upon it for an hour or so. We are very sure they will find the exercise a profitable one, in a sense higher than they will have anticipated. Having then stopped the *Tribune*, they will meditate at leisure on the abhorrence and execration with which one of the Hebrew Prophets must have regarded any kind of an Agrarian or Anti-Renter; that is, one opposed to perpetuating and extending the relation of Landlord and Tenant over the whole arable surface of the earth. Perhaps the contemplation of a few more passages of Sacred Writ may not be unprofitable in a moral sense— for example :—

'' 'Woe unto them that join [add] house to house, that lay field to field, till there be no place, that they may be placed alone in the midst of the earth.'—Isaiah, v. 8.

'' 'One thing thou lackest : go thy way, sell whatsoever thou hast, and give to the poor, and thou shalt have treasure in heaven; and come, take up the cross and follow me.

" 'And Jesus looked round about, and saith unto his disciples, How hardly shall they that have riches enter into the Kingdom of God!'—Mark, x. 21–23.

" 'And all that believed were together, and had all things common; and sold their possessions and goods, and parted them to all men, as every man had need.'—Acts, ii. 44, 45.

"We might cite columns of this sort from the Sacred Volume, showing a deplorable lack of Doctors of Divinity in ancient times, to be employed at $3,500 a year in denouncing, in sumptuous, pew-guarded edifices costing $75,000 each, all who should be guilty of 'loosening the faith of many in the *established order of things.*' Alas for their spiritual blindness! the ancient Prophets—GOD's Prophets—appear to have slight faith in or reverence for that 'established order' themselves! Their 'schemes' appear to have been regarded as exceedingly 'disorganizing' and hostile to 'good order' by the spiritual rulers of the people in those days.

"That Dr. Potts, pursuing (we trust) the career most congenial to his feelings, surrounded by every comfort and luxury, enjoying the best society, and enabled to support and educate his children to the hight of his desires, should be inclined to reprobate all 'nostrums' for the cure of Social evils, and sneer at 'labor-saving plans' of cooking, washing, schooling, etc., is rather deplorable than surprising. Were he some poor day-laborer, subsisting his family and paying rent on the dollar a day he could get when the weather permitted and some employer's necessity or caprice gave him a chance to earn it, we believe he would view the subject differently. As to the spirit which can denounce by wholesale all who labor, in behalf of a Social Reform, in defiance of general obloquy, rooted prejudice, and necessarily serious personal sacrifices, as enemies of Christianity and Good Morals, and call upon the public to starve them into silence, does it not merit the rebuke and loathing of every generous mind? Heaven aid us to imitate, though afar off, that Divinest charity which could say for its persecutors and murderers, 'Father, forgive them, for they know not what they do!'"

The American Tract Society filled with Puritan horror at the increase of sinfulness owing to the "tripping of the light fantastic toe," offered a prize of fifty dollars for the best tracts, which it proposed to publish, "On the Impropriety of Dancing." Horace Greeley, thinking he would help matters a little, improved the occasion by offering a few premiums for other tracts that he considered might be in order. He wrote :—

"The notice, copied above, suggests to us some other subjects on which we think Tracts are needed—subjects which are beginning to attract the thoughts of not a few, and which are, like dancing, of practical moment. We would suggest premiums to be offered, as follows :—

"$20 for the best Tract on 'The rightfulness and consistency of a Christian's spending $5,000 to $10,000 a year on the appetites and enjoyments of himself and family, when there are a thousand families within a mile of him who are compelled to live on less than $200 a year.

"$10 for the best Tract on the rightfulness and Christianity of a Christian's building a house for the exclusive residence of himself and family, at a cost of $50,000 to $100,000, within sight of a hundred families living in hovels worth less than $100.

"$5 for the best Tract on the Christianity of building

Churches which cost $100,000 each, in which *poor* sinners
can only worship on sufferance, and in the most out-of-the-
way corners.

"We would not intimate that these topics are by any
means so important as that of Dancing—far from it. The
sums we suggest will shield us from that imputation. Yet,
we think these subjects may also be discussed with profit,
and, that there may be no pecuniary hindrance, we will pay
the premiums if the American Tract Society will publish
the Tracts."

Believing as Greeley did in the Communistic Socialism
of the New Testament, he never allowed an opportunity to
escape him of personally endeavoring to make Christians
recognize that under the veneer of alleged religion much
hypocrisy existed. He lashed with a scourge, as it were,
divines of the Potts and Hawks type. When in Congress,
upon the question coming up of the salary of the chaplain
he said, if either House had one "who dared preach of
the faithlessness, neglect of duty, iniquitous waste of time,
and robbery of the public by Congressmen, there would be
some sense in the chaplain business; but any ill-bred
Nathan or Elijah who should undertake such a job would
be kicked out in short order."

Horace Greeley had very often in mind these verses,
from the Epistle of St. James, which have not yet been
printed at the head of the New York *Mail and Express*
by its editor, the brother-in-law of the Vanderbilts, Colonel
Elliott F. Shepard, who once for one hour publicly tried
to argue the New York Socialists into believing that he,
personally, was a Socialist too : —

"Go to now, ye rich men, weep and howl for your
miseries that shall come upon you. Your riches are corrupted, and your garments are moth-eaten. Your gold and

silver is cankered; and the rust of them shall be a witness against you, and shall eat your flesh as it were fire. Ye have heaped treasure together for the last days. Behold, the hire of the laborers who have reaped down your fields, which is of you kept back by fraud, crieth: and the cries of them which have reaped are entered into the ears of the Lord of Sabaoth.''

And Greeley carried such apostolic arguments directly home to those who in his day were of the same character, as St. James the Apostle had alluded to eighteen hundred years before. In his lecture on ''The Aims of Life'' he said :—

''In truth, wealth, employed only or mainly to subserve personal ends, is in its nature incompatible with a true life, or with the purpose of such a life. The man of substance, who regards his riches as means of luxury, of elegance, of power, (other than the power to relieve and bless,) or of continuing such advantages to his descendants, is inevitably, palpably beclouded as to the very purpose for which life was given him. His aims are selfish and groveling, his understanding darkened, his faltering, grudging, feeble efforts at goodness, are tainted by the sin of Ananias and Sapphira. His fealty to Mammon will ever clash with his duty to God.

''I do not know that I am more strongly moved by any ordinary spectacle than by that of the assembling for worship of a fashionable and wealthy congregation in one of our great cities. As the rich and the great roll up in their carriages to engross the superbly adorned pews, the poorer and humbler shuffle in on foot, and take the less desirable seats, leaving the worst of all to the crushed children of Africa, whose understanding, it would seem, is deemed so acute, that they need not hear more than half the service in order to comprehend it thoroughly. The same equivocal compliment is paid to the decrepit, the deaf, the superannuated, if they happen to be hopelessly poor. But the great man's coachman is not even supposed to hear at all. Were he at liberty, he would not venture to present himself at the door of the family pew—such a stretch of presumption would cost him a lecture on manners to superiors, and very likely his means of subsistence. *His* business in that solemn hour is not to worship God, but to take care of horses. While he assiduously fulfills this function in the shadow of the church outside, and the gilded prayer-books are in requisition within, half a dozen other human implements are busy at home preparing the sumptuous meal. For these, 'Sunday shines no holyday'; it hardly witnesses a relaxation of their labors. They may have some vague idea that the obligations, duties, and hopes of religion are divinely intended for all, but the whole atmosphere, the daily necessities of their life condemn such a notion. It may be their masters' duty to obey God; it is theirs to obey their masters; and in this service conscience is well nigh superfluous, and would often be an embarrassment and obstruction. Thus they wear out their lives in mere brutishness and serfdom, with no more mental exercise nor development than the domesticated animals which are their fellow servants and daily companions. How many families contribute annually to send the gospel to the heathen, without once reflecting that their practice and example made a great many more heathen than their money will ever convert."

"The Unfulfilled Mission of Christianity, a Letter to the Reader," is the heading in *Hints Toward Reforms,* to the following powerful series of Christian Socialist arguments :—

"WASHINGTON CITY, May 4, 1842.

", . . . IT was but yesterday that I stood in the great Commercial Emporium, and listened pensively to the rustling tread of its hurrying thousands.   Here passed the slave of commerce, the devotee of gain, with vacant gaze and introverted perception, his brow working unconsciously as he pondered over the thousands he hoped to win, yet dreaded to lose, by some casual turn of the wheel of fortune ; scanning, perchance, the sky, to note what prospect of tempest or favoring gale awaited his vessel now approaching the coast, hurrying to the bulletin for news, or to the price current to learn the chance of profit or loss on his ventures.   Beside him trudged unheededly the laborer, with his swart brow and stooping frame, toiling on sturdily, though wearily, through the rugged day, with thoughts of the wife and little ones whose narrow domicile and scanty comforts his arduous, unremitted exertions barely suffice to provide, and thinking sadly, shudderingly, of the period just at hand when his present employment shall cease, to be succeeded, he knows not how or whence. And now, there pass me the lawyer and the broker, each weaving in his brain the spider-web in which some poor unfortunate shall soon be enclosed, and gloating joyously over the anticipated triumph which to another shall be ruin.   But list ! a longer stride, a more heedless air : here rushes by a reckless, half-intoxicated sailor, just landed from a voyage around Cape Horn, and hastening to spend, in a few days' riot and debauchery, the hard-won earnings of as many years, and then return to his monotonous round, as penniless as ever, and one degree more debased and brutal than before.   There prances knavish Bankruptcy in its chariot, spattering the threadbare garb of some ruined creditor, who goes before on foot ; here trips Fashion in lace; there hobbles Beggary in rags, as, with counterfeited limp and loathsome travesty of the human form, it whines out its petition for alms. . . . And now 'tis evening, and the great avenues blaze with light, as the windows of the palaces of Traffic flash with gems and are radiant with the display of costly fabrics. The entrances to the haunts of dissipation are luminous and inviting to their victims, and, from the dark purlieus where they have shunned the glare of day, the votaries of sin come forth to flaunt their little season. In the narrower and less frequented paths, darkness holds partial dominion, and riot, crime, dissipation, and fierce contention, have recommenced their reign, destined, it may be, to outwear the night. Such is a rude and hasty presentment of the moral aspects of a day in *Christian* New York, where thousands are assembled (very properly and laudably, I doubt not) to devise the ways, and contribute the means, to carry the GOSPEL and its attendant blessings into all parts of the globe.

"And now I sit in Washington, where the great and the honorable of the land are assembled to shape its destinies. Their voices reach me in my narrow chamber; the rattle of their wheels is borne freshly to my ear, as they roll over the broad avenue.

"The commanding might of Mind is here. The orator, whose fervid utterance in the Senate has reverberated through the vast extent of our country, rocking the hearts of millions from the Aroostook to the Sabine, is here. The demagogue, base idol of a multitude's thoughtless hosannas, flatterer and flattered, corrupter and corrupted, is here— the enchantment lent by distance, dispelled by contact— his essential nothingness and selfish aims gleaming out abundantly through the paint and patchwork of counterfeit patriotism, in which he has arrayed himself. The gaudy

blazonry of military pomp, of naval prowess, is here. Here
the sleek and satisfied official jostles the shrinking and
cringing office-hunter from the walk. Still, as ever, amid
the shows of luxury and waste, stalks the gaunt form of
penury and want, pining for a crust, as it gazes through
blazing windows upon the superfluous banquet on which
thousands have been squandered. Gliding through, check-
ering all, are the dark figures of the low-browed children
of Cain, bearing ever their unmistakable badge of servitude
and degradation. Here, the gambler and the debauchee—
honorable and eminent, it may be—are preparing to waste
the midnight hours in orgies whereof the speedy issue is
shame, debasement, and death. Such is the spectacle
presented by the enlightened metropolis of this *Christian*
land, whence missionaries are radiating to every corner of
the world, in this nineteenth century since the advent of
the Savior. In the long interval, the Christian faith and
worship have widely diffused themselves, but where is the
CHRISTIAN IDEA? Where lingers the kingdom of universal
holiness and love which Jesus came to establish ON EARTH?

"Where is it? I see around me the stately and costly
edifices in which Herod and Dives proceed weekly, with
scrupulous punctuality, to worship God in pomp and
luxury, as followers of the Carpenter of Nazareth, the fisher-
men of Galilee. Christian forms and observances are thick
around me: where is the Christian spirit? I recognize it
not in that lordly pile; not within the folds of that ample
surplice; not within those richly-cushioned pews, which an
humble, threadbare stranger may not enter without encoun-
tering a frown, nor an African without provoking a curse
on his amazing presumption. Yet, possibly, in that poor
Ethiop's heart the divine emotion has found unsuspected
welcome; it may glow there as he shrinks tremblingly into

some obscure corner of the edifice, and listens rapturously to truths which not even the preacher comprehends. Perhaps, in some dingy conventicle, its material utterance drowned beneath discordant ejaculations of folly and frenzy, of fanaticism and absurdity, the incense of a genuine devotion is ascending, unmarked, to the throne of the Everlasting Father. But is this the fullness of the kingdom which Christ came to establish? Shall such occasional and solitary instances be held to overbear and set at naught the sad reality of a world lying in wickedness? Do we not know that evil and anguish, oppression and wretchedness, wrong and despair, are abundant, nearly as ever, among the children of men? And is not the world yet prepared to realize that, in the fullness of the Christian dispensation is contained the remedy for *all* evil—for all that is not incident to our mortality, even here? How long shall it be practically regarded as a form of worship and a code of difficult observances? Why not rather accept it as a divinely appointed means of entire and immediate emancipation from the ills of our earthly condition? Let not the idea be hastily condemned as extravagant; let us soberly consider it.

"When Christ directed the inquirer to sell all his goods, and give the avails to the poor—when He declared that the rich should with extreme difficulty enter the kingdom of heaven—when he related the parable of the pearl of great price, etc., did he merely utter extravagant hyperboles? The disciples did not so understand him, as we learn by their having 'all things in common,' even after his death. Did he propound these rules in exclusive reference to some imminent exigency? So it does not appear ; nor can it, unless the command to love our neighbor as ourself be understood to have a like limited and now lifeless significance. Why, then, should the Church, or assemblage of believers, prefer the interpretation of Ananias and Sapphira to that of Peter and Paul? Why should Christians famish—nay, why should *men* perish for lack of food, while in Christendom is abundance? Why should believers be driven to solicit and subsist on the freezing charity of our political Organizations, while within the Church is ample wealth? This, surely, is directly contrary to the precept and example of the Apostolic age. I have not traced the history minutely, yet I am confident that the first idea of a universal and permanent provision for the poor and destitute originated in that age, with Christ and His apostles; that it continued a work of the Church, and not at all of the State, down to a comparatively recent period; and that it lapsed into the hands of the latter through the increase of temporal knowledge and wisdom, and the decline of Christianity as a distinct and substantive power over the hearts and actions of men. If so, what is the obvious deduction?

"But a mere provision for the destitute is not all that is contemplated by the idea of Christianity. In that idea I clearly recognize the germ of a Great Social Renovation. In teaching mankind no longer to hate, distrust, and destroy, but to love and cherish each other as themselves, a stupendously beneficent Revolution was involved. Alms-houses for the destitute go but a short way toward the fulfillment of the great law of love. Not merely insurance against extremest misery, but provision for positive and essentially equal happiness, is implied. And why may not this be realized? Why should not the Christian dispensation become the basis of a new and benignant Social Order, from which want and woe, fraud and wrong, discord and antagonism, shall be banished, and the highest attainable good of each member be striven for and secured? Why may not such an order be formed, which shall secure to each individual, not only abundant food, and clothing, and shelter, but education, also—intellectual development, and all the means of rational enjoyment—requiring of him, in turn, that equal and just contribution of his efforts toward the general weal, which the community or church shall require, and which his own capacities and preference (very rarely, if unperverted, at variance) shall indicate? And why may not our race thus emancipate themselves from the bondage of constraint, and privation, and suffering, in which they so long have labored and groaned; and, guided and upheld by the law of Universal Love, rise speedily and surely to the primal condition, while the long scourged and desolate earth shall grow verdant and beauteous again?

"This is a vast and inspiring theme. I should not venture to speak so confidently on the hopeful side of it, had not loftier and serener spirits sounded its depths, and vanquished its difficulties. These have shown that the renovation of society on the basis of the Christian idea is not visionary, is not fantastic, is not impracticable. Nay, undoubted EXPERIENCE, not merely in the repeated and enduring instances of the Shakers and other ascetic communities, but in those of many of larger faith and clearer knowledge, has demonstrated this cheering truth. There is no longer a necessity, there is hardly an excuse for Social evil and degradation. The means of avoiding or vanquishing them are within the reach of nearly all. The system of ASSOCIATION, or sharehold property, blended with Attractive Industry, promulgated by FOURIER, does away with the last objection, that a Social Order adverse to the present must generate improvidence and idleness, and so perish through human infirmity. Its vast economies will bring wealth within the reach of all, while affording them the amplest means and opportunities for intellectual, moral, and social elevation and enjoyment.

"Carlyle * casually remarks, that a man, able and willing to work, yet unable to find employment, and thence lacking the means of subsistence, is the saddest sight under the sun.' What shall we say of a Christian famishing in a land of Christian affluence, because the means of earning bread is not afforded him in our chaotic and warring Social Order? Surely the soul of such a one must appear as an accusing angel at the bar of Eternal Justice against the Community in which such a tragedy was enacted. Yet such a calamity has taken place, even in this country. Let us hope that the time when it *could* be, is nearly at an end, and that the knowledge of its possibility will soon linger only as a fearful tradition in the homes of the children of men."

Horace Greeley, we learn from his own words, thus saw in Fourierist Socialism, simply the carrying out of the teachings of the Nazarene, who was born in a stable and had no place to rest his weary head. Greeley took an equally strong position in what he wrote on *The Church and the Age*, from which are here quoted a few passages :—

"I have as little taste as faculty for fine writing ; as little appetite as aptitude for mere sentimentality : if I were to attempt even a love-story, I have no doubt it would insensibly grow into a Socialist harangue or a dissertation, on the causes and cure of human destitution. This life, on which we have been launched, seems a problem so grave

---

* A collection of Carlyle's writings, more particularly of interest to students of the economical questions of the present time, has been published in the Social Science Library, by the Humboldt Publishing Company, with the title:, *The Socialism and Un-Socialism of Thomas Carlyle.*

and earnest as to afford little time or thought for idyls or madrigals. We awake in it to find ourselves members of the great body of Humanity—and in what condition is that body with which we are so indissolubly blended? Of the one thousand millions of human beings on earth, how large a proportion—certainly more than half—pass through life sufferers from want;—want of opportunity, of education, of shelter, and of food! Millions annually perish prematurely, through ignorance and the resulting evils—victims of famine, of excess, of evil habits, unfit aliment, or lawless passions, from which a better training, a juster idea of the laws of the universe, would have saved them. 'The people perish for lack of vision,' and so have done from the first. Ignorance of the inexorable laws of cause and effect which bind together virtue and happiness, vice and misery, has ever been a chief source of the woes under which 'the whole creation groaneth and travaileth together in pain until now.'

"Into the midst of this lazar-house of sin and sorrow, comes the angel Religion—and for what? Even granting that the paramount object of the Savior's mission and the Christian dispensation is salvation beyond the grave, is not the parallel design to mitigate the sufferings and rectify the errors of this present life still obvious, undeniable? The evils and woes over which Christ sorrowed were plainly temporal—the tender concern manifested by the Gospel for the destitute and desolate, is not confined to the future life. I have erringly read the Scriptures, if the solicitude therein expressed for the well-being of our race is at all confined to their condition in the world beyond the grave. . . . .

"We are brought face to face with the primary question, modified (or rather, fortified) as follows: Since evil exists, and *will* exist, what can we do to limit its blighting influences? Admit that the transgressor is irreclaimable, or that no benevolence can render him less wretched until he abandons his vicious courses, and still it may be quite feasible to mitigate the sufferings of those he has dragged down with him to perdition. Nay, more! We might, by patient, loving inquiry into his past history and circumstances, discover causes of his aberration, as yet unsuspected, which would serve to soften the abhorrence with which we have learned to regard him. We might bring to light facts showing that his infatuation is not so wanton as we have deemed it, but that influences preceding his birth, and by no means confined to his own narrow family circle, have powerfully aided to make him what he is. Having been drawn thus far in exploring the individual case, we may see before us a broad ocean of inquiry, stretching away to an unexplored continent of duty. We may now be impelled to consider how far the external influences which have conspired to make some men drunkards or outcasts, and others felons, are controllable, and whether it be not practicable to place even the less fortunate in such relations, and train them under such influences, as will assuredly preserve them from the contaminations and perversions of which the fruits are so deadly. . . . . Why shall not the preservation of the unborn from the depressing and debasing circumstances which have impelled and are still dooming so many millions all around us to perdition, become the paramount idea of the Christian, no less than of the philanthropist? Do you demur that saving men's souls from corruption in the present, or from perdition in the future life, is the chief end of the Gospel? Admit this, and still the question recurs, Can you hope to save the souls immured in bodies subjected to every debasing influence, without removing or counteracting those influences? How shall you hope to regenerate the denizens of the darker haunts of depravity and wretchedness in all our great cities, without removing them to purer homes and enabling them to eat the bread of Useful Industry and Virtuous Independence?

"It is not long since the London thieves—that is, a very large number of them—were called together by a philanthropist, who had obtained a clue to their haunts and the means of commanding their attention and confidence. Treating them in all things as erring, misguided, unfortunate, sinful brethren, he addressed them on the flagrant iniquity of their lives, the more palpable ruin to which such courses inevitably tended, and closed by exhorting them to instant, thorough reformation. All were affected; many melted to tears. At last one found words to express the general perplexity, substantially thus : 'Good sir, what shall we do? As thieves, we have employment and obtain some sort of a livelihood; as thieves, we have companions, friends, homes. *Will you insure us these as honest men?* We ask no reward for becoming honest and useful; but we cannot consent to starve. Show us how to live honestly and avoid starvation, and we will instantly abandon our wretched vocation. But your reputable tradesmen will not hire us; your reputable workmen will not tolerate our presence in the same shop with them ; the naked choice afforded us is to steal or starve.' And thus the conference ended, the good Samaritan baffled, puzzled, discouraged. He could of himself do nothing, and the Church was too busy decorating the palaces of its bishops, sending dissenters to prison for non-payment of tithes, and punishing its own ministers for preaching in heretical chapels, to trouble itself with so vulgar a novelty as the reformation of whole battalions of thieves, by enabling them to earn honest bread.

"But what is the Church to do? What duties are incumbent on her, which for ages have lain unrecognized and neglected? I answer, Many; but this first of all—To shield, at least, her own members from the temptations and woes which are inseparable from unwilling idleness and consequent destitution. Every church or society of believers should be, to its own members, at least, as beneficent as an Odd-Fellow's Lodge or Temperance League. It should, at least, so remotely, faintly approximate the first church* at Jerusalem as to say, 'So long as it shall be within our ability to prevent it, no member of this body shall be idle or destitute, who is willing to work cheerfully and faithfully at whatever innocent employment may be offered him, which will afford him a subsistence. To this extent, at least, the idea of Brotherhood shall be actualized in our relation as fellow Christians.' This would be found in practice a prodigious step in the right path, leading on to others. Let it once be established, as the common law of Christendom, that no believer may stand idle and famishing amid a Christian Community, including many who possess, in ample measure, the means of employing and rewarding the needy, and a broad foundation will be laid for a gradual and enduring reform in the relations of wealth to want, of Capital to Labor. What the world pressingly needs is, not mere alms-giving, but less necessity therefor; not bread in idleness, but opportunity and just recompense for Industry secured systematically to all. If political economy and the advancing tide of Democracy can secure or promote these, so be it; let us welcome any helps or hints that the progress of knowledge or invention may afford us; but let not the Church seek to excuse herself

---

* Acts, ii. 44, 45.

from her proper responsibility. In the spirit of that divine appeal, 'Lead us not into temptation,' she is bound to take care that her members are not subjected to the trial of Esau, but that each one of them is secured against vagrancy and famine, not in the world's cold, degrading poor-house, but under the paternal guardianship of Christian love. When she shall have risen to the altitude of this duty, she will be fitted to contemplate, without disrelish or dismay, the broader horizon of paternal obligation that stretches away beyond it. Heaven grant her wisdom early to apprehend and joyfully to accept her benignant destiny !''

There was nothing remarkable in the fact of Horace Greeley having been a Christian Socialist, for he was well aware that other literary men of international fame had taken the same position and that Lord Macaulay, reviewing in the *Edinburgh Review* of January, 1830, *Sir Thomas More, or Colloquies on the Progress and Prospects of Society,* by Robert Southey, LL.D., Poet Laureate, stated:—"The cure which Mr. Southey thinks that he has discovered is worthy of the sagacity which he has shown in detecting the evil. The calamities arising from the Collection of Wealth in the hands of a Few Capitalists are to be remedied by collecting it in the hands of ONE GREAT CAPITALIST, . . . THE STATE." But Robert Southey was a Sociocrat,—in the sense of Auguste Comte,—and somewhat of the Economic School of Robert Owen, whom, the whilom Jacobin author of *Wat Tyler* eulogized ;—as did also his brother "Lake Poet," Samuel Taylor Coleridge, who, Taine asserts, "had thought of founding in America (on the banks of the Susquehanna), a Communist Republic, purged of Kings and Priests," and, we learn elsewhere, "there, in pastoral peace and plenty, to bring back the Golden Age to Man." Coleridge, Southey and their friends,—one of whom was William Wordsworth, the personal associate of many of the French Girondists,—denominated their scheme—"THE PANTISOCRACY."

Horace Greeley always saw beyond the mere exigencies of the present. He looked forward to a future for the race when it would be Emancipated both socially and industrially. It was in this spirit he wrote that beautiful essay of his, so often quoted, *Glimpses of a Better Life.*

The result of the agitation of Greeley and the school of Social Reformers to which he belonged, as well as other agitations which have developed since his day, has forced the Church from its apathetic position. Henry Ward Beecher was one of the first to fall in line, and one eventful Sunday startled the "society christians," in Plymouth Church by saying, with all the force of his eloquence :—

"Listen not to the everlasting Conservative, who pines and whines at every attempt to drive him from the spot where he has lazily cast his anchor. . . . . Every abuse must be abolished. The whole system must be settled on the right basis. Settle it ten times and settle it wrong, you will have the work to begin again. Be satisfied with nothing but the complete enfranchisement of Humanity, and the restoration of man to the image of his God."

The Christian Socialists of Boston are another proof of the fact that reformatory ideas have struck home in this country, equally with the positions taken in Europe by Count Leo Tolstoi, the Christian Communist, and Archbishop Ketteler of Mayence, who for many years not only preached Christian Socialism from the high altar of his cathedral, but went among the working-people and organized many of those who accepted Roman Catholicism into Christian Trades Unions, or Socialistic Industrial Guilds. But His Grace "followed Schultz-Delitsch rather than the

Marx and Lassalle school." And Prince Bismarck, who was at that time master of Germany, justified his semi-Socialist legislation on the ground that his "Christian solicitude for the poor justified his taking a Christian position," saying further in the Reichstag : "If you will give the laborer the right to labor as long as he is in health, secure to him care when he is sick, and his support when he is old, the Social Democrats will blow their whistles in vain." Upon Eugene Richter criticising him for making this statement, "the man of blood and iron" responded : "I recognize the right to labor without qualification, and shall maintain it as long as I am in this place. In this I do not stand on the ground of Socialism, but on that of the municipal law of Prussia."

The Cardinal Archbishop of Baltimore did not hold long conferences with General Master Workman Terence V. Powderly of the Knights of Labor for nothing, when later he wrote to Cardinal Simeoni urging, with great force, that the Roman Catholic Church should not only be a mother, but a friend to the millions in America who live by labor.

And Father McGlynn was excommunicated !

Even Pope Leo XIII. is stirred up by the agitation, issues a Socialistic Encyclical from the chair of the poor fisherman Peter, and shows himself, in many passages of that document, to be mentally of the same opinion and in the same position economically, in denouncing Capitalist abuses and advocating Proletarian reforms,—as the Socialists of America and Europe, and the Socialists alone, have been agitating for over half a century in vain. But alas ! that Encyclical is centuries and centuries behind time. It should have been addressed to the great feudal lords of Europe who held men, women and children in villeinage, bought and sold them like sheep and cattle for hundreds of years, and trans-

mitted Human Slavery as an hereditary curse to the nineteenth century. In medievalism, when the Papacy was a
preponderating spiritual power, Emperors, Kings, Princes
and Barons, with whom she was in alliance, feared the
excommunications thundered from the Vatican ; now, the
gross materialism of the age superinduced by the Plutocrats,—the Kings of Capital and Feudal Lords of our
time,—have made men,—Anarchists and Capitalists alike,—
scoff at all laws, human or divine, and worship, what is the
only God known to them—Mammon, the Almighty Dollar.

But the Papal Encyclical will do good in certain quarters,
and it most certainly has been splendid agitation for the
Socialists of both hemispheres ; for it will bring some of
earth's children back to the realization of the fact that the
words of the Nazarene addressed directly to the rich and
the poor, were not spoken in parables after all.

And a kind of Protestant Episcopal Encyclical has also
been issued by Bishop Henry C. Potter from his "Episcopal Rooms," "to the Reverend Clergy of the Diocese of
New York." He told his "Dear Brethren" that—

"In New York centers the Capital that controls the
traffic and largely the manufactures of this New World. In
your congregations are many of those who control that Capital. In all our parishes are people who employ Labor or
reap the benefits of it. To these it is time to say that no
Christian man can innocently be indifferent to the interests
of workingmen and women ; that Wealth brings with it a
definite responsibility, first to know how best to use it to
serve others, as well as ourselves, and then resolutely to set
about doing it ; that luxury has its decent limits, and that
we, in this land, are in danger in many directions of over-
stepping those limits ; that class churches and class distinctions of kindred kinds have nearly destroyed in the hearts

of many of the poor all faith in the genuineness of a religion whose Founder declared, 'All ye are brethren,' but whose disciples more often seem by their acts to say, 'Stand thou there,' 'Trouble me not,' when their brethren remind them not merely of their manifold needs, but of their just rights."

The Protestant Lord Bishop of New York further said :

"The growth of Wealth among us has resulted not in binding men together, but in driving them apart. The Rich are further from the Poor, the Employer from his Workmen, Capital from Labor, now than ever before. Too many know less and less how the poor live, and give little time or none at all to efforts to know. The wage of the Laborer may be, doubtless, in most cases, it is, larger than it was thirty years ago ; but his wants have grown more rapidly than his wages, and his opportunities for gratifying them are not more numerous, but less. He knows more about decent living, but his home is often not more decent, and daily grows more costly. His mental horizon has been widened, but fit food for it is no more accessible. Instincts and aspirations have been awakened in him, which are certainly as honorable in him as in those more favorably situated, but Wealth does little either to direct or to satisfy them. The manners of the Poor, it is said, are more insolent and ungracious than of old to the Rich, and this discourages efforts to know and serve them. I do not see why Poverty should cringe to Wealth, which is as often as otherwise an accidental distinction, and quite as often a distinction unadorned by any especial moral or intellectual excellence. But we may be sure that the manners of the Poor, if they be insolent, are learned from those of people whose opportunities should, at least, have taught them that no arrogance is more insufferable or unwarrantable than that of mere Wealth. And if we are reaping to-day the fruits of these mutual hatreds between more and less favored classes, we may well own that the fault is not all on one side, and that it is time that we awaken to the need of sacrifices which alone can banish them.

"These sacrifices are not so much of money as of ease, of self-indulgent ignorance, of contemptuous indifference, of conceited and shallow views of the relations of men to one another. A Nation whose Wealth and Social Leadership are in the hands of people who fancy that day after day, like those of old, they can 'sit down to eat and drink and rise up to play,' careless of those who earn the dividends that they spend and pay the rents of the tenement houses that they own, but too often never visit or inspect, has but one doom before it, and that the worst. We may cover the pages of our Statute Books with laws regulating strikes and inflicting the severest penalties on those who organize resistance to the Individual Liberty whether of employer or workman; we may drill regiments and perfect our police; the safety and welfare of a State is not in these things, it is in the contentment and loyalty of its People. And these come by a different road. When Capitalists and Employers of Labor have forever dismissed the fallacy, which may be true enough in the domain of political economy, but is essentially false in the domain of religion, that Labor and the Laborer are alike a commodity, to be bought and sold, employed or dismissed, paid or underpaid as the market shall decree; when the interest of workmen and master shall have been owned by both as one, and the share of the laboring man shall be something more than A MERE WAGE; when the principle of a joint interest in what is produced of all the brains and hands that go to produce it is wisely and generously recognized; when the well being of our fellow men, their homes and food, their pleasures and their higher moral and spiritual necessities shall be seen to be matters concerning which we may not dare to say, 'Am I my brother's keeper?' then, but not till then, may we hope to heal those grave Social Divisions concerning which there need to be among all, as with Israel of old, 'great searchings of heart.'"

American Socialists have seen the results of the work of Horace Greeley, and their Agitators, on Christianity, not only in the Church itself, but in the very ranks of Labor. Thus, in the local assemblies of the Knights of Labor in New York city, it is not unusual to see the cassock of priests like Father Huntington, and the clerical attire of clergymen with the enthusiasm of Rev. Dr. Benjamin F. Da Costa, who there unite with the working people and telling them to "organize," call their attention to the prophecy of Isaiah :—

"The isles saw it and feared, the ends of the earth drew near and came. They helped everyone his neighbor and everyone said to his brother, 'Be of good courage.' So the carpenter encouraged the goldsmith, and he that smote with hammer him that smote the anvil. Let the people renew their strength, let them come near, let them speak, let us come together to judgment."

But over all and around all, hover the echoes of the eternal ideals taught by the Carpenter's Son, who was crucified by wealth and power, and Socialists, whether they be Jew or Gentile, Agnostic or Positivist, Christian or Buddhist, accept his mission to the race as having been on behalf of the Proletariat and in opposition to the Plutocracy. And so the majority of the men and women of the Progressive Movement can repeat with Ernest Renan that :—

"Humanity as a whole presents an assemblage of beings, low, selfish, superior to the animal only in this that their selfishness is more premeditated. But in the midst of this uniform vulgarity, pillars rise toward heaven and attest a more noble destiny. Jesus is the highest of these pillars which show to man whence he came and whither he should tend. In him is condensed all that is good and lofty in our nature. He was not sinless; he conquered the same passions which we combat; no angel of God comforted him, save his good conscience; no Satan tempted him, save that which each bears in his heart. And as many of the grand aspects of his character are lost to us by the fault of his disciples, it is probable also that many of his faults have been dissembled. But never has any man made the interests of Humanity predominate in his life over the littleness of self-love so much as he. Devoted without reserve to his idea, he subordinated everything to it to such a degree that toward the end of his life, the Universe no longer existed for him. It was by this flood of heroic will that he conquered heaven. There never was a man, Sakya-Mouni perhaps excepted, who so completely trampled under foot family, the joys of the world, and all temporal cares. He lived only for his Father, and for the divine mission which he believed it was his to fulfill.

"As for us, eternal children, condemned to weakness, we who labor without harvesting, and shall never see the fruit of what we have sown, let us bow before these demi-gods. They knew what we do not know: to create, to affirm, to act. Shall originality be born anew, or shall the world henceforth be content to follow the paths opened by the bold creators of the ancient ages? We know not. But whatever may be the surprises of the future, Jesus will never be surpassed. His worship will grow young without ceasing; his legend will call forth tears without end; his sufferings will melt the noblest hearts; all ages will proclaim that among the sons of men there is none born greater than Jesus."

CHAPTER VII.

GREELEY, A FARMER SOCIALIST.

FARMERS, planters and ranchmen alike, whether they pursue the agricultural life out west, down south or in New England, are one and all complaining of the "hard times" caused by the merciless exactions of Capitalism, or as they call it "Wall Street." Matters have come to such a pass—and their murmurs are just—that strong ameliorative methods have been endorsed and are now being tried. The agricultural class, whether "bosses" or "help," are combined together, to the number of some 3,500,000, for political purposes in the People's Party, for Coöperation in the Patrons of Husbandry, otherwise Grangers, and for general defense in the Farmers' Alliances. And they are following, more or less, in "the footprints on the sands of time" made by Horace Greeley for their predecessors forty to fifty years ago.

The teachings of the Founder of the *Tribune* are bearing fruit, for the conditions they complain of now were seen clearly by him then, and they are simply symptoms of the disease from which the whole Civilized World has ever suffered. That disease is the Capitalist system of production and distribution which Greeley proposed to cure by the substitution of Fourierist Socialism, as already explained.

Horace Greeley, a descendant of farmers, a farmer's son, a farmer boy in his youth and a farmer for relaxation in his manhood's prime, was thoroughly well aware of what ailed the agricultural class. He knew the tribulations of his forefathers, the hardships of his own boyhood and the chronic state of the impecunious farmer who was always battling with his creditors and winding up in bankruptcy, such as drove the Greeley family from being "boss" farmers in New Hampshire to be farm laborers in Vermont, when their homestead was sold over their heads by sheriff's sale.

He was always thinking and acting for the farmers, his own peculiar people. It was in this spirit he wrote in 1853 *What the Sister Arts Teach as to Farming?* and still later *What I Know About Farming?* a text book to this day throughout the length and breadth of the United States. He made the *Tribune* brim over with farming lore, and theoretical, practical and scientific information for the benefit of those who lived by and tilled the soil, and his lectures and writings teem with suggestions for palliative means and definitive plans for the Emancipation of the Farmer and Farm Laborer.

Horace Greeley's co-workers in the field of agitation and who believed in the same remedies that he proposed, also recognized the same causes and effects. Thus Parke Godwin in his *Democracy—Constructive and Pacific*, after entering fully into the necessary measures, clinches his arguments by endorsing as facts what Farmer S. Denton communicated in 1844 to the Michigan State Farmers' Convention concerning "The Vampyre of Commerce," as that rural genius termed the cause of agricultural distress. Farmer Denton after asserting—"That Wealth is but the accumulated creations of Labor, is a candid and obvious truth, which none will pretend to deny," then asks—"How is it, that those who create it all, are enabled to retain so little for their own share, is a phenomenon which requires explanation." And he does explain, by demonstrating that the non-producing class,—lawyers, bankers, merchants, etc.,—received annually out of the aggregate products of American industry, at the time he wrote,—$889,087,409, leaving for distribution among the laborers $157,097,591. This was the laborers' portion over and above such necessaries as a prudent master would provide for a slave, when acting in conformity to his own interests. The Plutocrats "got" it all then, exactly as they own and control everything now.

This is the view of United States Senator Peffer of Kansas, who has shown how Capitalism stands relatively to the whole farmer class, which he claims is to-day absolutely insolvent, with its property mortgaged far above its actual value, and simply the spoil of the modern Feudal Lords of Capital, who are further doing their best to entirely destroy the same class by investing much of their ill-gotten wealth in bonanza farms, upon which laborers are herded together in barracks like cattle. Theodore F. Cuno, the Sociological writer, lately showed that farmer bankruptcy is not peculiar to the West, and that New England also suffers, by stating: "There are over 1,460 farms in Massachusetts, comprising about 125,500 acres. Every one of these farms is worth about $3,500, but their owners could no longer make their living upon them, because they could not compete with the bonanza farmers of the West, who cultivate many square miles by means of costly machinery. Thus the American farmer is slowly but surely driven into the ranks of the Proletarians by the Capitalistic System."

Horace Greeley was one of the earliest American Land Reformers, and helped, along with his friend George Henry Evans, to carry into practical effect the Fourth and Tenth

Demands, made by the New York Political Socialists of 1826–30, for "Homestead Exemption" and "Homesteads for Actual Settlers." He introduced into Congress the first Free Homestead Bill, of which the following is the text :—

"1. That any citizen, and any alien who has declared his intention of becoming a citizen, may file a pre-emption claim to 160 acres of Public Land, settle upon it, improve it, and have the privilege of buying it at any time within seven years of filing the claim, at the Government price of $1.25 per acre : *provided*, that he is not the owner or claimant of any other real estate.

"2. That the Land office where a claim is filed, shall issue a Warrant of Pre-emption, securing the claimant in seven years' possession.

"3. That, after five years' occupancy, a warrant-holder who makes oath of his intention to reside on and cultivate his land for life shall become the owner of any forty acres of his claim which he may select; the head of a family eighty acres.

"4. That the price of public lands, when not sold to actual settlers, shall be five dollars per acre.

"5. That false affidavits, made to procure land under the provisions of this bill, shall be punished by three years' hard labor in a State prison, by a fine not exceeding $1,000, and by the loss of the land fraudulently obtained."

Well, indeed, was Greeley styled "the Farmers' Friend," and his arguments half a century ago on "Land Reforms" are still pertinent and good reading. The following is what he urged upon one occasion between forty and fifty years since :—

"The Rights of Man—his natural, unchanging, inalienable Rights *as* Man—have fitly become, in our day, the theme of general and earnest discussion. We find little of this in the world's early ages and their enduring monuments—in Homer, or Plato, or Cicero, in Magna Charta, or the Constitutions, so called, of ancient Republics, or more modern Limited Monarchies. Only since Paine met the Crisis of our Revolutionary struggle with those brief, terse, vigorous essays which brought the whole philosophy of Government into the strong clear sunlight of Common Sense—only since Jefferson condensed the truths so enunciated into the Declaration of our Independence—have the Rights of Man been prominently considered and discussed. And, when Jefferson and the Continental Congress proclaimed, in tones to which the world, however unwilling, has been compelled to listen, that 'all men are created equal,' and that among the 'inalienable rights' with which their Creator has endowed them are those of 'Life, Liberty, and the pursuit of Happiness,' they uttered truths of whose fullest import even they were not clearly conscious, and whose ultimate influences on Human well-being and destiny no man can even yet conceive.

"Let us consider their bearings on the newly agitated Land Question—on the Right of Man to the Soil. The Earth's surface undoubtedly contains good arable land enough to give to every family in existence a farm of ample dimensions, even though all the unhealthful or inhospitable portions of the globe were left utterly uninhabited. But of the One Thousand Millions of human beings who are supposed to be in existence, what proportion practically enjoy the Right to any Soil except that with which their lifeless bodies are finally covered? What proportion are at liberty to obey God's command, 'Six days shalt thou labor,' save in the contingency that some one else knows that he can buy that labor and sell its product on such terms that he may realize a pecuniary profit on the speculation?

"Now these deductions can hardly seem far-fetched: Man, having a conceded right to live, has a necessary right also to a reasonable share of those means of subsistence which God has provided for and made virtually necessary to the whole human family: Having a right to Liberty, he must have consequently the right to go *somewhere* on earth and do what is essential to his continued existence, not by the purchased permission of some other man, but by virtue of his manhood: having the right to pursue his own happiness by any means not inconsistent with the welfare and happiness of others, he has the right to do so *somewhere*, and to be protected and justified in so doing. In short, the terrestrial Man, possessing the well-known properties of matter as well as of spirit, can only in truth enjoy the rights of 'Life, Liberty, and the pursuit of Happiness,' by being guaranteed some *place* in which to enjoy them. He who has no clear, inherent right to live *somewhere*, has no right to live at all.

"But look at the question from the side of Labor: God expressly commands men to labor six days of every seven, and has made obedience to this command a vital condition of healthful and comfortable existence. (Alas! that one man should obey and another enjoy the reward of his obedience!) Here, in a State or County, are fifty thousand persons able and willing to labor, with an abundance of arable land to employ them all constantly and reward them generously: but the land mainly belongs to a few dozens or hundreds of this population, (or, still worse, of absentees,) who virtually say to the twenty or thirty thousand would-be laborers who own no land, 'You can only be allowed to 'work here on condition that you will allow us [in the

'shape of rents, price of land, or depressed wages] one-half
'to three-fourths of the entire product of your toil.' Is
not here a heavy tax levied by man upon obedience to the
laws of Nature and of God? Who does not see that Labor
is discouraged and Idleness immensely increased by this
exaction, and the power vested in the few to impose it?

"Yet the most appalling feature of our present system
of Land-holding is the manifest tendency of its evils to
become more and more aggravated and intolerable—nay,
the inevitable necessity that they *should* become so, if the
system itself be endured. If the population of the British
Isles were this day no more dense than that of Indiana or
Russia, the average recompense of its Labor would doubtless
be increased, the condition of its laboring people greatly
improved. The gradual increase of population therein
from three or four millions to thirty or forty, has, in connection with the monopoly of the Soil by a class who are
not its cultivators, gradually carried up the market value
and the yearly rental of arable land to prices, which enable
the land-owning few to riot in unparalleled luxury, and
doom the landless many to toil evermore for the barest
necessaries of life, while hundreds of thousands vainly beg
from door to door, an opportunity to earn the blackest
bread by the most repulsive and meagerly recompensed
drudgery. Like causes will produce like effects here and
elsewhere. It is not the fact that the landlords are few
that is so baneful. If they were ten times as many, the evil
would hardly be mitigated. So long as the millions, whom
God has doomed in the sweat of their faces to eat bread,
shall be constrained to solicit of others the privilege of so
doing, and to propitiate the land-owning class by such a
share of their products as Cupidity may exact and Necessity
must concede, the increase of population will be paralleled

by the depression of Labor and the Laborer. Other influences may come in to modify or counteract this—new inventions which vastly increase the efficiency of Labor ; improved
processes, more scientific culture, etc., may do something
to mitigate the ills of poverty ; but the master evil, a
monopoly of land by those who do not use it, tends ever
to sink the landless multitude into a state of more abject
dependence, while it restricts the demand for and the price
of their sole commodity and resource.

"Suppose the usage and the law were so changed that
no man was permitted, in this boasted land of equal rights,
to hold as his own more than half a square mile of arable
soil (which is enough for fifty men to cultivate), so long as
a single person needing land in the Community should
remain destitute of any, what a mighty and beneficent
transformation would be effected in the reward of Labor and
the condition of the Laboring Class ! Then, instead of a
constant increase in the proportion of landless seekers for
something to do, resulting in a constant jostling and under-
bidding among laborers wanting employment, we should
see a continual division and subdivision of large estates,
with a steady increase in the number and proportion of
small proprietors, each his own employer and his own
laborer, whereby the mass of landless seekers for work as
hirelings or tenants would be rapidly diminished. It is
not proposed to disturb any individual in the full enjoyment
of his possessions, but to make the operation of the proposed reform wholly prospective, so that, while each
proprietor or landlord, at the enactment of the Limitation,
should retain his estates until death, all future aggregation
shall be sternly forbidden, and the principle applied to
each existing estate on the decease of its present owner.
Even the right to transmit property to heirs or devisees

would not be interfered with, except so far as to say, ' Man
' of Millions! bequeath your wealth as you choose; but
' that part of it which consists of the Soil can only be
' inherited and held by any one to the extent of the limit
' prescribed by law.   If you see fit to devise more than
' this to any one person, he may select from your bequest,
' and any he may previously own, so much as the law
' allows him to retain, and sell the rest: or, if he does not
' do this within a year, the State will do it for him, holding
' the proceeds of the portion sold subject to his order.'

"That this will seem arbitrary and impracticable to
many is a matter of course, and the hardship of not allowing a man to *do as he likes with his own* will doubtless be
dilated on in tones of moving eloquence.   But the principle here involved has already been asserted in our Usury
Laws and many others which tend to fetter or check the
spirit of personal acquisition when it is found encroaching
upon the domain of public good.   A man may *not* 'do as
he likes with his own' money, nor even with his own house—
he is forbidden to burn the latter, though built with his own
hands, and entirely unconnected with any other.   Many, if
not most States already limit the area of land which may be
acquired and held by a Bank or Moneyed Corporation;
probably none allow Aliens freely to acquire and enjoy it.
Coeval with the great Hebrew Lawgiver and very thoroughly enforced by him, reäppearing in the noblest periods
of Roman republicanism, but gradually sapped and overthrown by an ever-grasping Aristocracy, the principle of
Land Limitation has received the approval of some of the
most gifted and philanthropic of ancient or modern times.
Its triumphant establishment, wherever Popular Education
and Universal Suffrage shall have preceded it, is well nigh
inevitable.

"A ready objection of those who have scarcely thought on the subject, imports that any attempt to remedy by law the inequalities of fortune in the matter of Land involves the principle of an arbitrary distribution of Property equally to everybody. But this is an egregious error. What Nature indicates and Justice requires is *Equal Opportunities* to all. To maintain that he who has idly frolicked through the summer, has an equal right to food and clothing in the winter with his frugal neighbor, who by patient toil has produced five hundred bushels of grain and some hundreds of pounds of flax and wool, is to contravene the Apostle's precept, 'He that will not work shall not eat.' But Land Limitation contemplates a gentle and gradual restoration of that equal right to the Soil which was ordained by the Creator in the constitution of the globe. Instead of giving to the idle the products of other men's labor, it is intended to countervail that dispensation of human policy whereby millions labor ceaselessly for scanty and bitter bread, while thousands revel sumptuously on the lion's share of the products of the toil so meagerly recompensed. Not to transfer the toiler's earnings to the idler, but to *prevent* such transfer, is the object of Land Reform.

"But if it be possible to resist the force of the considerations which dictate the enactment of laws, looking to a more equal apportionment of the Soil now private property, how *can* it be to oppose, with even plausibility, the application of the Land Reform principles to our vast and bounteous National Domain? Here we have a public patrimony equal to the habitable portion of Europe, and calculated to support in generous abundance a population of Two Hundred Millions of People. Under our present system, (the best the world has known since the overthrow of the Hebrew Commonwealth), this Domain is becoming private property at the rate of some Three to Five Millions of Acres per annum. Making a reasonable allowance for the steadily increasing demand, arising from the enlargement of our population and the swelling tide of immigration, we may safely calculate that in fifty years our Public Lands will have been diminished by at least Three Hundred Millions of their very choicest portion, namely, that bordering or approaching the navigable waters of the Mississippi, the Columbia, and their tributaries. The remainder must be far inferior in soil and natural advantages generally. What then will be the condition and prospects of the landless millions among our people, pressed upon by European competition and European immigration on the one side, and deprived in great measure of the present safety-valve of Western migration on the other? But look forward another half-century, and judge what will then be the state of 'the disinherited classes,' should no change be made meantime in our land-laws. Look to Saxony, to Belgium, to Ireland, for a parallel.

"National Reform is the broad and sure basis whereon all other Reforms may be safely erected. A single law of Congress, proffering to each landless citizen a patch of the Public Domain—small but sufficient, when faithfully cultivated, for the sustenance of his family, and forbidding further sales of the Public Lands except in limited quantities to actual settlers, with a suitable proviso against future aggregation, would promote immensely the independence, enlightenment, morality, industry, and comfort of our entire laboring population evermore. It would improve the condition of the Laboring Class in our cities, not by drawing away all to the new lands of the West, but by so enlarging the stream of emigration thither, as to diminish the pressure of competition in the Labor market throughout the country, and enable the hireling to make terms with his employer as to the duration of his daily toil and the amount of his recompense. It would render settlements more compact and continuous, insuring a more rapid establishment of Roads, of Schools, of Divine Worship, etc. It would enlarge immensely the demand for the products of our manufactories and workshops, and thus aid the laborers remaining in the Old States by increasing the demand for their labor as well as diminishing the competition to supply it. It would hardly be possible to exaggerate the ultimate benefits of the proposed Reform, and the day of its triumph should be hailed by the poor and lowly as the birthday of *their* Independence, as the Fourth of July is celebrated as that of the Nation."

Horace Greeley, in accordance with the "Fourth Demand" of the "New York Workingmen's Party," always agitated for "Homestead Exemption." Here is a brief essay of his written on that imperative measure, about 1845, with a due remembrance of his own family's experience in New Hampshire, when he was a boy :—

"The general policy of exempting certain necessaries of life from seizure and confiscation for debt no longer stands in need of vindication. The Roman barbarism of selling the debtor to satisfy the demand of his creditor and the more absurd and recent enormity of shutting him up in jail, to be an expense to the creditor and no benefit to himself nor anybody else, are now generally exploded. Instead of depriving the debtor of all chance to earn a livelihood, or to support his family, it is the wiser effort of our time to encourage him to work and earn by reserving of his property certain household articles of prime necessity and his implements of labor from the clutch of the sheriff. And I feel very sure that these exemptions, though sometimes

abused, have in the main operated justly and beneficently.
A man, hitherto, in easy circumstances is often rendered
bankrupt by misplaced confidence, by endorsing for friends,
by a commercial revulsion, or by a mistaken estimate of his
own resources, by a fire, a flood, or some other calamity.
Of course, as soon as it is known that he is unable to pay,
everybody insists on being paid, and his remaining property is sacrificed for less than half its worth, just when he
most needs that it should command its full value. The law,
as it has been, steps in, not to protect and comfort, but to
harass and skin him, until he finds himself not merely destitute of property, but of the ability to earn any. His
implements of labor, the shelter of his family, their bedding, clothes and cooking-ware, are dragged away and
sold for a song; and he has the pleasant prospect before
him of seeing anything that he may henceforth be able to
earn, carried off and sacrificed in like manner, without paying his debts or contributing sensibly toward that consummation. Law costs eat up pretty much all that such small
matters will fetch, and he is, if left out of prison, hardly
better off than if in it. Discouraged, despairing, avoided by
his sunshine friends, he is, in the expressive language of
the street, *ruined.* He sinks in stupid lethargy under the
crushing load weighing upon him, and becomes feeble,
heartless, inefficient—very often a dependent on the
grudged charity of kindred, an idler, a pauper, a drunkard.

"Public sentiment, enlightened by observation and
reflection, has outgrown this policy and subjected it to
many important modifications. Imprisonment for debt is
nearly extinct; liberal exemptions of implements of labor
and household furniture have been enacted in most States;
and now the question is fairly presented—'Shall a shelter
for wife and children, a piece of ground wherefrom to grow

their food, be added to the present list of exempted articles?'
To this question I most emphatically answer, 'Yes! Let
the bankrupt's wife and children have a shelter in spite of
his misfortunes.   Let him still have an assured opportunity
to labor on and produce from the soil now that his other
resources are cut off.   In our diseased and unstable social
condition, the banker of to-day may be the bankrupt of
to-morrow.   Let us all in prosperity remember the teachings
of adversity and be merciful.'

"Now, I know all that may be said, and have said a
part of it against the selfishness, the dishonesty, the gross
culpability, of a large proportion of the debtor class.   I
know that no man has a moral *right* to give entertainments,
to buy fine clothes and jewelry, to inhabit a costly house
and live sumptuously, while he is, or pretends to be, unable
to pay his honest debts.   Such a man is a swindler, no
matter though 'Hon.' is prefixed to his name or 'D. D.'
appended to it.   I will go as heartily and as far as any
man for punishing him *as* a swindler, but not for turning
his family into the street on a simple allegation of debt.
Indeed, it is one of my reasons for urging the further
prosecution of the Exemption policy that I wish to see
loose, idle livers deprived of the facilities they now enjoy
for running into debt.   Credit, credit everywhere—credit
to men of doubtful character or principles—credit for
articles that never should be bought except by those who
have the money to pay for them and more behind it—
credit absorbing half the movable capital of the country in
channels where it is least useful—such credit is among the
sorest evils of our time.   Credit should be given to the
upright, the frugal and the industrious only—to farmers
for farms, implements or stock ; to mechanics or artisans
for machinery or material ; to forwarders and exchangers

to enable them to purchase produce with cash and market it advantageously for all parties. But credit for silks, pianos and Brussels carpets—for wines, liquors and perfumes—this is about as common and as extensive as the right sort, and it is bad policy to encourage such by legislation. I did hope that a mortal blow had been struck at such credit by the National Bankrupt Law; but faction and folly destroyed that law just when its evils had been all encountered and its blessings were about to be experienced. I shall rejoice if the same end is reached, to a more limited extent, by Homestead Exemption.

"The soundness of the principle of Homestead Exemption is not generally questioned by the adversaries of the policy. They have a safer mode of warfare than that. No bill can be drawn so as to hit their several tastes—if the amount exempted is high enough for one, it is too high for another; and if you reduce it to the pattern of the latter, the former will vote against it as a mockery and worse than nothing. If a House passes a bill notwithstanding, the Senate will amend, or postpone, or fail to act upon it, and the measure fails. Yet already Wisconsin, Georgia, Texas, New York, and I believe some other States, have Homestead Exemption laws, and nobody even suggests their repeal. Those States would as soon think of going back to the cast-off atrocity of stripping a man of all he has and shutting him up in jail without trial on a mere allegation or suspicion of debt. A secure though humble home to every family is one of the generous aspirations of our age, and it will yet be established as one-of the cardinal principles of a Republican polity. It will prove a potent element of a true and genial Conservatism. The timorous people who used to declaim against the unsafety of a Government swayed by all manner of vagrants and

loafers, were not so very wrong as to the evil, though griev-
ously mistaken as to the remedy, which is to be found in
supplying these vagrants with Homes and not in depriving
them of Votes. A Republic in which every man shall feel
that he has interests to protect, rights to defend, must be
the strongest government on earth, and such will ours be
when every inhabitant shall have his own secure Home.
Now Homestead Exemption will not directly provide any
one with a freehold who is without it, but it will secure one
to each man or woman who has it, and thus strongly impel
every man to acquire one. The young man will naturally
say, 'If I work for and pay the price of a dwelling and
piece of land while I am single and can save, I may be
very sure that no misfortune in after-life can deprive me
of a home so long as I choose to retain it.' That the end
of this will be frugality in youth and independence in after-
life to thousands, who otherwise would stumble on to
maturity heedless and improvident, I cannot doubt. And,
in spite of distrust, timidity, indolence and avarice, the
good work will go on, until the enjoyment of Inviolable
Homes shall be commensurate with the existence of
Republican Freedom.''

Those farmers, who are now secure in their Homesteads
from legal Capitalistic sharks, have to thank the Pioneer
Socialists for it.

Horace Greeley, although insisting that temporary
alleviation should be rendered through soothing remedies
to the farmer, believed in perpetuating a continuously
normal state of vigorous health. This, he could see in
Socialism alone. On his return from Europe in 1851, after
studying agricultural conditions there, he said: ''If Universal Labor is ever to be constantly employed and fairly
rewarded, it must be through a more direct and intimate

relation of laborer with laborer; not through the system
of complexity, aggregation, and needless expense, wherein
the grain-grower of Illinois hires, through half a dozen
intermediates, his Iron made in Wales, and sends his grain
thither to pay for the work, instead of having it done at
the ore-bed in his township, with the coal which underlies
the whole County. I know how strong is the current
against this view of Labor's true interest, but the world
will refuse to be ruled by names and plausibilities forever."

He believed, as the Grangers, for instance, have ever
done, in getting rid of the middle-man, the agents and all
the other species of cormorants, who feed upon the farmer.
There would be no need then for Produce Exchanges
on the present gambling basis, with "Old Hutches," and
Armours, first cornering farm products themselves and
leading the way for the Trusts to gobble up all eventually.
Producer and Consumer would meet face to face, and deal
together, each helping the other, without the Capitalistic
intermediates and sweaters of all kinds,—who are altogether
unnecessary.

Greeley knew further, as as he says in one place, that
"Until some marked change shall have been wrought in
the general condition of our rural Industry, so as to render
it less repulsive than it now is, our cities must continue
over-crowded and full of misery. The naked truth that,
as a general rule, no one lives by *bona fide* physical labor
who can obtain a living without, and very few live by farming or the like who can live by what are esteemed the
lighter and more genteel avocations mainly pursued in
cities and villages, explains much of the misery so prevalent all around us. Doubtless, the Monopoly of Land
is one of the ultimate causes of this deplorable state of
things; thousands annually quitting the country for cities

who would cling to the homes of their infancy if they were
not the property of others, and would cultivate the soil like
their fathers if they had any soil to cultivate.   Having
none, they are tempted to seek in some city the employment and independence which seem denied them where
they were born.''

Industrial monopolies, he insisted, should make way
for a Universal Coöperative Civilization, as outlined in the
beneficent schemes of the various projects for Socio-Economic Reform.   He knew the success of the Shakers and the
Harmonists, who under the Community Socialistic system
are worth, to-day, millions upon millions of dollars, and
willingly he gave his time and put out his money to assist
similar undertakings.   Thus, according to Noyes's *History
of American Socialisms*, he wrote in 1845:—"As one
Associationist, who has given his efforts and means freely
to the cause, I feel that I have a right to speak frankly.
I know that the great number of our believers are far from
wealthy; yet I know that there is wealth enough in our
ranks, if it were but devoted to it, to give an instant and
resistless influence to the cause.   A few thousand dollars
subscribed to the stock of each existing Association would,
in most cases, extinguish the mortgages on its property,
provide it with machinery and materials, and render its
industry immediately productive and profitable.   Then
manufacturing invention and skill would fearlessly take up
their abode with our infant colonies; Labor and thrift would
flow thither, and a new and brighter era would dawn upon
them.   Fellow Associationists! I shall do whatever I can
for the promotion of the common cause; to it whatever I
have, or may hereafter acquire, of pecuniary ability is
devoted: may I not hope a like devotion from you?—
H. G.''

Greeley never regarded such sacrifices of his money as speculations. To him they were bona-fide investments of capital for the good of others, not of himself. He wished to teach practice by precept. Like Elder Frederick W. Evans he was aware that people had to be brought back to first principles and taught by past experiences, as well as by present experiments. It was in this spirit, the good old Shaker Elder informs us in his "Autobiography," that

"Moses was a land reformer. The Jews held land as do the people of Vineland, by allotment, each one having his little family homestead. The early Christians, being all Jews, easily went one step further, and held their land 'in common;' and thus did the Shakers, viewing them as a body politic complete in themselves. For all the principles of Materialistic Socialism were in practical operation,— their 'works;' where is possessed and enjoyed 'freedom of the public lands,' and of all lands, and 'land limitation,' and 'homesteads inalienable;' where is fully carried out 'abolition of slavery, both chattel and wages,' including poverty and riches; monopoly in all its forms, together with speculation, usury, and competition in business; where is abolished 'imprisonment for debt,' or for any other cause, for in this Community (or Nation) not only are there no 'laws for the collection of debts,' but debt itself (as must be the case in a perfect Community) is impossible; where 'Woman's Rights' are fully recognized, where equal suffrage for men and women, and equal participation in the government of an order founded by a woman, was an inevitable necessity."

Horace Greeley was a sanguine Socialist. He was always charged full with optimism. In May, 1843, he wrote and truthfully wrote :—

"The Doctrine of Association is spreading throughout

the country with a rapidity which we did not anticipate, and of which we had but little hope. We receive papers from nearly all parts of the Northern and Western States, and some from the South, containing articles upon Association, in which general views and outlines of the System are given. They speak of the subject as one 'which is calling public attention,' or 'about which so much is now said,' or, 'which is a good deal spoken of in this part of the country,' etc., showing that our Principles are becoming a topic of public discussion. From the rapid progress of our Doctrines during the past year, we look forward with hope to their rapid continued dissemination. We feel perfectly confident that never, in the history of the world, has a philosophical doctrine, or the plan of a Great Reform, spread with the rapidity with which the Doctrine of Association has spread in the United States, for the last year or two. There are now a large number of papers, and quite a number of lecturers in various parts of the country, who are lending their efforts to the cause, so that the onward movement must be greatly accelerated.

"Small Associations are springing up rapidly in various parts of the country. The Sylvania Association in Pike county, Pa., is now in operation; about seventy persons are on the domain, erecting buildings, etc., and preparing for the reception of other members.

"An Association has been organized in Jefferson county. Our friend, A. M. Watson, is at the head of it; he has been engaged for the last three years in spreading the principles in that part of the State, and the result is the formation of an Association. Several farmers have put in their farms and taken stock; by this means the Domain has been obtained. About three hundred persons, we are informed, are on the lands. They have a very fine quarry on their

Domain, and they intend, among the branches of Industry
which they will pursue, to take contracts for erecting buildings out of the Association. They are now erecting a
banking-house in Watertown, near which the Association
is located.

"Efforts are making in various parts of this State, in
Vermont, in Pennsylvania, Indiana, and Illinois, to establish
Associations, which will probably be successful in the course
of the present year. We have heard of these movements;
there may be others of which we are not informed."

But many of these Coöperative experiments died from
inanition, on account of the utter impracticability of the
men starting them, most of whom were Utopians, who
knowing nothing whatever of agriculture, wanted to be
farmers. Prof. Richard T. Ely, quoting Noyes's *History
of American Socialisms*, says there were eleven Communities
founded during the Owenite period, commencing about
1826; and thirty-four under the Fourierist revival between
1842–46; and adds:—

"It is safe to say that considerably over one hundred,
possibly two hundred, communistic villages have been
founded in the United States, although comparatively few
yet live. There are perhaps from seventy to eighty communities at present (1886) in the United States, with a
membership of from six to seven thousand, and property
the value of which may be roughly estimated at TWENTY-
FIVE or THIRTY MILLIONS OF DOLLARS."

John Humphrey Noyes, whose work was just referred to,
and who was a first cousin of Rutherford B. Hayes, once
President of the United States, wrote, in 1862:—"Horace
Greeley was Treasurer of the Sylvania Association, formed
in 1843, and signed a declaration of the manner in which it
proposed to reconstruct 'the present defective, vice-engen-

dering, and ruinous system of society, with the wasteful complication of its isolated households.' . . . . Having earnestly studied the system of Industrial Organization and Social Reform propounded by Charles Fourier, and been led to recognize in it a beneficent, expansive, and practical plan for the melioration of the condition of man and his moral and intellectual elevation, they most heartily adopted that system as the basis and guide of their operations. The Sylvania Association is the first attempt in North America to realize in practice the vast economies, intellectual advantages and social enjoyments resulting from Fourier's System.''

But Horace Greeley himself relates in his *Recollections*, under the caption of ''Socialistic Efforts,'' the economic history of the Sylvania Association and of the famous Brook Farm, to which a special chapter will be devoted in this volume, relative to ''Greeley's Fourierist Associates.'' He said :—

''Of the practical attempts to realize our Social Utopia, I believe that known as 'Brook Farm,' in Roxbury, Mass., ten miles from Boston, was first in the order of time, and notable in many other respects. Its projectors were cultivated, scholarly persons, who were profoundly dissatisfied with the aims, as well as the routine, of ordinary life, and who welcomed in Theoretic Socialism a fairer and nobler ideal. So they bought a cold, grassy farm of two hundred acres, added two or three new buildings to those which had served the last preceding owner, and bravely took possession. New members joined from time to time, as others left; the land was improved, and, I believe, some was added; boarders were taken occasionally; a school was started and maintained; and so the concern fared on through some five or six years. But, deficient in capital, in agricultural skill, and in many needful things besides, it was never a pecuniary success, and was finally given up about 1847 or '48,—paying its debts, I understood, to the last dime, but returning nothing to its stockholders. I believe this was the only attempt made in New England.

"From this city, two bands of Socialist Pioneers went forth,—one to a rugged, lofty region in Pike county, Pa., five miles from the Erie Railroad at the mouth of the Lackawaxen, which they called 'Sylvania,' after the State. The domain here purchased was ample,—some 2,300 acres; the location was healthy, and there was abundance of wood and water. But the soil was stony and poor; the altitude was such that there was a heavy frost on the 4th of July, 1844; the members were generally very poor, and in good part inefficient also; and the crops harvested were slender enough. I think 'Sylvania' was founded early in 1843, and gave up the ghost—having little else to give up—some time in 1845. Its domain returned to the seller or his assigns, in satisfaction of his mortgage, and its movables nearly or quite paid its debts, leaving its stock a total loss."

Of another enterprise, the North American Phalanx, founded in 1843 and wound up in 1850, Greeley says that it "had more vitality and a better location. The nucleus of its membership was formed at Albany, in the State of New York, though it drew associates from every quarter. Several of them were capable mechanics, traders and farmers. It was located at Shrewsbury, Monmouth county, in the State of New Jersey, on a farm of 673 acres, but the soil was altogether worn out."

"Here," Greeley wrote, "we few, but zealous Associationists of New York and its vicinity for a time concentrated our means and our efforts; each subscribing freely to the capital and then aiding the enterprise by loans to nearly an equal amount. I think the capital ultimately invested here (loans included) was fully $100,000, or about one-fourth the amount there should have been."

The North American Phalanx was well equipped, had a good farmhouse,—not one of the Phalansteries so gorgeously depicted by Fourier and Brisbane, by any means,— large orchards and a fruit house. Upon the last named being destroyed by fire, the Community disbanded. Greeley insisted that " there was no pecuniary failure, in the ordinary acceptation of the term. The property was sold out at auction,—the domain in tracts of ten to eighty acres,—and though it brought not more than two-thirds of its cash value, every debt was paid, and each stockholder received back about 65 per cent. of his investment with interest. I reckon that not many stockholders in gold mines or oil wells can show a better result."

These were the principal Agricultural Fourierist Phalanxes, but the idea was not limited to mere organization alone in America. Horace Greeley did a vast amount of educational work among his personal friends. As an evidence of this, the executor of his will, the philanthropist Charles Storrs, of Brooklyn, New York State, with his brother, Augustus Storrs, the Treasurer of Plymouth Church, founded and donated in perpetuity to the State of Connecticut, the Storrs Agricultural College, at Mansfield, the well-managed farm of which shows its students what careful skill and tillage will do for the fields of the "Nutmeg State." Nor have the results of Greeley's Economic Work, nor of the work of the school of thinkers to which he belonged, been limited to his own native New England. There has been successfully accomplished on the Pacific Slope within the past few years, a miniature republic. This is the Kaweah Community, from which Anarchists and

Free Lovers are rigorously excluded because it is based upon the Socialism of Greeley, "plus" modern principles and practice. And even into that practical Utopia the subsidized emissaries of the California Lumber Trust sneaked, using capitalistic scribblers, and even Congress and the troops of the United States, to destroy this attempt to realize on a small scale, the Coöperative Commonwealth.

We have shown in a previous chapter how Greeley's views on Socialistic Farming had very little changed in 1868, when he composed his *Social Creed*, given in the preceding pages of this work. Agriculturists can read with profit and instruction, relative to the exigencies of the present day, his lecture on the "Emancipation of Labor," which bears, particularly in parts, on man's connection with the soil. He shows therein, more strongly than in the passages already quoted, the dangers of Land Monopoly and Bonanza Farming, though the lecture was written half a century ago. But his advice was always given or opinion expressed with a regard solely to Socialistic development.

Horace Greeley never lost faith in Community Economics, and this is clearly shown by the following passage, written four years before his death and published in his *Recollections*: "The fact stares us in the face, that, while hundreds of banks and factories, and thousands of mercantile concerns managed by shrewd, strong men, have gone into bankruptcy and perished, Shaker Communities, established more than sixty years ago, upon a basis of little property and less worldly wisdom, are living and prosperous to-day. And their experience has been imitated by the German Communities at Economy, Pa., Zoar, Ohio, the Society of Ebenezer, etc., etc. Theory, however plausible, must respect the facts."

Some Socialists hold that the Grangers, who are purely

indigenous in origin, came into existence during the administration of President Grant, mainly through the teachings
of Horace Greeley and his associates on the New York
Tribune. And why not? From the very foundation
of the *Tribune* until after Greeley's death, forty years afterwards, he hardly ever failed in its columns when discussing
economic questions, to treat them from his own Socialistic
standpoint. Americans well know what the *Tribune* was to
the farmer. Hence, whatever the future may develop
through the acts of farmers' sons, the fundamental principles
upon which such acts will be based, will be such as were
inculcated by Horace Greeley.

The Patrons of Husbandry with their thirty thousand
Granges in the States and Territories of this Republic,
aggregating over 3,500,000 of members, inclusive of the
Farmers' Alliance, which first came into existence in the
State of Texas, stand firmly upon the platform of "the
education of the agricultural classes in the Science of Economic Government;" "the development of a better state
mentally, morally, socially and financially;" and the securing of "entire harmony and good will among all mankind
and brotherly love among ourselves." The rise of these
organizations may be in part due to the pressing needs of
the agricultural class in this age, but a good deal of the
inspiration must be certainly attributed to the propagandist
work of Horace Greeley.

Not long ago the author of these pages had a conversa-
tion on the subject of the farmers' new movement with
Professor Daniel De Leon, lately the occupant of a Chair
of Political Economy at Columbia College, and who, in the
Spring of 1891, visited the West and South, on a tour of
propaganda under instructions from the National Executive
Committee of the Socialist Labor Party of the United
States of America. He told the writer :—

"My tour extended through Northern Pennsylvania,
Ohio, Indiana and Illinois, Michigan, Wisconsin, Iowa,
Minnesota, and across in a straight line to the Pacific, down
through Washington, Oregon, and California, and back
again over Arizona, New Mexico, Colorado, Kansas,
Missouri, Southern Illinois, Indiana, Ohio, and Pennsyl-
vania, including the coke regions, and northward through
Maryland, Delaware and New Jersey.

"As to the Single Tax, there is none of it.   There are
some Capitalists' Free Trade Clubs, who talk a sort of
Single Tax, but don't amount to anything *quâ* Single
Taxers.   The only Workingmen's Single Tax Club I came
across was at Evansville, Ind.   They are K. of L., and
Socialists to a man.   Since I was there they dropped the
silly misnomer, have re-organized as a Socialist Section
and joined the Party.

"As to the Farmers' Alliance, to use the expression of
one of its members, all that the Socialists have to do is to
push their wagon up into the Alliance districts and they
will capture the whole movement.   The leaders in the
Alliance seem to be afraid, as yet, to speak boldly.   The
Cincinnati Platform does not express the opinion of the
rank and file ; and in so far as it does express it, it only
indicates some of the floating notions among them.   To
predict the exact outcome of the movement would be risky.
On the whole, I hail the movement.   To say the least, it
will remove political apathy—the greatest difficulty we
have had to contend against.

"As to the prospects of Socialism, my tour has satisfied
me that it is coming with rapid strides.   The rantings of
'plutogues' like Gen. Ordway can only do us good.
Socialism can no longer be condemned by name in
America.   Some of my friends think the ball will be set

rolling in Europe first. I believe, on the contrary, that America will lead in the establishment of the Social Democracy, the same as she led in the establishment of the Political Republic."

But whatever the criticisms "doctrinaire" Socialists may make, the whole trend of the present movement is altogether Socialistic.

It is high time for the people of the United States of America,—the Capitalist and Politician Classes especially,—to put on their thinking caps, when a large number of the representatives of Organized Labor of the cities meet in convention with the delegates of the Farmers' Alliances, Grangers, etc., and assert that :

"In view of the Great Social, Industrial, and Economical Revolution now dawning upon the civilized world, and the new and living issues confronting the American people, we believe that the time has arrived for a crystallization of the political reform forces of our country."

And more particularly when such men assert or demand the fulfillment of the doctrine of equal rights for all with privileges to none ; the passage of laws prohibiting the alien ownership of land ; a graduated income tax ; an eight hour legal day's work for all corporations ; "the most rigid, honest, and just National control and supervision of the means of public communication and transportation, and if this control and supervision does not remove the abuses now existing, we demand the Government ownership of such means of communication and transportation ;" and in addition thereto, sent for referendum vote to, and agitation among all Labor Organizations and Farmer Bodies represented, this resolution offered to the National Convention by a native American Nationalist, who represented the very acme of Native American Socialism ;

"RESOLVED. That when in the course of business consolidations in the form of Trusts or private syndicates it becomes evident that any branch of commerce is used for the behoof and profit of a few men at the expense of the general public, we believe that the people should assume charge of such commerce, through their National, State, or Municipal Administration."

CHAPTER VIII.

GREELEY'S SOCIALISTIC ASSOCIATES.

HORACE GREELEY was not alone in his crusade against the Competitive System, and therefore did not have single handed, as he vowed in his early manhood, to wage—

> " War on Fraud entrenched with Power,
> On smooth Pretense and specious Wrong."

He was neither infallible, nor a genius, in the real meaning of the word, and it would be utterly un-Socialistic to transform a plain blunt man into a demi-god, in connection with an Altruistic Movement, the members of which have always repudiated leaders. Greeley lived mentally on the one hand, on the inspirations of the founders of the American Republic, and of the truly great men of history ; and on the other, in association with many of rare intellectual gifts. Some of these have been already mentioned, such as Robert Owen, Albert Brisbane and Parke Godwin. There were others who developed out of the Brook Farm Socialists. Greeley hints at some of these in the extract quoted in the last chapter, but they and their confreres were something more than simply " cultivated, scholarly persons."

Ralph Waldo Emerson was the spiritual father of this coterie, which developed out of the Boston Symposium or Transcendental Club. The Club came into existence in the home of George Ripley, the counselor, guide and friend of the Brook Farm Socialists.

The Concord Philosopher tells the story of how Dr. William Ellery Channing "opened his mind to Mr. and Mrs. Ripley, and with some care they invited a limited party of ladies and gentlemen. I had the honor to be present. Though I recall the fact, I do not retain any instant consequence of this attempt, or any connection between it and the new zeal of the friends who at that time began to be drawn together by sympathy of studies and of aspiration. Margaret Fuller, George Ripley, Dr. Convers Francis, Theodore Parker, Dr. Hedge, Mr. Brownson, James Freeman Clarke, William H. Channing, and many others gradually drew together, and from time to time spent an afternoon at each others' houses in a serious conversation. . . . These fine conversations, of course, were incomprehensible to some in the company, and they had their revenge in their little jokes. One declared that 'it seemed to him like going to Heaven in a swing ;' another reported that, at a knotty point in the discourse, a sympathizing Englishman with a squeaking voice interrupted with the question, 'Mr. Alcott, a lady near me desires to inquire whether Omnipotence abnegates attribute?' . . . . Nothing more serious came of it than the modest quarterly journal called *The Dial*, which, under the editorship of Margaret Fuller, and later of some other (Emerson), enjoyed its obscurity for four years. All its papers were unpaid contributions, and it was rather a work of friendship among the narrow circle of students, than the organ of any party. Perhaps its writers were its chief readers ; yet it contained some noble papers by Margaret Fuller, and some numbers had an instant exhausting sale, because of papers by Theodore Parker."

The Brook Farm Socialistic Community evoluted, in the Spring of 1841, directly, as stated, from the Sympo-

sium, through Albert Brisbane, who had already converted
Horace Greeley, finding the Transcendental Club a good
field for missionary work. Brisbane managed to make
a considerable number of proselytes, and George Ripley
fulfilled the dream long entertained, and suggested to him,
by Dr. Channing, of "an Association in which the members instead of preying on one another and seeking to put
one another down, after the fashion of this world, should live
together as brothers, seeking one another's elevation and
spiritual growth." "The Brook Farm Institute of Agriculture and Education," as this proposed association was
baptized, duly came into existence. We have, in the
previous chapter, given Horace Greeley's brief account of
its economic history. Almost every member of the *Tribune*
editorial staff, during its first decade of existence, graduated from Brook Farm ; and all were out and out Socialists,
at least so far as the Progressive Movement had then entered
into practical action that could be seen and heard of men.

Ralph Waldo Emerson never personally belonged to
this Fourierist Community, but what he thought of its
Social Philosophy has been already narrated. He is as
yet the only historian of the Brook Farm experiment
worth the name, and what he had to record was told
in some six pages. He summed it up as "a noble and
generous movement in the projectors to try an experiment of better living. They had the feeling that our
ways of living were too conventional and expensive, not
allowing each to do what he had a talent for, and not
permitting men to combine cultivation of mind and heart
with a reasonable amount of daily labor. At the same
time, it was an attempt to lift others with themselves, and
to share the advantages they should attain with others
now deprived of them." In another place, Emerson calls

Brook Farm "a perpetual picnic, a French Revolution in small, an 'Age of Reason' in a patty-pan."

But this Socialist Community is generally known throughout the civilized world, on account of the *Blithedale Romance* of Nathaniel Hawthorne, the greatest of American novelists, whose *Scarlet Letter* places him in the front rank of the world's writers of fiction,—with Hugo, Thackeray and Cervantes. Yet Emerson has raised his protest against Hawthorne's sketches of Brook Farm, which he thought were done "not happily," and were "quite unworthy of his genius." Hawthorne had, however, already met this possible objection, himself, in the preface to his volume, where he states :

"In the 'Blithedale' of this volume many readers will probably suspect a faint and not very faithful shadowing of Brook Farm, in Roxbury, which (now a little more than ten years ago) was occupied and cultivated by a company of Socialists. . . . He begs it to be understood, however, that he has considered the institution itself as not less fairly the subject of fictitious handling, than the imaginary persons he has introduced there. His whole treatment of the affair is altogether incidental to the main purpose of the romance ; nor does he put forward the slightest pretensions to illustrate a theory, or elicit a conclusion, favorable, or otherwise, in respect to Socialism. In short, his present concern with the Socialistic Community is merely to establish a theater a little removed from the highway of ordinary travel, where the creatures of his brain may play their phantasmagorical antics without exposing them to too close a comparison with the actual events of real lives."

Hawthorne speaks in the same preface, of the "good fortune" he had, in being "personally connected" with Brook Farm, and styled it "his old affectionately remembered home," which was "the most romantic episode of his own life,—essentially a day dream and yet a fact." Those who desire to know how Hawthorne skillfully interwove Fourierism into that novel must read it for themselves, as well as the introduction to recent editions, by his son-in-law George Parsons Lathrop, as well as the fifth chapter of *A Study of Hawthorne.*

Nathaniel Hawthorne, as if to reiterate his strong objection to being considered the historian of Brook Farm, further says in his preface, dated "Concord, Mass., May, 1852:" to the *Blithedale Romance*:—"The author cannot close his reference to this subject without expressing a most earnest wish that some one of the many cultivated and philosophic minds, which took an interest in that enterprise, might now give the world its history. Ripley, with whom rests the honorable paternity of the institution, Dana, Dwight, Channing, Burton, Parker, for instance,—with others whom he dares not name, because they veil themselves from the public eye,—among these is the ability to convey both the outward narrative and the inner truth and spirit of the whole affair, together with the lessons which those years of thought and toil must have elaborated, for the behoof of future experimentalists. Even the brilliant Howadji (Curtis) might find as rich a theme in his youthful reminiscences of Brook Farm, and a more novel one,—close at hand as it lies,—than those which he has since made so distant a pilgrimage to seek, in Syria and along the current of the Nile."

The author of the *Marble Faun* really thought Brook Farm and its intellectual dissipation all very prosaic; yet he was a good Socialist, accepting in full along with his fellow laborers there, the same basic principles and pursuing the same great objects, as do now the followers of the

practical or rather the political side of the Progressive
Movement of America and Europe, as enunciated by
Edward Bellamy, Lawrence Gronlund, Karl Marx, Ferdinand Lassalle and the rest of their brother reformers.
But Hawthorne put his time into the Brook Farm experiment, working sixteen hours a day at agriculture.   He
also added to the Common Fund the whole of his savings,
which had amounted to one thousand dollars. Yet after all,
like Miles Coverdale, "he was a spectator, not a partici-
pant."   His after life and his personal association at Concord with Ellery Channing the poet, Emerson and Thoreau,
are matters appertaining to, and a part of the literary
history of this country.

George Ripley was the founder of the Brook Farm
Community, as already stated, and he regarded it as a
practical continuation of his own work as a minister of the
Gospel, its fundamental thought being the carrying out
literally, of Christ's words recorded in the New Testament,
relative to the economic life of man.   Fourierist Socialism
meant to Ripley's followers :—

"The freedom from care, the spontaneousness of labor,
the absence of all toil and anxiety, the sense of equality
in condition and the abolition of all class distinctions
(which) made work a delight.   There was exhilaration, joy,
gayety. Wealth was nothing ; fame was nothing ; natural
development was all."

Ripley was the "deus ex machinâ" of Brook Farm
and was "over, in, and through the whole," teaching
"intellectual and moral philosophy and mathematics." He
"admonished, wrote letters, milked cows, drove oxen,
talked, lent a cheerful temper to every part of the arrangement, animated the various groups, and sent his ringing
laugh to all quarters of the institution."   He is best known

in connection with Charles A. Dana in conjunction with *Appleton's Encyclopedia,* which they projected and edited. But Ripley's greatest work until the end of his well-spent life, work which helped to elevate the intellectual standard, taste and sentiments of the people of the United States, was due to his position, which he occupied from 1849, as literary editor of the *Tribune.*

In mentioning this distinguished literateur, it is well to note here that Horace Greeley induced, as far as he could, the staff and employés of the *Tribune* to become actual partners in the *Tribune* Association. The idea was suggested in no friendly spirit by the New York *Express*: "If the editor of the *Tribune* believed a word of what he says, he would convert his profitable printing establishment into a Fourier common-stock concern." And he and his partner Thomas McElrath, who like Greeley, accepted Fourierism, did. But before doing so, however, and making the *Tribune* property into a Coöperative concern, its editor publicly said in its columns: "As to 'carrying out his theories of Fourierism,' etc., he (the editor of the *Tribune*) has expended for this specific purpose some thousands of dollars, and intends to make the same disposition of more as soon as he has it to expend. Whether he ought to be guided by his own judgment or that of the *Express* man respecting the time and manner of thus testifying his faith, he will consider, in due season. He has never had a dollar which was not the fair product of his own downright labor, and for whatever of worldly wealth may accrue to him, beyond the needs of those dependent on his efforts, he holds himself but the steward of a kind Providence, and bound to use it all, as shall seem most conducive to the good of the Human Race. It is quite probable, however, that he will never satisfy the *Express* that he is either honest, sincere, or well-meaning, but that is not material. He has chosen, once for all, to answer a sort of attack which has become fashionable with a certain class of his enemies, and can hardly be driven to notice the like again.''

A nephew of the great Dr. Channing, William Henry Channing, who as an orator was never surpassed in this country, was another of the Brook Farm Socialists. This eminent man, who "created a new era in American oratory,'' absolutely accepted Socialism as a cure for all human evils, editing his magazine *The Present*, in the interest of that philosophy. Of him Ralph Waldo Emerson wrote in 1883: "Rev. William Henry Channing, now of London, was from the first a student of Socialism in France and England, and in perfect sympathy with this experiment.'' Channing died abroad in 1884. His son is a member of the British House of Commons, and his daughter was the wife of Sir Edwin Arnold, the author of *The Light of Asia*, who seems to have, through this association, had imparted to him in that wondrous Buddhistic poem, some of the Transcendentalism of his father-in-law. And here comes in a strange coincidence. The English and American Theosophists, who accept considerable of the teachings of the "Buddha of Buddhas,'' are many of them Socialists. Colonel Henry S. Olcott was once agricultural editor of the *Tribune*. Annie Besant is both a leading Theosophist and a Socialist. In New York city we discovered the same thing, when Nationalism, that indigenous form of American Socialism, found a resting place on Manhattan Island. Almost the first to join it, were some of the officers of the American Theosophical Society, who also accepted office in the Nationalist organization, among them being John W. Lovell, the publisher, and General Abner Doubleday, the hero of Antietam and Gettysburg, who fired the first gun on the northern side in the Civil War. There were also a stray millionaire or two, who equally believed in *The Light of Asia* and in Socialism. And why should not a millionaire be a Socialist, when we remember that Courtlandt Palmer, the idealistic Positivist, announced himself one, over and over again, from the rostrum?

But the highest form of religious enthusiasm in the Christian sense, was to be found among the Brook Farmers. If, on the one hand, the Unitarian orator and author, Theodore Parker, was among the Socialist brothers, there was also Isaac Thomas Hecker, who, some years after leaving Brook Farm, became a Roman Catholic, was ordained a priest by Cardinal Wiseman, joined the Redemptorist Fathers, and later, with the sanction of Pope Pius the Ninth, founded the Monastic Missionary Order of St. Paul the Apostle, which had much of the Socialism in it, that Hecker learned in the Consociate Family at Fruitlands, with which were connected Henry D. Thoreau and Amos Bronson Alcott.

Theodore Parker, Emerson says, "was our Savonarola, an excellent scholar, in frank and affectionate communication with the best minds of his day, yet the tribune of the people, and the stout reformer to urge and defend every cause of Humanity with and for the humblest of mankind." Theodore Parker, who was buried in the Protestant Cemetery at Rome, near the last remains of Shelley and Keats, we are informed "met at Brook Farm, which lay close to him at West Roxbury, the finest, most cultivated, and most ardent intellects of the day; he had made the acquaintance of delightful people; he had studied and talked a great deal; he had been brought face to face with practical problems of Society."

And if there be one thing for which Theodore Parker

will ever remain in the memory of humanitarian Americans, it will be the noble work he did in the Abolition Movement, side by side with William Lloyd Garrison and Wendell Phillips, even at one time being tried "for the misdemeanor of a speech in Faneuil Hall against kidnapping" negro slaves.

George Ripley had as his predecessor in the literary editorship of the *Tribune*, the celebrated Margaret Fuller, Countess D'Ossoli, who fills a large place in American literary history in connection with Emerson, Greeley and the other choice spirits, who either were members of the Brook Farm Community, or temporary residents there, in which latter category she must be placed. Outside of her position in the belles-lettres of the United States, she has had achieved for her by the genius of Nathaniel Hawthorne, an international reputation, owing to the fact of her having been supposed to be the "Zenobia Fauntleroy" of the *Blithedale Romance*. George Parsons Lathrop, editor of Hawthorne's complete works, says :—

"Zenobia, the other daughter, who holds so important a place in the romance, it has been thought was suggested by Margaret Fuller, or by a lady who was actually domiciled at Brook Farm while Hawthorne was staying there. Both these theories are doubtless incorrect, so far as they assume that Hawthorne consciously drew from either of the persons in question. Margaret Fuller was not a member of the Community at all, any more than was Ralph Waldo Emerson, who, in popular estimation has been identified with it."

Margaret Fuller has already been referred to in a passage from Emerson, who also says, speaking of her supposed identity with Hawthorne's Zenobia, that "no friend who knew Margaret Fuller could recognize her rich and brilliant genius under the dismal mask which the public fancied was meant for her in that disagreeable story." Her life and tragic death at sea, with her husband and child, off the coast of New Jersey on her return home from Europe, have been fully described in separate volumes devoted to her, which should be read in conjunction with the chapters on her, in James Parton's *Life of Horace Greeley* and Greeley's own autobiographical *Recollections.*

George William Curtis was one of the prominent Brook Farm Socialists who has achieved a foremost place in American annals as a brilliant author, editor and orator. Emerson says : "George W. Curtis, of New York, and his brother, of English Oxford, were members of the family from the first." Curtis was chosen by Horace Greeley as a member of his editorial staff in 1850, and his famous papers on "Lotus Eating" originally appeared in the *Tribune.* It is needless to specify here all his other works, and "all the world and his wife" almost personally know George W. Curtis through the "Editor's Easy Chair" in *Harper's New Monthly Magazine.*

Horace Greeley selected the best managing editor the *Tribune* ever had, from among the Brook Farm Socialists. This was Charles Anderson Dana, the present editor of the New York *Sun.* It has been asserted in Appleton's *Cyclopædia of American Biography*, upon the authority of one of the survivors of the Brook Farm Community, that Dana was the "only man of affairs connected with that Unitarian, Humanitarian and Socialistic experiment." While there, it was not unusual for Dana to drive in from West Roxbury to Boston, eight miles, with the big market cart containing that portion of the vegetable produce of the Community which was disposed of at Faneuil Hall Market. Old friends of his remember his keen chaffering and dickering there over the potatoes, carrots, turnips, etc., and his general appearance, which was decidedly rural with his "billy-cock" hat, fustian coat and high boots into which were tucked his trousers.

Charles A. Dana, before joining the *Tribune* in 1847, was on the staff of the *Chronotype*, a paper advocating Social Reforms, edited by Elizur Wright. He won his editorial spurs, however, at Brook Farm while editing the community organ, the *Harbinger*. The following is a contemporary advertisement of that Socialistic newspaper while Dana was editor, after the disbandment of Brook Farm :—

"The *Harbinger*. A Weekly Newspaper, Devoted to the Principles of Associative Science.

"The *Harbinger* is the advocate of a Social Reform, which shall embrace, reconcile, and do justice to the various interests that are essential to the true life of Humanity— which, in maintaining the rights of Labor, shall not overlook the legitimate claims of Capital—which seeks to combine the elevation of the working classes, by the introduction of a natural, efficient and attractive system of industry, with the widest developments of Art and universal, spiritual culture—and which shall destroy the fruitful sources of antagonism, oppression and inhumanity that now exist in the relations of men, by the establishment of such organic arrangements as will necessarily produce a comprehensive and harmonious unity.

"The *Harbinger* will discuss all questions relating to the progress of society, the past history of the race, the present aspects of civilization, the great humanitary reforms of the day, and the political movements of Europe and America, in the light of Associative Science ; but with a sincere and fraternal recognition of all elements of truth, goodness and beauty, in whatever institution or doctrine it may be called on to consider.

"Terms. Invariably in advance. For one year, $2.00; For six months, $1.00; Six copies for one year to the same address, $10.00; Ten copies for one year to the same address, $15.00.

"☞ Address all communications, and all subscriptions and letters on business, to '*The Editor of the Harbinger*, 9 Spruce Street, New York.'"

Dana was on the *Tribune* for fifteen years, and when the Civil War broke out he was suggested by President Abraham Lincoln, and Secretary of State William H. Seward, as the Assistant Secretary of War to Edwin M. Stanton, which position he occupied with honor to himself and chief. It is also not uninteresting to know that Arthur Brisbane, the New York *Sun's* former European correspondent, and the son of Horace Greeley's Socialistic mentor, was once the editor-in-chief of the New York Evening *Sun*.

That Charles A. Dana has had a strong mental influence over his associates on the New York *Sun*, which he re-organized in 1867, is shown by the position taken by one of his editors, in the Labor Movement,—"Brave and Noble" John Swinton, who once was the candidate of the Socialist Labor Party for the Mayoralty of the city of New York. John Swinton is a Socialist now, as Charles A. Dana was formerly, and a year or two ago made this declaration:—

"The greater part of the work of the world is now done, not in the old fashion of handicraft, but by machinery, through which new industrial forces have been let loose upon mankind. The working people must find some means of dealing with these transforming and revolutionary forces. I hold that they must become the possessors and control-

ers of these new forces which they have brought into play ;
and that the time must come to an end in which they are
to be of advantage mainly to a capitalist class."

John Sullivan Dwight was also a Brook Farm Socialist
and lived there five years teaching Latin, Greek, German
and Music, "at the same time farming, cutting wood,
cultivating trees and other industries." He assisted Dana
in the editorship of the *Harbinger*, and Emerson on the
Dial, but made his great reputation later as a musical critic
through the columns of the *Tribune*, as did another journalist who occupied the same position. This was William
Henry Fry, the composer of the American opera of
"Leonora."

Warren Burton, a well known Massachusetts clergyman and author, but a native of New Hampshire, was also
at Brook Farm. In later life he figured somewhat in New
England as the advocate of "true culture for all," through
the proposed raising of the condition of the public schools.

We have the record of a nobleman as one of the Brook
Farm Socialists. Emerson says: "An English baronet,
Sir John Caldwell, was a frequent visitor, and more or less
directly interested in the leaders and their success." There
is no question about his title, as he is duly recorded in
Burke's *Peerage and Baronetage* as "Sir Henry John
Caldwell, Sixth Baronet, of Castle Caldwell, county Fer-
managh, Ireland, and Count of Milan, in the Holy Roman
Empire." There was nothing of the revolutionary Prince
Kropotkin about him, any more than there was of the
bogus Lord Gordon, whom Jay Gould utilized to decoy
Americans into his Erie Railroad schemes ; much less was
he an alleged French Marquis with a cockney accent, on
the hunt for rich widows ; or an Italian Baron who gradu-
ated from a Parisian barber-shop before developing into a
Delmonico waiter and marrying a Murray Hill heiress.

Those we have named, were the principal Brook Farm Socialists and of them Emerson says :—

"The founders of Brook Farm should have this praise : that they made what all people try to make, an agreeable place to live in. All comers, even the most fastidious, found it the pleasantest of residences. It is certain that freedom from household routine, variety of character and talent, variety of work, variety of means, of thought and instruction, art, music, poetry, reading, masquerade, did not permit sluggishness or despondency ; broke up routine. There is agreement in the testimony that it was, to most of the associates, education ; to many, the most important period of their life, the birth of valued friendships, their first acquaintance with the riches of conversation, their training in behavior."

And Charles A. Dana, in the *Harbinger*, extended this eulogium of the charms of Brook Farm in these words :—

"The life which we now lead, though to a superficial observer surrounded with so many imperfections and embarrassments, is far superior to what we were ever able to attain in common society. There is a freedom from the frivolities of fashion, from arbitrary restrictions, and from the frenzy of competition. . . . There is a greater variety of employments, a more constant demand for the exertion of all the faculties, and a more exquisite pleasure in effort, from the consciousness that we are laboring, not for personal ends, but for a Holy Principle ; and even the external sacrifices which the Pioneers in every enterprise are obliged to make, are not without a certain romantic charm, which effectually prevents us from envying the luxuries of Egypt, though we should be blessed with neither the manna nor the quails, which once cheered a table in the desert."

But they were *bona fide* American Socialists all the same, as were also the members of the Community at Fruitlands, near Harvard, Worcester county, Massachusetts, of which Father Hecker was a member. The founders of the "Consociate Family," as it was designated, were Amos Bronson Alcott and two Englishmen, Charles Lane and H. G. Wright. This Community derives much of its interest from the tact that Louisa May Alcott, the author of *Little Women* and other volumes of great social value, was brought up there and had as her teacher Henry David Thoreau, the hermit naturalist, who was for a time a member of her father's Socialist fraternity.

Nathaniel Hawthorne and Ralph Waldo Emerson were two of Thoreau's greatest friends, and Emerson thus analyzes him : "Since the foxes and the birds have the right of it with a warm hole to keep out the weather, and no more, a pent-house to fend the sun and rain is the house which lays no tax on the owner's time and thoughts, and which he can leave, when the sun is warm, and defy the robber. This was Thoreau's doctrine, who said that the Fourierists had a sense of duty which led them to devote themselves to their second-best. And Thoreau gave in flesh and blood and pertinacious Saxon belief the purest ethics. He was more real and practically believing in them than any of his company, and fortified you at all times with an affirmative experience which refused to be set aside. Thoreau was in his own person a practical answer, almost a refutation, to the theories of the Socialists. He required no phalanx, no government, no society, almost no memory. He lived extempore from hour to hour, like the birds and the angels ; brought every day a new proposition, as revolutionary as that of yesterday, but different : the only man of leisure in his town ; and his independence made all others look like slaves."

Horace Greeley always considered Thoreau too much of an Individualist and objected to his "defiant Pantheism." Thoreau carried his hatred of human slavery so far as to refuse to pay taxes to a government that sustained it, and was consequently imprisoned for his obstinacy upon one occasion. Emerson made the oration at Thoreau's funeral, saying among other things: "His soul was made for the noblest society; he had in a short life exhausted the capabilities of this world; wherever there is beauty, he will find a home."

There were other Fourierist Socialists on the staff of the *Tribune.* Among these was Ellery Channing the poet, who married Margaret Fuller's sister. Then there was Robert Carter who was the *Tribune's* Washington correspondent, and a devoted Free Soil Abolitionist, who edited with James Russell Lowell, the *Pioneer,* before the poet made his reputation with the *Biglow Papers.*

One of the most interesting of Horace Greeley's staff was Count Adam Gurowski, the Russian Slavophile, who had suffered in prison, in his native land, for his revolutionary doctrines, and being a Fourierite, found a natural home on the *Tribune.*

Many others were there, who graduated from the side of Horace Greeley, taking with them the inspirations which actuated the life of their former chief. Some of these are editors of national reputation, and represent that power referred to by Carlyle in *Sartor Resartus* when he said: "The Journalists are now the true kings and clergy: henceforth historians, unless they are fools, must write not of Bourbon Dynasties, and Tudors, and Hapsburgs; but of stamped, broadsheet dynasties, and quite new successive names, according as this or the other able editor, or combination of able editors, gains the world's ear."

Horace Greeley's memory and life-work are, however, kept fresher among New York working journalists,—like the reporters who founded the Horace Greeley Labor Club of the Knights of Labor, many of whom were strong Socialists,—than among those whom he especially selected long years ago, as members of his editorial staff, because they were Fourierites, but some of whom, have through the achievement of wealth and other causes repudiated their former views. Of such as these the founder of the *Tribune*, in 1867, wrote :—

"It is a lamentable spectacle to see men whose best days of manly maturity and mental power were devoted to the cause of freedom departing from consistency in their old days, to the disheartening of those upon whom the better example of their early life might exert an inspiriting influence. These painful aberrations cannot be explained on the ground, that age has a tendency to chill enthusiasm for freedom, for we have many examples to the contrary. Must we look for the explanation of them in some natural defect of character, developed by circumstances?"

CHAPTER IX.

GREELEY'S INDUSTRIAL SOCIALISM.

THE founder of the New York *Tribune* never forgot that he had once been a journeyman printer and belonged to the ranks of the working people. This is a marked characteristic of all his speeches, lectures and writings. His continuous endeavor was to raise his former proletarian associates, through the means of Socialistic Coöperation, to the position of being their own masters and employers.

We have seen, by the aid of his own narration, what his own condition was, as a journeyman printer, while tramping from town to town, fruitlessly hunting from job office to newspaper office, and back again, in search of work. He knew that these conditions had always been chronic for wage earners, not only in his own craft, but in almost every other field of industrial activity.

Horace Greeley could look back fully fifty years, that is from 1831 when he arrived in New York city, to the period of the American Revolution, and there was always the same state of affairs,—long hours, small wages and an army of unemployed, occasionally employed by Capitalism, to keep up a state of competition for work between the wages slaves. Yet, bad as things were for the American Proletariat, they were not sufficiently oppressive and degrading, in the opinion of wealthy men of the type of John Jay, who was Governor of the State of New York

before he was Chief Justice of the United States. We find
this landlord aristocrat, who was one of the authors of the
Federalist, the gospel of American Republicanism, grumbling in 1784 that "the wages of mechanics and laborers are
very extravagant."

Let us see what the very extravagant hire and condition
of these wages slaves after the Revolution were—the period
which frothy orators of the politician and bourgeois classes
depict as a very "golden age," and we can perhaps then
understand how, crushed down as they were, they did not
care for political rights, any more than their descendants
seem to care now. It is well to note also the condition of
"free labor" with "freedom of contract" over a century
ago, as all our present low wage and long hour labor
difficulties are attributed to recent foreign immigration or
"disaffected agitators" from Europe, who have settled
down in this happy Paradise of ours, and have described
it as Sheol itself,—just as Horace Greeley, Parke Godwin,
Albert Brisbane and the Fourierist Socialists did half a
century ago.

In 1784 there were in the State of New York not only
wages-slaves, but chattel-slaves—negroes, just as there were
in the Southern States, but not in such large numbers.
The Declaration of Independence and the Constitution were
to the last-named a mere jest, until 1827, when the colored
chattel-slaves were emancipated in the State of New York.
Though the dark-skinned brethren were "created free and
equal," yet the law denied to them those "certain inalienable rights" of "life, liberty and the pursuit of happiness."
Yet some writers have insinuated that these chattel-slaves
from "Afric's burning sands," were better off in 1784 than
the white wages slaves in New York city, for the reason that
a planter, or any other owner, was bound to keep his chattel

in health and strength, otherwise there would be a depreciation of so much per pound of working capital, when it
might, perchance, be necessary to bring it to the slave
mart.

Unskilled laborers, at the end of the 18th century and
commencement of the 19th, were generally hired by the
day, and in cities they boarded and lodged themselves. On
farms, laborers were fed and lodged and given a few dollars
a week. The hours of work were usually from sunrise to
sunset, both in Summer and Winter. It is asserted that in
Pennsylvania canal diggers ate the coarsest diet and were
housed in the rudest sheds. They received $6 a month
from May to November, and $5 a month from November
to May. They were given lodging, but had to supply
their own blankets. Hod-carriers, mortar-mixers, diggers
and choppers, who labored on public buildings and cut the
streets and avenues of Washington, were paid $70 a year,
or $60 for all the work they could do from March 1 to
December 20. Wages at New York city and at Albany,—
and it must be remembered there was only one city in the
United States in 1790 with over 40,000 inhabitants,—were
$3 a week, or 40 cents a day; at Lancaster, $8 to $10 a
month; in Pennsylvania, workmen got $6 a month in
Summer and $5 in Winter; and at Fredericksburg, $5 to $7
a month.

Virginia working people received about £16, in currency
a year, and slaves when hired out, realized to their masters
about £1 a month. The average rate of wages in the
whole United States was $65 a year, with food and perhaps
lodging,—and out of this an operative had to keep his
wife and family, if he were so unfortunate as to have them.

Type setters were about the best paid wage earners, as
they received 25 cents a thousand ems, or an average of

about $8 a week. They were organized, too, on Manhattan Island in 1817, for then, Peter Force was their President and the old political lobbyist, Thurlow Weed, was a member. Weed states in his *Autobiography* that he aided in incorporating them in 1818. He writes: "I remember with what deference I then ventured into the presence of distinguished members of the legislature, and how sharply I was rebuked by the two gentlemen, who were quite shocked at the idea of incorporating journeymen mechanics."

And similar ideas were entertained by nearly all other lawmakers of the period; all of their statutory enactments were in the interest of their own classes, the large capitalists and bourgeoisie of the period. Hence, to-day, the existence of Labor Conspiracy Laws on our Statute Books and the presence of the old English Common Law of the British colonial period in our law courts, and quoted in nearly every decision or summing up of our Judges.

This position is defined more specifically in one of the Declarations of the Trades Unions and Local Assemblies of the State of New York meeting in State Convention at Troy, on September 17th and 18th, 1888, to devise ways and means for securing the repeal or modification of the Industrial Conspiracy Laws :—

"We insist that a direct descent can be traced from the edicts of the Roman Emperors to the Penal Code of the State of New York. Laws of Nero and Vespasian were codified into the *Institutes* of Justinian, which is still a common law text-book ; thence, after members of the Craft Guilds were burned alive for conspiring in trades' unions on the continent of Europe, they found their way into the English Common Law under the Plantagenet, Tudor, Stuart and Guelph monarchs, and thence became embodied in the

Colonial laws of New York, upon the Dutch making way
for the British in the seventeenth century. The English
Common Law and Statutes were transplanted to this colony,
including the Conspiracy and Combination Laws. The
framers of the Constitution of the State of New York after
the Revolution, although conceding political and religious
liberties, did not change the Statutes concerning the industrial masses. This is the reason that when David Dudley
Field codified the Statutes of this State, he incorporated the
spirit and substance of the Mediæval Conspiracy Laws.

"Among these laws was one which is still quoted in our
law courts and which was passed nearly 250 years ago, in
the reign of Edward VI, and was directed against the 'Con-
federacies of Artificers, Handicraftsmen and Laborers,' also
a law of the reign of George I., in which the combinations
of workingmen were prohibited. Our judges on every
occasion, as well as the State prosecuting officers, quote
and make rulings upon precedents which have been made
in the English Courts since the American Revolution and in
the reigns of George III. and George IV. Our judges
still quote the decision of the British Colonial Judiciary in
1741, when some New York bakers were tried for alleged
Conspiracy."

Here is a decision of just 150 years ago and thirty-five
years before the Declaration of Independence was signed,
and yet in 1836 in the Court of Oyer and Terminer in New
York city, in the case of twenty-one journeymen tailors,
tried and convicted for striking for higher wages, Judge
Edwards said:—

"Let these societies only arise from time to time, and
they will at last extend to every trade in the city, and there
will be as many governments as there are societies. Combinations were not necessary in this country for the protec-

tion of mechanics or any other class.   They were of foreign
origin, not in harmony with our institutions or the character
of the people.''

Notwithstanding this dictum we find, as shown, that in
1741, native born American journeymen bakers combined in
a strike "not to bake bread but on certain terms," and
were indicted and tried as criminals for this heinous offense.
Also that in the years 1796, 1798, 1799, 1805 and 1815,
there were five different strikes of native born American
journeymen shoemakers in Philadelphia, of which the three
first were successful and the two latter resulted in conspiracy trials and the conviction of members of the union.   In
1809 New York city saw a general strike of all the shoemakers.   Ship carpenters and caulkers struck over and over
again between 1817 and 1830; tailors in 1827, some of
whom were tried for conspiracy ; and printers at Albany,
N. Y., in 1821, because, as they put it, there was employed
in one of the printing offices a "rat."

About the year 1802 also occurred the famous strike of
the New York sailors, who had been receiving $10 a
month, but were so ungrateful as to demand $14 instead
from their masters.   We are informed that they formed in
a body, marched around the city, and compelled other
seamen who were employed at the old rates to leave their
ships and join the strike.   But, as McMaster narrates,
"the constables were soon in pursuit, arrested the leader,
lodged him in jail, and so ended (one of) the earliest of
labor strikes.''

Horace Greeley knew that strikes were quite unnecessary, for the working people had it in their own hands to
get rid forever of their causes by combining together on a
Socio-Economic basis—as he pointed out half a century
ago, in the following brief essay on "Strikes and their
Remedy :"—

"The recent Strikes for Wages in different parts of the country, but especially those of the Iron-Puddlers of Pittsburgh, suggest grave and yet hopeful thoughts. In reading the proceedings of the Strikers, an observer's attention will be arrested by their emphatic though unconscious condemnation of our entire Social framework as defective and unjust. Probably half of these men never harbored the idea of a Social Reconstruction—never even heard of it. Ask them one by one if such an idea could be made to work, and they would shake their heads and say, 'It is all well in theory, but it will never do in practice.' But when they come to differ with their employers, they at once assume the defectiveness of our present Social polity, and argue from it as a point by nobody disputed : 'We *ought* to be paid so much, [thus runs their logic] because we *need* and they can *afford* it.' ' *Ought,*' do you say, friends? Don't you realize that the whole world around is based upon *must* instead of *ought*? Which one of you, though earning fifteen dollars per week, ever paid five cents more than the market price for a bushel of potatoes, or a basket of eggs, or a quarter of mutton, because the seller *ought* to be fairly paid for his labor, and couldn't really *afford* to sell at the market rate? Nay, which of you well-paid puddlers ever gave a poor widow a dollar a piece for making your shirts when you could get them made as well for half a dollar, even though at the dollar you would be getting three days' work for one? Step forward from the ranks, you gentlemen that have conducted *your own* buying and hiring through life on the principle of '*ought,*' and let me make my obeisance to each of you ! I shall do it right heartily, and with no fear of being rendered neck-weary by the operation.

"Yet that '*ought*' is a glorious word when applied to

the relations of Business and of Labor—we must not let it
be forgotten.   There is in it the seeds of a Revolution more
gigantic and pervasive than any Vergniaud* or Kossuth
ever devised.   Heaven speed the day when, not only in
Iron but in all branches of Industry, the reward of Labor
shall be regulated not by 'must,' but by 'ought.'   .   .   .

"The most melancholy feature of these strikes is the
apparent indisposition on either side to discover any law
whereby these collisions may be terminated for the present
and precluded in future.   It seems so natural for the workmen to say, 'You tell us that you can pay but three-fourths
of our former wages because of the low price of Iron ; now
suppose we accept your terms, *will you agree that our
wages shall advance whenever and so fast as the price of Iron
shall improve ?*'—'Yes,' would be the natural and proper
answer of the masters, '*if you will agree that they shall be
reduced whenever and so fast as Iron shall decline still further.*'   This being accepted, the entire relation of Capital
to Labor in this particular department is reädjusted on the
basis of Proportion or Common Interest instead of that of
arbitrary Wages, evolving contrariety of interests.   Now
the puddler gets so much, although the Iron should not sell
for enough to pay him, and cares very little whether the
business is prosperous or depressed, save as its suspension
may turn him out of work.   But with the establishment of
Proportion as a law of the trade, every worker's interests

* Peter Victurnien Vergniaud, the famous Girondist leader, was
condemned to death on October 30th, 1793, and was executed on
the Place de Grève, Paris, whither he and his fellow patriots
marched to the guillotine singing the "Marseillaise" in the spirit
of true republicanism.   The crime of these moderate republicans
was the endeavor to prevent the further possibility of such outrages
against Humanity as the September Massacres, and above all to
procure the punishment of that fiend in human shape, Danton, and
the other blood-thirsty Terrorists.

would be on the side of prosperity, and his wages every week depend on the price which Iron should bear at the end of it.

"But from neither party to this controversy do I hear one fruitful or reconciling word. From the journeymen's side, we have all manner of Jacobinic clamor against the oppressions of Capital, Wealth, Monopoly, etc., but no practical suggestion for their removal. No one says, 'Let us hire Iron-works [of which there are abundance shut up] and go to making Iron as our own masters.' Even in Wheeling, where there has been a great meeting of Iron-workers to sympathise with and encourage the Pittsburgh puddlers, no voice uttered the creative words, 'Stop depending on masters, and go to making Iron for yourselves!' How is it that a course so obvious, so decisive, and now rescued from the fatal taint of novelty by a signal success, should remain unadopted and even unconsidered?"

Incidental to the question of Strikes is the fact that a brief period before Horace Greeley wrote these lines, Robert Rantoul, Junior, the educational reformer, who had edited a "Workingman's Library," issued "by the Lyceums," successfully defended some Massachusetts journeymen bootmakers. Rantoul, who was an advocate of the abolition of all Human Slavery, pleaded for these men, who had been indicted for a conspiracy to raise wages, and "procured their discharge on the ground that a combination of individuals to effect, by means not unlawful, that which each might legally do, was not a criminal conspiracy."

Horace Greeley was always urging ameliorative and definitive measures for the freedom from wages slavery of his whilom class. Workingmen, to-day, can have no better reading for their own instruction, than his three lectures on "The Organization of Labor," "The Emancipation of Labor," and "The Relations of Learning Toward Labor,"— the last named of which was an address delivered July 23d, 1844, before the Literary Societies of Hamilton College, Clinton, in the State of New York.

Exception may be taken by some, relative to Greeley's position on the limitation of the hours of labor in his lecture on "The Emancipation of Labor." He should not be misunderstood. That lecture was written in December, 1846, that is forty-five years ago. At that time men, women and children, in the factory and on the farm, invariably worked from sunrise to sunset. This meant sixteen hours a day in the summer. An agitation, at the period when Greeley made this statement, in favor of amelioration solely, was in progress against "sun to sun" slavery. There was a ten hours movement. One result was that President Van Buren on April 10, 1840, signed a general order introducing the ten hour system thereafter into the Navy Yard at Washington, D. C., and in "all public establishments." Prof. Richard T. Ely, of Johns Hopkins University, from whose *Labor Movement in America* these statements are taken, asserts that "within this year (1886) seventeen and eighteen hours have been a common length of a day's labor on the street railways of the United States. . . . . Once a week in Baltimore they (the bakers) have worked steadily for twenty-five hours, and in New York for twenty-six—a normal working day considerably larger it is seen than the solar day!" The first national action taken in favor of eight-hours was on June 24, 1869, when "a bill for an eight hour day was introduced into Congress by General Banks, whose wife, by the way, was once a factory girl at Lowell."

The founder of the *Tribune* was always the printer-editor, and he was the first President of Typographical Union No. 6 of New York city. James Parton records that on January 7th, 1849, the Printers' Festival was held at Washington in the District of Columbia, and "Mr. Greeley attended it, and made a speech. His remarks were designed to show, that 'the interests of tradesmen generally, but especially of the printing and publishing trade, including authors and editors, were intimately involved in the establishment and maintenance of high rates of compensation for labor in all departments of industry. It is of vital interest to us all that the entire community shall be buyers of books and subscribers to journals, which they cannot be unless their earnings are sufficient to supply generously their physical wants and leave some surplus for intellectual aliment. We ought, therefore, as a class, from regard to our own interests, if from no higher motive, to combine to keep up higher rates of compensation in our own business, and to favor every movement in behalf of such rates in other callings.'

"He concluded by offering a sentiment :—

"' The Lightning of Intelligence—Now crashing ancient tyrannies and toppling down thrones—May it swiftly irradiate the world.'"

Horace Greeley delivered the following address on "The Union of Workers," to the organized journeymen printers of New York city, then known as "The New York Typographical Society," at their celebration of the birthday of Benjamin Franklin, January 17th, 1850 :—

"The ancient Egyptians had a custom of seating at their feasts the robed skeleton of some departed friend, whose stern silence contrasted strikingly with the mirth and hilarity of his living companions. I believe scholars are not agreed as to the purpose and meaning of this strange

custom—whether the rigid, silent guests were intended to
say to the festal throng—'Enjoy and revel while you may,
for Time flies, Man perishes; in a few years all is dust, is
nothing—therefore, make haste to quaff the wine while it
sparkles, to seize pleasure while the capacity of enjoyment
remains to you'; or rather to impress the opposite sentiment—'Life is short; Life is earnest; stupendous consequences hang suspended on your use or abuse of the speck
of time allotted you; therefore, be temperate in your indulgence, moderate in your festive mirth, and, seeing in what
I am what you soon must be, consider and beware!' I
shall not of course pretend to decide this grave question,
though I shall assume for the occasion that the latter is the
true rendering; and, in accordance with the elemental idea,
I venture to assume among you to-night the functions of
the Egyptians' silent monitor, and while others stir you
with lofty eloquence or charm you with dulcet flatteries—
with pictures of the grand achievements of our Art in the
past and its brilliant prospects for the future, I shall speak
to you frankly of our deficiencies, our failings, and the
urgent demands upon us for new and more arduous
exertions in yet unrecognized fields of duty.

"It is now some four centuries since the discovery or
invention of our Art. fully three since our continent began
to be the home of civilized men, and more than two since
the Pilgrim fugitives first landed on Plymouth Rock.
Since that landing, and even within the last century, what
amazing strides have been made in the diffusion of Knowledge and the perfection of the implements and processes
of Industry—in the efficiency of Human Labor and the
facilitation of intercourse between country and country,
clime and clime! The steam-engine, the spinning-jenny,
the power-loom; the canal, steam-ship, power-press, rail-

road and lightning telegraph—these, in their present perfection and efficiency, are a few of the trophies of human
genius and labor within even the last century.

"But while Labor has thus doubled and quadrupled its
own efficacy in the production of whatever is needful to
the physical sustenance, intellectual improvement and
social enjoyment of Man, I do not find that there has been
a corresponding melioration in the condition of the
Laborer. That there has been some improvement I do
not deny; but has it been at all commensurate with the
general progress of our race in whatever pertains to physical
convenience or comfort? I think not; and I could not
help pondering this matter even while our orator's silvery
tones were delighting our ears with poetical descriptions
of the wonders which Science and Invention have achieved
and are achieving. I could not help considering that,
while Labor builds far more sumptuous mansions in our
day than of old, furnishing them far more gorgeously and
luxuriously, the laborer who builds those mansions lives
oftenest in a squalid lodging, than which the builders of
palaces in the fifteenth century can hardly have dwelt in
more wretched; and that while the demands for Labor, the
uses of Labor, the efficiency of Labor, are multiplied and
extended on every side by the rush of invention and the
growth of luxury around us, yet in this middle of the
Nineteenth Century (call it the last year of the first half or
the first year of the last half as you please) Labor is a drug
in the market—that the temperate, efficient, upright
Worker often finds the comfortable maintenance and proper
education of his children beyond his ability—and that, in
this thriving Commercial Emporium of the New World, this
trophy and pride of Christian Civilization—there are at
this day not less than Forty Thousand human beings

anxious to earn the bread of honest industry but vainly seeking, and painfully, despairingly awaiting opportunity for so doing. This last is the feature of our condition which seems to me most important and commanding, and it is to this, on occasions like the present, and in listening to such orations as that which has just delighted us, that my thoughts are irresistibly turned.

"What can be the reason of this? Why is it that these Forty Thousand strong-handed, willing Workers stand here thus fixed, enchained, in loathed, despairing idleness? Why are they compelled to wear out our pavements in hurrying hither and thither in anxious, heart-sick quest of. something to do?—with downcast looks and trembling voice beseeching some fellow man to give them leave to labor for their bread? I trust no one here gives any heed to the mumbling of self-styled Political Economists about 'Over-Production' and the kindred phrases with which counsel is darkened. 'Over-Production'—of what? Where? Can there be Over-Production of Food, when so many, even in our midst, are suffering the pangs of famine? "Over-Production' of Clothing and Fabrics, while our streets swarm with men, women and children who are not half-clad, and who shiver through the night beneath the clothing they have worn by day? 'Over-Production' of Dwellings, when not half the families of our city have adequate and comfortable habitations, not to speak of that large class whose lodgings are utterly incompatible with decency and morality? No, friends! there is *no* 'Over-Production,' save of articles pernicious and poisonous, like Alcoholic Liquors, Lewd Books, implements of Gaming, etc. Of whatever conduces to human sustenance, comfort or true education, there is not and never has been too much produced, although, owing to imperfect and vicious arrangements for Distribution, there may often be a glut in the warehouses of Trade, while thousands greatly need and would gladly purchase if they could. What the world eminently requires is some wise adjustment, some remodeling of the Social Machinery diminishing its friction, whereby *every person willing to work shall assuredly have work to do, and the just reward of that work in the articles most essential to his sustenance and comfort.* It may be that there is indeed a surplus of that particular product which some man's labor could most skillfully or rapidly produce, —Pianos, Watches, or Gauzes, for example—and therefore it may be advisable to intermit for a season the production of these—yet the skill, the faculty, the muscular energy not required in that particular department of production might nevertheless be made available, even though in a subordinate degree, in the fabrication of some kindred product for which there *is* a demand among the general mass of consumers. I maintain, then, that in our day no man should be compelled to stand idle or wander vainly in search of employment, even though that particular calling for which he is best fitted has now no place for him, but that the palpable self-interest of the Community should prescribe the creation of some Social Providence expressly to take care that no man, woman or child shall ever stand uselessly idle when willing and anxious to work. Even the most injudicious application of the Labor now wasted through lack of opportunity could not fail to increase the National Wealth to the extent of millions on millions per annum, while its effect on the condition of the Laboring Class, in preserving them from temptation, dissipation and crime, would be incalculably beneficent.

"Now what I stand here to complain of is the indifference and inattention of the Laboring Mass, and especially

of those entitled to a leading position in it, like the Printers,
to the discussion of a truth so grand and so fruitful as the
Right to Labor. It is more discussed, more pondered,
to-day, by Merchants, Capitalists, Scholars, and men who
are called Aristocrats, than by the mass of those who earn
their living by the sweat of the face. It is now eighteen
years since I came to this city a journeyman printer, during
which years I have been intimately connected with our
craft in one capacity or another, and yet I have never
heard of a meeting of Printers to consider and discuss the
Rights generally of Labor, the causes of its depression, the
means of its advancement. During these eighteen years
there have been hard times and good times, so called ;
seasons of activity and seasons of depression—in the course
of which the country has been 'saved,' I forget how often—
our city has doubled in population and more than doubled
in wealth—and yet the Laboring Class *as* a Class is just
where it was when I came here, or, if anything, in a worse
condition, as the increased valuation of Property has caused
advance in Rents and in some other necessaries of life.
Individuals have risen *out* of the Laboring Class, becoming
buyers of Labor and sellers of its Products, and grown rich
thereby ; but the condition of the Laboring Class, as such,
has not improved, and I think is less favorable than it was
twenty years ago. Why should it not investigate, determine and develop the causes of this? Why not consider
the practicability of securing Work and Homes to all
willing to work for them? Can we imagine that improvement is to come without effort or even inquiry? Is it the
order of Nature or of Providence that it should? Do
blessings come to other classes without foresight or calculation? I have heard complaints that Machinery and
Invention do not work *for* the Laboring Class, but rather

against them. Concede the assumption, and is not the inquiry a fair one, What has the Laboring Class ever done to *make* Machinery work in its favor? When has it planned, or sought, or calculated, to render Machinery its ally and aid rather than its enemy and oppressor?

"I am here to-night to tell you that you, and our Trade, and the Laboring Class of our city have been glaringly unfaithful in this respect to yourselves, your posterity, and your Race, and that the Workers of Paris, for example, are in advance of their brethren here in knowledge of and devotion to the interests and rights of Labor. And I am here, not to find fault merely, but to exhort you to awake from your apathy and heed the summons of Duty.

"I stand here, friends, to urge that a new leaf be now turned over—that the Laboring Class, instead of idly and blindly waiting for better circumstances and better times, shall begin at once to consider and discuss the means of controlling circumstances and commanding times, by study, calculation, foresight, union, We have heard to-night of a Union of Printers and a Printers' Library, for which latter one generous donation has been proffered. I have little faith in giving, as a remedy for the woes of mankind, and not much in any effort for the elevation or improvement of any one section of Producers of Wealth in our city. What I would suggest would be the Union and Organization of *all* Workers for their mutual improvement and benefit, leading to the erection of a spacious edifice at some central point in our city to form a LABORERS' EXCHANGE, just as Commerce now has its Exchange, very properly.*

* Lucien Sanial informed the author that during his recent visit to Europe while attending the International Socialist Congress at Brussels, he found that the Municipal authorities of Paris,—not the "ouvriers,"—were erecting, at the expense of the city, for the workingmen of Paris, a magnificent building, the "Bourse du Travail" or Labor Exchange, to take the place of that now allotted to their use by the municipality.

Let the new Exchange be erected and owned as a joint-stock property, paying a fair dividend to those whose money erected it; let it contain the best spacious Hall for General Meetings to be found in our city, with smaller Lecture-Rooms for the meetings of particular sections or callings—all to be leased or rented at fair prices to all who may choose to hire them, when not needed for the primary purpose of discussing and advancing the interests of Labor. Let us have here books opened, wherein any one wanting work may inscribe his name, residence, capacities and terms, while any one wishing to hire may do likewise, as well as meet personally those seeking employment. These are but hints toward a few of the uses which such a Labor Exchange might subserve, while its Reading-Room and Library, easily formed and replenished, should be opened freely and gladly to all. Such an edifice, rightly planned and constructed, might become, and I confidently hope would become, a most important instrumentality in the great work of advancing the Laboring Class in comfort, intelligence and independence. I trust we need not long await its erection "

James Parton, in his *Life of Horace Greeley*, speaks in the highest terms of commendation of the position taken by the founder of the New York *Tribune*, as soon as he had achieved wealth and success. Greeley never forgot the class to which he had belonged, and referring to the volume, *Hints Toward Reforms*, Parton, when both were alive, wrote as follows :—

" It shows Horace Greeley to be a man whose interest in human welfare is sincere, habitual, innate and indestructible. We all know what is the usual course of a person who—as the stupid phrase is— '*rises*' from the condition of a manual laborer to a position of influence and wealth.

If our own observation were not sufficient, Thackeray and Curtis have told the whole world the sorry history of the modern snob; how he ignores his origin, and bends all his little soul to the task of cutting a figure in the circles to which he has gained admittance.

"Twenty men are suffocating in a dungeon—one man, by climbing upon the shoulders of some of his companions, and assisted up still higher by the strength of others, *escapes*, breathes the pure air of heaven, exults in freedom! Does he not, instantly and with all his might, strive for the rescue of his late companions, still suffering? Is he not prompt with rope, and pole, and ladder, and food, and cheering words? No—the caitiff wanders off to seek his pleasure, and makes haste to remove from his person, and his memory too, every trace of his recent misery. *This* it is to be a snob. No treason like this clings to the skirts of Horace Greeley. He has stood by his Order. The landless, the hireling, the uninstructed—he was their Companion once—he is their Champion now."

Plutocracy may roar and howl, through its subsidized agents, as much as it pleases against the armies of Organized Labor, battling for their rights, but it should never forget that it is because of the labors of men belonging to its own order, who were not selfish capitalists, that the wage workers are to-day organized in powerful and multitudinous bodies. To Robert Owen, once a cotton mill owner, the organizations of the Old World owe their origin,—for what has been done, of late years, in Germany and France, is only the repetition of what he did in the years 1833–1834, when he organized a national body of British proletarian wages slaves. But Owen was a Socialist, as was likewise Horace Greeley,—a newspaper proprietor,—to whom the Solidarity of American working people, in certain modern developments, must be, in a great measure, attributed.

The American Federation of Labor, which is only a few years old, in the preamble to its Constitution tells identically the same story as did Horace Greeley, when it recites:—

"WHEREAS, A struggle is going on in all the nations of the civilized world, between the oppressors and the oppressed of all countries, a struggle between the Capitalist and the Laborer, which grows in intensity from year to year, and will work disastrous results to the toiling millions, if they are not combined for mutual protection and benefit;

"It therefore behooves the Representatives of the Trades and Labor Unions of America, in Convention assembled, to adopt such measures and disseminate such principles among the mechanics and laborers of our country as will permanently unite them to secure the recognition of the rights to which they are justly entitled."

But the American Federation of Labor, in action goes so far only and no further and not the whole length, so that the waves of Labor should come rolling in to sweep away the Capitalistic System. It thoroughly recognizes the evils, but refrains from applying the proper remedies, and for the simple reason, that a large number of organizations, united in the American Federation of Labor, are in theory and principle as Capitalistic as Capitalists themselves. They are willing to continue the present competitive system, which to them is all right, as long as a few victories or supposed triumphs are gained from their "masters." Others may starve as long as they get fair wages.

The spirit of the "New Trades Unionism," is fortunately becoming the inspiration, which is rallying the workers to Final Emancipation. It is high time that the "Pure and Simple Trades Unionists" should go. But in relegating them to the rear, Organized Labor might well adopt for its own the words spoken by *The People's Press*, of London,

with regard to the "Pure and Simple" ex-workingmen,—
who are now members of the British House of Commons
and are paid annual salaries by their Trades Unions to
represent them—as follows :—

"They have each and all of them done good work in
their time for the Cause of Labor. It is not their fault
that they have been left hopelessly behind by the course
of events. Men, measures, problems, and methods have
all altered enormously since they first made their bow upon
the political boards. Full-grown and well-tried men, long
before things assumed their present shape, hardened by
the blows they have given and taken in past battles, it is
no wonder that they have lacked the adaptability of younger
men. When long-accepted creeds have crumbled, and
venerable war cries fail to elicit a ready response, there is
need of new men to meet the new demands. And though
there is no reason that those who have sustained the dangers and faced the toil which came to them, without flinch-
ing, should be condemned or denounced, there is strong
reason why their advice and direction should be sparingly
relied upon when novel and unfamiliar questions—to
them—are under discussion."

The "*laissez faire*" or let alone policy which would
linger for years over the limitation of the hours of labor
alone, as it has done for over fifty years, has been a
loss of potential energy to Organized Labor. The force
expended might have been devoted to carrying out through
political and economic measures, a genuine treatment for
the entire eradication of the disease, and not mere palliative
remedies diverting attraction from the main cause of the
trouble,—the Competitive Capitalistic System.

But the American Federation of Labor, it must be
remembered, claims to have a membership of nearly 700,000

workingmen, who, if they would only combine politically
with the Knights of Labor, as well as with the Farmers'
Alliances and Grangers, would sweep this country, and
elect a Proletarian President of the United States and Proletarian Governors, legislatures and State and municipal
officials in every State of the Union.

The Order of the Knights of Labor, that native American organization in origin, seems to bear the possibility
of more potentiality within it, as it is most certainly
based in its principles, upon the position taken by Horace
Greeley and other Socialists, from whom the tailor-
founder Uriah S. Stevens must have obtained them. This
position is very plainly pointed out in the admirable history
of American *Woman in Industry* by Alice Hyneman Rhine,*
whose sixty pages give more essential facts than Carroll D.
Wright's mastodon volume issued by the National Bureau
of Labor, with its perplexing columns of figures, leading
one away from the true facts in order apparently to make
a good case for the Capitalist class. Mrs. Rhine, speaking
of the Coöperative factories and industries organized by
the Knights of Labor, right in the line of Horace Greeley's
suggestions, says :—

"This departure from the custom prevailing among
the Proletariat to sell their services for wage hire, was due
largely to the demand made in the nineteenth plank of the
platform of the Knights of Labor for the abolition of the
wages system and a National System of Coöperation in lieu
thereof. The insertion of such a demand proved the
founders of the order to have been thinkers radical enough
to go a step beyond the old idea of trades organizations,

---

* *Woman's Work in America*, edited by Annie Nathan Meyer,
with Introduction by Julia Ward Howe, 12mo. N. Y., Henry Holt
& Co., 1891. (Mrs. Rhine was married to Mr. Sotheran Oct. 17, 1893.)

with their petty notions of each trade working solely in its own interests. In comparison with the broad and lofty conception of the Knights of Labor, which sought to include in its benefits all women and men engaged in every department of industrial work, other organizations, such as the American Federation of Labor, which is a mere rope of sand, showed themselves away in the rear-guard of Progressive Civilization, by placing themselves solely on the old competitive and selfish trades union basis."

The Knights of Labor,—who, a few years ago, numbered in the neighborhood of a million members,—in the "Preamble" to their Constitution take the position that :—

"The alarming development and aggressiveness of great capitalists and corporations, unless checked, will inevitably lead to the pauperization and hopeless degradation of the toiling masses.

"It is imperative, if we desire to enjoy the full blessings of life, that a check be placed upon unjust accumulation, and the power for evil of aggregated wealth.

"This much-desired object can be accomplished only by the united efforts of those who obey the divine injunction, 'In the sweat of thy face shalt thou eat bread.'

"Therefore, we have formed the Order of the Knights of Labor, for the purpose of organizing and directing the power of the industrial masses, not as a political party, for it is more—in it are crystallized sentiments and measures for the benefit of the whole people ; but it should be borne in mind, when exercising the right of suffrage, that most of the objects herein set forth can only be obtained through legislation, and that it is the duty of all to assist in nominating and supporting with their votes only such candidates as will pledge their support to those measures, regardless of party ; but no one shall, however, be compelled to vote with the majority. And calling upon all who believe in securing 'the greatest good to the greatest number' to join and assist us, we declare to the world that our aims are :—

"I. To make industrial and moral worth, not wealth, the true standard of individual and National greatness.

"II. To secure to the workers the full enjoyment of the wealth they create, sufficient leisure in which to develop their intellectual, moral and social faculties ; all of the benefits, recreation and pleasures of association ; in a word, to enable them to share in the gains and honors of advancing civilization."

The Knights are strong radicals politically on the land question, and their two last political demands read :—

"XVII. That, in connection with the Post-office, the Government shall organize Financial Exchanges, Safe Deposits, and facilities for deposits of savings of the people in small sums.

"XVIII. That the Government shall obtain possession, by purchase, under the right of Eminent Domain, of all Telegraphs, Telephones, and Railroads ; and that hereafter no charter or license be issued to any corporation for construction or operation of any means of transporting intelligence, passengers, or freight."

Here we find nothing but demands in the trend of *bona fide* Socialism, and, out of their twenty-two demands in all, six only are economic, the remainder being purely political and obtainable by legislation alone. It has been truthfully asserted, that in some particulars, the Knights of Labor are more Socialistic than the Socialists themselves.

Yet, through general apathy or other causes, except as Organizers, they have not advanced beyond having a platform, which they have only sporadically attempted to carry into effect. There is no reason why they should be in this

Rip Van Winkle condition, individual ecclesiastics, such as
Cardinal Gibbons of Baltimore and Cardinal Manning of
Westminster, having indorsed their demands as just and
righteous, the last-named having said upon one occasion
that he, mentally, was "a good Knight of Labor."

Knights of Labor do not study enough. Some of their
own agitators, like Victor Drury, for instance, whose *Polity
of the Labor Movement* should be a text-book,—have
written enough and to spare to put them on the right track.
What Horace Greeley said about Coöperation, already
printed in these pages, should be household words to the
Knights, and books bearing on such Coöperative Labor as
the Godin experiment, Howland's *Papa's Own Girl*, and
the like, which can be obtained for a few cents, should afford
the favorite occupation of their moments of leisure.

When two of the modern feudal Lords of Capital,—
Andrew Carnegie and Abram S. Hewitt,—give wage earners
advice on Coöperation, endorsing its main features,—the
Proletarians must be very dull and laggard indeed if they
do not accept it, after their very enemies point it out to
them.

Andrew Carnegie, the boss puddler of Pittsburgh, Pa.,
a year or two ago, made this statement:—

"Whatever the future may have in store for Labor the
evolutionist, who sees nothing but certain and steady progress for the race, will never attempt to set bounds to its
triumphs, even to its final forms of complete and Universal
Industrial Coöperation, which I hope is some day to be
reached."

And Abram S. Hewitt, who, while Mayor of the city
of New York, was charged publicly by Secretary Ernest
Bohm of the Central Labor Union with being a Socialist,
told the Church Congress, at Cincinnati, on October 18th,
1878, that:—

"The present distribution of wealth does not conform to the principles of justice;" and that "in the nature of things it would seem that corporations must continue to grow and absorb the great bulk of the business of the world, but that these corporations will be organized upon a distribution of ownership among those who are engaged in them, so that in the end the business of the world will be conducted by men in association with each other, each being directly interested in the ownership of the enterprise in which he is engaged."

And as for Labor-Saving Machinery, we have demonstrated in these pages, how over sixty years ago, Thomas Skidmore, the New York Socialist, showed American workingmen that it was their imperative duty to obtain possession of what was under the Capitalist System such a curse to them, through Steam and Iron taking the place of Brain and Muscle.

Horace Greeley also, just forty years ago, in his lecture on "The Crystal Palace and its Lessons," spoke as follows:

"This is but one among a thousand noiseless agencies constantly preaching the advantages and economies of COMBINATION, and indicating the certainty that through Coöperation lies the way whereby Labor is to emerge from bondage, anxiety, and need, into liberty and assured competence. This truth, long apparent to the eye of Reason, threatens to be made palpable even to stolidity and stagnation, by the sharp spur of Necessity. Rude, rugged Labor must organize itself for its appointed work of production, or it will soon have nothing to do. It must concentrate its energies for the creation of commodious and economical homes, or it will have no home but the Union Work House. It must save and combine its earnings, for the purchase and command of Machinery; or Machinery, owned by and working for Capital alone, will reduce it to insignificance, want and despair. . . . .

"And so muscular force, or *mere* Labor, becomes daily more and more a drug in the market, shivers at the approach of winter, cringes lower and lower at the glance of a machine-lord or landlord, and vainly paces street after street, with weary limbs and sinking heart, in quest of 'something to do.'

"The only effectual remedy for this deplorable state, and still more deplorable tendency, is found, not in Destruction, but in Construction—not in Anarchy and War on the rights of Property, but in Order and the creation of more property by and for the Poor—not in envy and hatred of the Rich, but in general study and imitation of the forecast and frugality by which they were made rich, which are as potent this hour as they ever were, and which wise Coöperation will render effective for the Poor of to-day. In this country, where so much land is still unappropriated, and the legal right of Association is absolute and universal, the Laboring Classes are masters of their own destiny, and that of their brethren throughout the world. A thousand young men, inured to labor, and as yet unburdened with families, can save at least one hundred dollars each, in the space of two years, if they will ; and by wisely and legally combining this in a capital of $100,000, investing it judiciously in Land, Machinery, and Buildings, under the direction of their ablest and most responsible members, they may be morally certain henceforth of constant employment for each, under circumstances which will insure them the utmost efficiency and the full reward of their labor. To Woman, whose work is still more depressed and still more meagerly rewarded, the means of securing emancipation and just recompense are substantially the same. The workers, in every department of industry, may secure and own the Machinery best calculated to give efficiency to their labor, if they will but unitedly, persistently try. Through the Scientific Association of Labor and Capital, three-fourths of them may within five years accomplish this, while by heedlessness and isolated competition they are sure to miss it, and see their condition grow gradually worse and worse. Labor working *against* Machinery is inevitably doomed, as the present condition of the hand-loom weavers all over the globe sufficiently attests ; Labor working *for* Machinery, in which it has no interest, can obtain in the average but a scanty, precarious, and diminishing subsistence ; while to Labor working *with* Machinery, which it owns and directs, there are ample recompense, steady employment, and the prospect of gradual improvement. Such is one of the great truths confirmed by the lessons of the Crystal Palace.''

There is "balm in Gilead,'' however, notwithstanding the apathy in some quarters. Thus, the New York Central Labor Union recently said, that "After ten years of existence it has found that IT IS IMPOSSIBLE TO SECURE CONCESSIONS IN THE INDUSTRIAL FIELD UNLESS IT IS FULLY ARMED IN THE POLITICAL FIELD.'' And what did it say ten years ago? In its "Declaration of Principles'' it asserted :—

"We hold that the soil of every country is the social and common inheritance of the people of that country, and hence all should have free and equal access to the soil, without tribute to landlords or monopolists.

"We further hold that Labor produces all wealth, and therefore the laborer is in justice entitled to a full share of the wealth he labors to produce. But when wealth producers live in poverty and idlers roll in luxury, it is very evident that the Social and Industrial System which causes such conditions must be wrong and immoral, and requires a thorough change.

"It is self-evident that as the power of Capital combines and increases, the Political Freedom of the toiling masses becomes more and more a delusive farce.

"There can be no harmony between Capital and Labor under the present Industrial System, for the simple reason that Capital, in its modern character, consists very largely of rent, interest and profits wrongfully extorted from the producer, who possesses neither the land nor the means of production, and is, therefore, compelled to sell his arms, brains, or both, to the possessor of the land and means of production, and at such prices as an uncertain and speculative market may allow.

"Organization of Trade and Labor Unions is one of the most effective means to check the evil overgrowths of the prevailing system, and they contain in them the seed for a new and better system. But they must keep pace with the progress of the age and with the march of advanced ideas.

"While Trades and Labor Unions hitherto have struggled for higher wages or shorter hours of labor, they have partially protected themselves as producers, but not as consumers and citizens. The ruling moneyed classes have meanwhile obtained legal sanction to wring from the workers all the benefits that strikes and resistance gained, and this they have done by high rents, costly transportation, gigantic corners in grain and provisions, and by monopolizing the issue of money. They have used the Police, Militia, and even the Federal Troops against the workers whenever they felt their Capitalistic interests in danger. And yet Trades and Labor Unions went so far as to prohibit the discussion of such topics in their meetings, and on election day their members voted in favor of a

representative of the very class that oppressed them all the
year round.

"The Emancipation of the Working Classes must be
achieved by the working classes themselves, as no other
class has any interest in improving their condition.   The
combined wage-working class represents the great majority
of the people.   In their hands rests the future of our
free institutions, and it is in their destiny to replace the
present iniquitous Social System by one based upon equity,
morality, and the nobility of all useful Labor.

"We regard it as the sacred duty of every honorable
laboring man to sever his affiliations with all political parties
of the Capitalists, and to devote his energy and attention
to the organization of his Trade or Labor Union, and the
concentration of all Unions into one solid body for the
purpose of assisting each other in all struggles—Political
or Industrial—to resist every attempt of the ruling classes
directed against our liberties, and to extend our fraternal
hand to the workers of our land and to all nations of the
globe that struggle for the same independence."

The New York Central Labor Federation, which has
a like program, is on the road to carry it into effect, by
having become an active ally of the Socialist Labor Party.
So have some National organizations connected with the
American Federation of Labor.   The Machinists, for
instance, when they organized an International Union, a
month or two ago, followed in the line of the "International
Union of Journeymen Bakers and Confectioners," who
went so far in National Convention as to pass the following
Resolutions:—

"WHEREAS, it is becoming more evident every day
that the condition of the working class cannot be permanently improved by trades-organizations founded upon an
exclusive trade-union basis, the present productive system

swelling the army of the unemployed at an appalling rate, which reserve army threatens ruin to the best organized union ; and—

"WHEREAS, in order to secure a permanent improvement in the condition of the working class, it is imperatively necessary that the workers should take Political Action, and by the Ballot conquer the Political Power for the purpose of substituting for the present industrial system of exploitation, a Coöperative Productive System ; and—

"WHEREAS, the policy of asking concessions from the old parties, advocated by prominent trades-union leaders, will never secure to the workers their full rights ; and—

"WHEREAS, furthermore, we see in the realization of the Platform of the Socialist Labor Party, THE ONLY WAY OF SECURING OUR RIGHTS BY LAWFUL MEANS ; therefore be it—

"RESOLVED, by the Bakers and Confectioners' Journeymen International Union, in Convention assembled at Indianapolis, Ind., on March 2nd, 1891, that we fully endorse the platform of the Socialist Labor Party and urge our members, wherever a section of the Socialist Labor Party exists, to join the same ; and—

"Be it furthermore Resolved—

"That we most strongly condemn the action of Samuel Gompers, President of the American Federation of Labor, at the Convention held at Detroit, Michigan, from December 8th to 13th, 1890, in reference to the rejection of the Central Labor Federation of New York—for no other reason than that a section of the Socialist Labor Party is represented in said central body."

It is to be hoped that such great labor organizations, instead of taking "a crab step," will wake up the Conservative Trades Unionists and force them to make a similar forward move. There is no doubt about it, but that the

condition of Labor in the United States to-day is something
appalling.   According to the National Census of 1880 and
the statistics therein furnished by employers, we find that
the 2,800,000 Industrial Workers in this country only
received an average wage of $6.50 per week, whereas the
254,000 Factory Lords made a profit of $1,026,000,000.
This was only a portion of the profit made by Capitalism,
which to-day owns or controls through a few Plutocrats
the entire wealth of the United States, estimated at some
$60,000,000,000.

The horrors of what the New York *Sun* calls "Siberia
in Tennessee,"—and the condition of the miners in half a
dozen States of the Union is equally miserable—would
seem to surpass belief, were they not corroborated by anti-
proletarian newspapers.   These monstrous conditions most
certainly demand immediate and active measures for their
suppression.   Let any one read Henry D. Lloyd's work *A
Strike of Millionaires against Miners, or the Story of Spring
Valley*, and it is hardly possible to imagine but that even
the most stony-hearted of human beings would be won over
to the cause of these unfortunate children of Humanity,
now kept in degraded servitude by Capitalists Chauncey M.
Depew, Albert Keep, N. K. Fairbank, William K. Vanderbilt, F. W. Vanderbilt, John I. Blair, William L. Scott,
Marvin Hughitt, Horace Williams, John M. Burke, H. M.
Twombley, D. O. Mills, Samuel F. Barger, Percy R. Pyne,
A. G. Dulman, M. L. Sykes, D. P. Kimball, W. M. Scott,
E. N. Saunders, D. C. Shepard, and other railroad
magnates.

The arraignment of the Plutocratic Class was made
years and years ago by Horace Greeley, Albert Brisbane,
Parke Godwin, and the American Fourierist Socialists.
And it seems to the author of these pages hardly necessary
to enter into the present crimes of Capitalism, when not a

single day passes but that the morning newspaper brings to the breakfast table of nearly every one in the land, not only the record of the warfare between Organized Capital and Organized Labor, but of the fearful effects of Strikes and Lock-outs and their general results in sufferings added to the miseries of the poor. Let those who wish to know what is going on around them,—at least those who pretend to be ignorant—read the official Labor Reports of New York State compiled by Commissioner Peck, and there will be found described things quite as heartrending and awful as Dante told in his *Inferno,* or as the most lurid imagination could evolve out of a diseased brain.

Yet worse for future generations is the physical and mental "Slaughter of the Innocents," in factories and shops, and no wonder that Bishop Henry C. Potter in his righteous indignation against child labor exclaimed :—

"The Herods are not all dead, nor are the Murdered Innocents all buried."

There is also another phase of the savagery of the present war between Capitalism and Labor,—and that is the perpetual succession of murders committed by the Pinkerton "thugs" and the other armed mercenaries employed by the monopolizers of the wealth they did not produce. The blood of these martyrs cries aloud. If on the one hand such crimes are treasured up against the Plutocrats by the Proletariat, on the other hand, the Wages Slaves can console themselves with the thought of Byron in *Marino Faliero* :

"They never fail who die
In a great cause ; the block may soak their gore ;
Their heads may sodden in the sun ; their limbs
Be strung to city gates and castle walls—
But still their spirit walks abroad."

CHAPTER X.

SOCIALISM'S PRESENT AND FUTURE.

"THE time has passed when Socialism can be dismissed with curses, or threats, or sneers, or interjections."

So wrote Washington Gladden, who is one of the apologists of the present competitive system, in the pages of the ultra-respectable *Century*, not so very long ago. Then Mr. Gladden discusses a few books written "pro" and "con" the great Labor Movement, without apparently having the least information about the historic evolution of Modern American Socialism through the Communities; Owenism; the indigenous movement in the thirties in New York State; the later Fourierist development in the forties in Massachusetts, at Brook Farm, and in New York and elsewhere through Greeley and the *Tribune*, which, by the pens of Brisbane, Godwin, Dana, Curtis and numerous others, laid the foundation for various agricultural, and industrial economic and political movements.

Such writers as Mr. Gladden see certain effects, and never care to pursue them scientifically to their causes. They observe symptoms and believe they are the disease itself,—then they give the world the dubious benefit of their alleged diagnosis, with the result of making confusion worse confounded. These politico-economic empirics are regarded by the masses as "Sir Oracles" when they "open wide their hyper-critical mouths," and the result is, that the misanthropic public accepts "the sponsorial and patronymic appellations," with which Doctor Peter Pangloss, LL.D., A. S. S., and Co., meddle and muddle, mixing up as one and the same thing, such contrarieties as Anarchism and Socialism. They altogether misstate and mistake prior conditions. To return to Mr. Gladden, would it not be very funny to listen at the receiver of his Microphone for "the curses, or sneers, or threats, or interjections," which up to the present have never been heard of in American literary history as having been hurled at Emerson, Hawthorne, Parker, Godwin, Curtis and their cultured associates?

"Cave Canem!" There have been quite a host of such misinformants as Gladden, Hitchcock, Atkinson, Sumner, Walker and others, who have too evidently taken most of their economic observations from the wrong end of their mental telescopes, or with the caps on their microscopes, making them display such profound gloom as might lead one to imagine their owners had "in dark Cimmerian deserts ever dwelt."

But the day of such people is rapidly drawing to a close and they may gesticulate and shout Conservatism as long as they please, for we are gradually approaching the condition, through the spread of more general intelligence, that probably a few hundreds may accept their misinformation, while the 63,000,000 will proceed onward, leaving the infinitesimal minority much in the state that Horace Greeley described:—

"The stubborn conservative is like a horse on board a ferry boat. The horse may back, but the boat moves on, and the animal with it."

It will be a very long time indeed before American workingmen will be betrayed and side tracked as they were in New York city during what was called the "Henry George Movement." Here comes in a strange fact, not generally known, concerning that fungoid growth. The

public believe those 68,000 votes cast, were purely on a
Single Tax Land Reform issue. Nothing of the kind.
The Platform on which the Mayoralty candidate was nominated was the Socialistic Preamble and Demands of the
New York Central Labor Union, printed in the previous
chapter, which insist on nothing less than absolute Land
Nationalization. But demagoguery achieved a triumph
and the disastrous result was seen later, when the wages
slaves of Manhattan Island followed the "Will o' the
Wisp" Single Tax leaders and landed themselves in the
bogs of the corrupt Republican and Democratic parties
over supposititious tariff issues.

Now they are beginning to learn that either Protection
or Free Trade is for them, "a mockery, a delusion and a
snare." "Bad times" had been attributed to both tariff
and no tariff, and the wage earners discovered by sad experience that there can only be Protection for the Capitalists
and Free Trade for the Monopolists. The "iron law of
wages" stops the way and so the proletariat are neither free
nor protected as producers or consumers. When wages
are high the necessaries of life are as a rule high also, and
vice versa, low wages meaning low priced necessaries.
The Plutocracy owns or controls everything that is worth
having in "the land of the free and the home of the
brave." And if we look abroad, it matters not in what
foreign countries, whether protected or free trade, the
Proletarians are equally oppressed and wretched.

Socialism has assumed proportions of which many of
its sanguine advocates have not the slightest appreciation.
The blossom will quickly bloom on the trees, and the fruit
will soon be gathered. On the farms and ranches in the
West and South, the coming Coöperative Commonwealth is
talked over, and the working people are discussing, as they

never did before, economic and political questions. Even some of the middle class are considering Socialism as a remedy for the Trusts which are bankrupting them, and cultured and brainy people, many sitting in professorial chairs, have had their say in favor of Collectivist ideas in the great monthlies of America and Europe. The work of propaganda proceeding in America is not known to the Gladdens and that ilk. Wherever there is a Local Assembly, a Trades Union, an Alliance, a Grange or a Debating Society, there will the Socialist agitator be found, exhorting or disseminating his literature.

And that literature is worth consideration because it is not as a rule seen in the wonted places for books. It is carted around from meeting to meeting, — unless there be a permanent Labor Lyceum, — and laid upon side tables where volumes or tracts ranging in price from a dollar to a cent may be procured. It is in this way the agitation is principally done, — through the brain. Some of these works are worthy of mention. There is the *Labor Catechism* of Osborne Ward, a native American,—no German if you please,— and his history of the Labor Movement going back to the times of Romulus, Draco and Rameses. The former of these volumes has been in circulation from fifteen to twenty years. Then, there is the *Better Times* of Dr. Adolf Douai, who introduced the Kindergarten System into the United States ; as well as Helen Campbell's *Prisoners of Poverty*, which, strange to say, although depicting the horrors of the tenement sweating system, was originally published in the columns of Mr. Whitelaw Reid's *Tribune.* Nowadays no one wants *Progress and Poverty*. The cry is for Bellamy's *Looking Backward* or the *Coöperative Commonwealth* of Lawrence Gronlund. And here is an interesting evidence of progress. It is barely a month ago since the ablest of American literary critics, Mayo W. Hazeltine, devoted four columns in the New York *Sun* to that new book, *Our Destiny*, styling Mr. Gronlund, its author, who was once a Philadelphia lawyer :—"an American writer on Socialism, whose books are read by his opponents with keen interest if not with sympathy, owing to his gift of attractive exposition and the sincere benignity of his aims and teachings."

So Washington Gladden may be assured that if there were once curses for the Socialists, the cursing is now limited to Capitalistic blasphemy, for elsewhere it has "grown small by degrees and beautifully less."

And so the missionary work goes on, from the International Standpoint in America, and men who fought through the civil war as their ancestors did under Washington and Lafayette, have as much enthusiasm as had the "Sons of Liberty" before the Revolution,—only they regard what is going on in Europe as did the gallant foreigners who helped to give Independence to the United States of America. Nor are such persons limited to any one part of America. You find them all over, in New England, in the West, wherever there is a Section of Socialists, a Knights of Labor Assembly, a Farmers' Alliance, or a Grange, or wherever their literature or newspapers can reach.

The sentiment is marvelously growing in unexpected quarters,—that the Plutocracy are gradually un-Americanizing the United States, and that a return to the first principles of the Declaration of Independence must be brought about in order to save the Republic. This healthy symptom is in the trend of Socialism, for under the present modern feudal competitive system, individualism has been absolutely crushed. A few capitalists, the professional class and possibly a good number of merchants may have a considerable amount of individuality permitted them, but the great Trusts and Corporations are gradually transforming even them into mere automata, moving simply as Messieurs Gould, Vanderbilt, Rockefeller, Astor and Co. pull the strings.

As for the mass,—the sixty-three millions,—wages servitude controls almost every thought and act of the family and the individual. Under the competitive system the man employed by another is never a free agent. He is simply the slave of a master, and from the time that he gets up in the morning till he goes to bed at night he is as much a bondsman as any negro ever was, below Mason and Dixey's line before the war. He has independence, no,—freedom of contract, yes,—but more frequently than not, the black list or boycott put on him by Capitalism, if he makes himself antagonistic, may point the way to "misery, hunger and dirt," for the beloved ones dependent on him.

But this is not the place, to enter fully into Socialistic argumentation, and those who wish to inform themselves are referred to such easy expositions as J. Edward Hall's *Place of Individualism in the Socialist System*,—the author of which was a journeyman machinist of Long Island ancestry, who ran in 1887 as the Socialist Candidate for Secretary of State of New York ; or Alexander Jonas's *Reporter and Socialist;* or H. M. Hyndman's *Socialism and Slavery;* or J. L. Joynes's *Socialist Catechism,* * to say nothing of the larger works already alluded to in these pages.

Workingmen above all are studying and debating these questions within their Assemblies and Unions, and the feeling has grown in America, that no proletarian need be the wages slave of Capitalism under the Competitive System,

---

* Lassalle's *Working Man's Programme*, translated by Peters; Marx and Engels's *Manifesto of the Communists*, and Engels's *Development of Socialism from Utopia to Science*, can also be read with advantage.

when he might become a partner in production and distribution under the Coming Coöperative Civilization.

Such unfortunates as the Pennsylvania miners cannot help considering, when partaking of their meals of mush for breakfast, mush for dinner, and mush for supper, that their labor helps to pay the salary of a $10,000 a year cook for a Vanderbilt. The ranchman, bled by the Capitalists and Railroad Corporations, cannot understand how he has to dispose of the beef he raises for two cents a pound, when it is sold to the consumer in New York, Boston or Philadelphia for twenty cents per pound. Thinking it over with the planter and farmer who are equal victims, then he sees that the Capitalistic Transportation and Banking Systems stand between the producer in the West and the consumer in the East, and *vice versa*, and the only way out of it, he asserts, is that the Government shall run the railroads* —and also do his banking and storage for him, by the aid of Sub-Treasuries.

And it is another step for him as a tenant farmer to want the land of the country Nationalized so that he shall, along with the rest of the people, be his own landlord, instead, should he be supposed to own his land, of being the serf of mortgagees who drain the very life blood out of himself and family.

Socialists absolutely assert that before the first half of the Twentieth Century is over the Three Americas will be united in one great Social Republic and the United States of Europe confederated with them, thus carrying out the

---

* One of the ablest presentations of the arguments in favor of governmental ownership of railroads was penned some years ago for the *North American Review*, and printed therein under the title of "A Remedy for Railway Abuses." Its author, Prof. Isaac L. Rice, then of Columbia College, also wrote *What is Music?* published in the Humboldt Library of Science.

glorious future of Humanity outlined by Giuseppe Mazzini, Karl Marx and other statesmen philosophers.

The Socialist Movement now is absolutely Interna-. tional. It holds its periodic Congresses at various points on the civilized globe, repudiating the selfish national prejudices and demoniacal hatreds which have laved the earth with human blood, and proclaiming that when the Constructive Armies of Industry are organized, Destruction and War will be ended.

Great as is the future for America, that of other semi-civilized countries is equally hopeful. Take Germany for instance. It is barely a week or two since the New York *Herald's* European correspondent, Jacques St. Cère, cabled the following :—

"But there is another event really important, from which may result a political and social revolution. It is the meeting at Erfurt of the Congress of German Socialists—that is is to say, of people in Germany who have the courage to say that militarism is a misfortune and that the difference between Germany and France—namely, the Alsace-Lorraine question—should be settled otherwise than by war.

"Seeing that the progress of the Socialists is constant, they must be followed very closely; yet again this week they won in the elections to the Saxon Landtag. Last week they gained seats in an unexpected fashion in the Bavarian elections.

"It must be noticed how numerous they are, what they have obtained and what they want.

"The number of Socialists who voted at the elections in 1871 was 101,927. That was small, and since that time the following has been the increase :—In 1874, 351,670; in 1875, 493,447; in 1878, 437,158; in 1881, 311,961. At this period Prince Bismarck caused the anti-Socialist

laws to be passed. In 1884 the Socialist vote was 549,990;
in 1887, 763,128, and finally in 1890, 1,341,587.

"Never in Europe has a party progressed in such
a manner. In 1871 there was but one Socialist Deputy, M.
Bebel; in 1890 there are thirty-six. In 1871 Berlin alone
had Socialist electors; in 1890 they are everywhere—at
Hamburg, Munich, Mannheim, Leipsic, as also in the
rural districts.

"The Propaganda is conducted by agents chosen by
the Central Committee composed of twelve delegates.
They pass from town to town holding forth that the anti-
Socialist laws are abrogated, making speeches and distrib-
uting their newspapers; for the party has forty-nine
political journals, nineteen daily—one with 125,000 sub-
scibers—twenty four weekly and six bi-weekly publications.
The party has also a review and an illustrated and satirical
newspaper. In each workshop there is a member who
receives one of the party newspapers, and whose mission it
is to read these newspapers to his companions. Moreover,
there are Propaganda pamphlets, of which 200,000 are
distributed free each year.

"The funds are supplied by a weekly call of ten
pfennigs from each member, besides the voluntary dona-
tions. We have seen, for example, M. Singer, a rich dry
goods merchant of Berlin, giving 100,000 marks at one
time. He is now a Parliamentary Deputy. The party
has an income of 60,000 marks per annum, which is spent
in the expenses of the Propaganda. All the positions,
from that of the chief to that of the propagator, are
honorary. There is a special electoral fund to which the
extraordinary receipts are added. For condemned companions, whose families always live at the expense of the
party, special collections are made.

"The first article of the program is as follows :—The political and economical expropriation of the capitalist class and the social appropriation of the means of production. The German Socialists wish firstly an Economic Revolution and then a Social Revolution.

"Prince Bismarck has said that the Socialists are the only danger threatening the Empire.

"M. Bebel has said : 'Yet another twenty years of peace and we shall be the masters of Germany.'

"William II. has said : 'The interest of the monarchy compels us to do justice to the demands of the working classes.'"

The handwriting is on the walls of the royal palaces, and the castles and mansions of the capitalist aristocracy, and privileged classes of Great Britain and Ireland, where the Social Democracy conjoined to the "New Trades Unionism" is making marvelous headway, presaging there, within a few years, the certain construction of a new civilization on the ruins of an effete monarchy.

France hears the voice of the Socialist in the "Corps legislatif," where the once opposing factions, being united, will march onward for the final success of real "Liberty, Equality and Fraternity."

So with other nations in Europe, even little Belgium putting herself in the front.   With regard to that country Lucien Sanial recently reported :—

"The condition of the Socialist Labor Party in Belgium was especially remarkable.   In every city that he visited there was a 'House of the People' that belongs to the Socialist party, together with Coöperative stores, bakeries, butcher shops, etc., the profits of which serve in part to increase the plant while the balance is used to publish daily papers, books, pamphlets and other Socialist literature.

The bakeries of Ghent, Brussels, Liege and Verviers, each turn out from 140,000 to 160,000 pounds of bread per week. The bread is better and sold one cent cheaper per kilogram than that of any private bakery. The employees of the Coöperation work only eight hours, while other bakers work from fourteen to sixteen hours a day, and the salaries of the first are considerably higher than those of the latter. Under good management and in the hands of men thoroughly imbued with the spirit of Socialism, Coöperation had proved in Belgium a powerful means of Socialistic propaganda, whereas in England, where it had been applied on a larger scale still, but upon the purely Capitalistic principle, it had produced no Social effect worth considering."

Socialism has gained in a similar manner throughout the other countries of Europe and America, including the Argentine Republic, where the trickeries of Capitalism not only toppled over the great banking house of the Barings, the money rivals of the Rothschilds, but led to the formation of a Socialist Labor Party.

But if there be one thing more than another that gives Socialism the greatest force, it is, that the highest inspirations of men of the noblest genius are being devoted to its service. When Art and Song unite in building up the new structure for man, there are indeed outlined the most glorious and really altruistic possibilities for Humanity. When the Art Socialists,—such men as John Ruskin, William Morris, Walter Crane, E. Burne Jones, associate for the cause with poets of international reputation like the late Robert Browning. Surely the prospect is most cheering for the early coming of the time foretold by the Socialist poet Percy Bysshe Shelley, when, "in a proper condition of society," there will be "no pauperism"—

> "No meditative signs of selfishness,
> No jealous intercourse of wretched gain,
> No balancings of prudence, cold and long;
> In just and equal measure all is weighed;
> One scale contains the sum of human weal,
> And one the good man's heart."

Yes, before the Twentieth Century has ended its fourth or fifth decade, there will be held in America, along with the Fourth of July, the annual ratification and reaffirmation of the Emancipation of the Wages Slaves,—which will have been helped by the energies of coming Greeleys, Brisbanes and Godwins; and then in the favorite lines of Horace Greeley, from the pen of Charles Mackay, the Labor-poet—

> "Once the welcome Light has broken,
>   Who shall say
> What the unimagined glories
>   Of the day?
> What the evil that shall perish
>   In its ray?
> Aid the dawning, Tongue and Pen!
> Aid it, hopes of Honest Men!
> Aid it Paper! aid it Type!
> Aid it, for the hour is ripe!
> And our earnest must not slacken
>   Into play;
> Men of Thought, and Men of Action,
>   CLEAR THE WAY!"

FINIS CORONAT OPUS.

INDEX

345

Clinton, Col. Charles, 76
Clinton, De Witt, 76, 77
Clinton, George, 76
Coleridge, Samuel Taylor, quot-
ed, 244
Columbus, Christopher, 62
Comte, August, 220, 244
Conrad, E., quoted, 102–103
Considerant, M. Victor, 125
Cooper, Thomas, 117
Cuno, Theodore F., quoted, 254
Curtis, George W., 85, 192, 285,
291, 317, 333
Curtis, Joel, 87

D

D'ARUSMONT, FRANCES WRIGHT,
95, 96, 201, 202
Da Costa, Rev. Benjamin F., 250
Dana, Charles A., 27, 192, 285,
287, 291–293, quoted, 295
Danton, 306
Darthe, Augustin Alexander, 78,
82, 113
Davis, Jefferson, 94, 157
De Leon, Daniel, xx, xxx
Debs, Eugene V., xxxvii
Denton, "Farmer" S., quoted,
253–254
Depew, Chauncey, 142, 330
Dixon, Rev. Thomas, quoted, 51
Doherty, Hugh, 125
Douai, Dr. A., xiii, 61, 335
Doubleday, Gen. Abner, 288
Drake, Joseph Rodman, 96
Drury, Henry, 61
Drury, Victor, 326
Dulman, A. G., 330
Duquesnoy, 80
Duroy, 80
Dwight, John Sullivan, 294

E

EDWARDS (Judge), 303
Elliott, Jonathan, 23
Ely, Richard T., quoted, 7, 14,
63, 64–69, 272, 308
Emerson, Ralph Waldo, 192,
281, 282, 286, 290, 294, 297,

quoted, 41, 73, 74, 108, 128–
130, 283, 284, 288, 289, 297
Engles, Frederick, 113, 170, 337
Evans, Elder F. W., 65, quoted,
66, 67, 72, 83, 84–87, 89
Evans, George H., 65, 83, 95, 254
Everett, Edward, 108, 109

F

FAIRBANKS, N. K., 330
Fern, Fanny, 2
Fichte, Johann Gottlieb, quoted,
110–111
Field, David Dudley, 303
Ford, Ebenezer, 85
Ford, Patrick, 61
Forestier, 80
Fortuny, 111
Fourier, Charles, 11, 14, 19, 83,
122–126, quoted, 131–132, 136,
144, 217, 225, 273, 275
Francis, Dr. Convers, 282
Franklin, Benjamin, 1, 23, 309
Fraser, James, Bishop of Man-
chester, x
Froude, James Anthony, quoted,
15
Fry, William Henry, 184, 294
Fuller, Margaret, 192, 282, 290

G

GARRISON, William Lloyd, 57,
290
George, Henry, xviii, 66, 333
Gerard, James W., quoted, 17–
18, 111
Germain, 81
Gibbons (Cardinal), 323
Giles, Edward, 145
Girard, Stephen, 103
Gladden, Washington, 332, 333,
335, 336
Godwin, Parke, 19, 102, 136, 145,
192, 217, 281, 300, 333, quoted,
49, 137–141
Gompers, Samuel, xxi–xxiii, 329
Gonoud, 111
Goujon, 80
Graham, William H., 144